Gendering Civil War

Edinburgh Studies in Modern Arabic Literature
Series Editor: Rasheed El-Enany

Writing Beirut: Mappings of the City in the Modern Arabic Novel
Samira Aghacy

Women, Writing and the Iraqi State: Resistance and Collaboration under the Ba'th, 1968–2003
Hawraa Al-Hassan

Autobiographical Identities in Contemporary Arab Literature
Valerie Anishchenkova

The Iraqi Novel: Key Writers, Key Texts
Fabio Caiani and Catherine Cobham

Sufism in the Contemporary Arabic Novel
Ziad Elmarsafy

Gender, Nation, and the Arabic Novel: Egypt 1892–2008
Hoda Elsadda

The Arabic Prose Poem: Poetic Theory and Practice
Huda Fakhreddine

The Unmaking of the Arab Intellectual: Prophecy, Exile and the Nation
Zeina G. Halabi

Egypt 1919: The Revolution in Literature and Film
Dina Heshmat

Post-War Anglophone Lebanese Fiction: Home Matters in the Diaspora
Syrine Hout

Prophetic Translation: The Making of Modern Egyptian Literature
Maya I. Kesrouany

Nasser in the Egyptian Imaginary
Omar Khalifah

Conspiracy in Modern Egyptian Literature
Benjamin Koerber

War and Occupation in Iraqi Fiction
Ikram Masmoudi

Literary Autobiography and Arab National Struggles
Tahia Abdel Nasser

The Libyan Novel: Humans, Animals and the Poetics of Vulnerability
Charis Olszok

The Arab Naḥḍah*: The Making of the Intellectual and Humanist Movement*
Abdulrazzak Patel

Blogging from Egypt: Digital Literature, 2005–2016
Teresa Pepe

Religion in the Egyptian Novel
Christina Phillips

Space in Modern Egyptian Fiction
Yasmine Ramadan

Gendering Civil War: Francophone Women's Writing in Lebanon
Mireille Rebeiz

Occidentalism: Literary Representations of the Maghrebi Experience of the East–West Encounter
Zahia Smail Salhi

Sonallah Ibrahim: Rebel with a Pen
Paul Starkey

Minorities in the Contemporary Egyptian Novel
Mary Youssef

edinburghuniversitypress.com/series/smal

Gendering Civil War

Francophone Women's Writing in Lebanon

Mireille Rebeiz

EDINBURGH
University Press

To Baba

Edinburgh University Press is one of the leading university presses in the UK. We publish academic books and journals in our selected subject areas across the humanities and social sciences, combining cutting-edge scholarship with high editorial and production values to produce academic works of lasting importance. For more information visit our website: edinburghuniversitypress.com

Cover image: *Le cri du Cèdre (The Scream of the Cedar)*, print 71 × 61 cm
© Sandra Kheir Sahyoun

Edinburgh University Press Ltd
The Tun – Holyrood Road
12 (2f) Jackson's Entry
Edinburgh EH8 8PJ

Typeset in 11/15 EB Garamond by
Cheshire Typesetting Ltd, Cuddington, Cheshire,
printed and bound in Great Britain

A CIP record for this book is available from the British Library

ISBN 978 1 4744 9926 2 (hardback)
ISBN 978 1 4744 9928 6 (webready PDF)
ISBN 978 1 4744 9929 3 (epub)

Contents

Series Editor's Foreword

Edinburgh Studies in Modern Arabic Literature is a unique series that aims to fill a glaring gap in scholarship in the field of modern Arabic literature. Its dedication to Arabic literature in the modern period (that is, from the nineteenth century onwards) is what makes it unique among series undertaken by academic publishers in the English-speaking world. Individual books on modern Arabic literature in general or aspects of it have been and continue to be published sporadically. Series on Islamic studies and Arab/ Islamic thought and civilisation are not in short supply either in the academic world, but these are far removed from the study of Arabic literature qua literature, that is, imaginative, creative literature as we understand the term when, for instance, we speak of English literature or French literature. Even series labelled 'Arabic/ Middle Eastern Literature' make no period distinction, extending their purview from the sixth century to the present, and often including non-Arabic literatures of the region. This series aims to redress the situation by focusing on the Arabic literature and criticism of today, stretching its interest to the earliest beginnings of Arab modernity in the nineteenth century.

The need for such a dedicated series, and generally for the redoubling of scholarly endeavour in researching and introducing modern Arabic literature to the Western reader, has never been stronger. Among activities and events heightening public, let alone academic, interest in all things Arab, and not least Arabic literature, are the significant growth in the last decades of the translation of contemporary Arab authors from all genres, especially fiction, into English; the higher profile of Arabic literature internationally since the award of the Nobel Prize in Literature to Naguib Mahfouz in 1988; the growing number of Arab authors living in the Western diaspora and writing both in English and Arabic; the adoption of such authors and others by mainstream, high-circulation publishers, as opposed to the academic publishers of the past; and the establishment of prestigious prizes, such as the International Prize for Arabic Fiction, popularly referred to in the Arab world as the Arabic Booker, run by the Man Booker Foundation, which brings huge publicity to the shortlist and winner every year, as well as translation contracts into English and other languages. It is therefore part of the ambition of this series that it will increasingly address a wider reading public beyond its natural territory of students and researchers in Arabic and world literature. Nor indeed is the academic readership of the series expected to be confined to specialists in literature in the light of the growing trend for interdisciplinarity, which increasingly sees scholars crossing field boundaries in their research tools and coming up with findings that equally cross discipline borders in their appeal. The need for such a dedicated series, and generally for the redoubling of scholarly endeavour in researching and introducing modern Arabic literature to the Western reader, has never been stronger. Among activities and events heightening public, let alone academic, interest in all things Arab, and not least Arabic literature, are the significant growth in the last decades of the translation of contemporary Arab authors from all genres, especially fiction, into English; the higher profile of Arabic literature internationally since the award of the Nobel Prize for Literature to Naguib Mahfouz in 1988; the growing number of Arab authors living in the Western diaspora and writing both in English and Arabic; the adoption of such authors and others by mainstream, high-circulation publishers, as opposed to the academic publishers of the past; the establishment of prestigious prizes, such as the International Prize for Arabic Fiction, popularly referred to in the Arab world as the Arabic Booker, run by the Man Booker Foundation, which brings huge publicity to the shortlist and winner every year, as well as translation contracts into English and other languages; and very recently the events of the Arab Spring. It is therefore part of the ambition of this series that it will increasingly address a wider reading public beyond its natural territory of students and researchers in Arabic and world literature. Nor indeed is the academic readership of the series expected to be confined to specialists in literature in the light of the growing trend for interdisciplinarity, which increasingly sees scholars crossing field boundaries in their research tools and coming up with findings that equally cross discipline borders in their appeal.

The Lebanese civil war (1975–90) was one of the longest and most traumatic experiences of the Lebanese nation, a country torn by sectarian strife since the nineteenth century, long before its formation under the French mandate in 1920 and independence in 1943. Having had strong cultural and religious relations with France since Ottoman times and later under French colonisation in the aftermath of the First World War, relations which did not slacken after independence, it is not surprising that the French language became for some of the country's writers the chosen vehicle for self-expression, especially for those who emigrated to France. While the majority of Lebanese literature today is produced in Arabic, some output, especially in the diaspora, continues to be made in French. A monumental event like the civil war which raged for fifteen years with an unspeakable history of carnage and atrocity was bound to become a major preoccupation of writers, men and women, of older and younger generations, all trying to record, understand and come to terms with what they witnessed personally or was recounted to them by survivors. Each faction, each gender, each generation, those who lived through the conflict and those who fled it – all wrestled in their writing with the harrowing experience. The abundance of literature was matched by an abundance of critical and scholarly attention too. But the share of that attention of Lebanese women writers writing in French was meagre. The book in hand, dedicated to francophone Lebanese women writers treating the civil war, is an attempt to redress this imbalance with its focus on a selection of significant writers such as Vénus Khoury-Ghata, Etel Adnan, Evelyne Accad, Andrée Chedid, Hyam Yared and Georgia Makhlouf, who amongst themselves represent two generations of writers. Wider scholarship apart, this title will further enrich studies of Lebanese war literature in this very series joining ranks with the earlier titles of Syrine Hout's *Post-War Anglophone Lebanese Fiction* (2012), and Samira Aghacy's *Writing Beirut* (2015).

Rasheed El-Enany,
Series Editor,
Emeritus Professor of Modern Arabic Literature,
University of Exeter

Acknowledgements

I would like to express my deep and sincere gratitude to Mama and Baba for their love and support throughout this project. Baba believed in me even when I did not believe in myself. I am heartbroken that he will not get to see this book published as he left this earth; so, Baba, this one is for you.

I want to acknowledge family members who have been a solid presence in my life: my brothers Mike and Mario and their families in Lebanon, and my wonderful aunt Eglal Nasser and her family in New York. Every time I called Eglal she would ask me in French, 'Are you done with this book?' I can finally say 'yes' to her. I want to add a big thank you to my aunt and uncle in Normandy, and to Florence and Michel Guillemette and their family in Montpellier for housing me and feeding me the best French food during my summer research trips.

I also would like to say a special thanks to my pod family, Dean Danielle Conway and Emmanuel Quainoo, for helping us go through the pandemic, to my colleagues at Dickinson College, to the editorial team at Edinburgh University Press, and to the American Association of University Women for granting me the American Fellowship which allowed me to focus on my writing and move forward in my career.

I am grateful for my mentors, Dr Alec G. Hargreaves and Dr Michael S. Neiberg, for their availability, wisdom, friendship and guidance.

Finally, this book would not have been possible without my husband and child's unwavering support. Stacey Suver, my soulmate, read my manuscript several times, discussed ideas and offered suggestions. He made sure my

Oxford commas are where they should be, and he provided me with chocolate during my late writing hours. I am blessed to have a husband who strongly believes in women's rights and gender equality and who is proud of my successes.

Introduction

This is the first book-length analysis of Lebanese Francophone writings of women on the Lebanese civil war from the 1970s through the present time. Drawing on a corpus of writings by Vénus Khoury-Ghata (b. 1937), Etel Adnan (b. 1925), Evelyne Accad (b. 1943), Andrée Chedid (1920–2011), Hyam Yared (b. 1975) and Georgia Makhlouf (b. 1955), some of which has previously received little or no scholarly attention, this book examines the use of distinctive narrative forms in addressing interlinked questions of violence, war trauma and gender relations.

This book considers literature as a semiotic and a mimetic space. It is motivated by a lack of attention to narrative structure due to a general concern with stylistic expression, and it combines the study of the form and the content of the novel and examines ways by which Lebanese women writers of French expression constructed their war narratives. In doing so, this book seeks to answer the following questions: How are war stories told? In what way are war narratives constructed? Who is telling the story and why? In what way does the narrative voice participate in the structure and meaning building of a narrative? Is the narrative voice the only tool that tells war stories or can the body contribute to the narrative? If so, in what way does the body in general, and the female body more precisely, do so? What are the narrative roles assigned to the female body in the construction of war narratives? In what way does a woman's voice or a woman's body factor into the telling of war stories?

To answer these questions, I examine the intersection between the different fields of narratology (classical and post-classical), trauma studies, women's gender and sexuality studies and francophone studies. Narratology, in its narrow meaning, is generally understood as the theory that objectively studies the structure of a narrative. I adopt a broad definition of narratology which regards the narrative as a whole and includes the study of the narrative structure but also its meaning and context. In fact, and as Mieke Bal argues, there is a blurred line between the interpretation of a narrative and an analysis of its form (Bal 1997: 10–11). As such, I proceed to examine the ways by which both structure and meaning inform each other to construct a war narrative. To say it differently, I seek to examine what James Phelan calls the ethics of the telling (or the way by which the author relates to the audience using certain tools), and the ethics of the told (or what is being experienced or represented) (Phelan 2011: 56).

Drawing on a wide range of critical theories in the fields mentioned above, I elucidate the deeply rooted relationship between the narrative strategies, structures and meaning in Lebanese women's war stories of French expression. The intersection between narratology with the other fields imposes a shift in the agenda of literary analysis as the narrative form now plays a role in its own interpretation. It not only aids the content, but it also helps transmit the meaning of war narratives.

Traditionally in what is called classical structural narratology, the voice is examined 'scientifically' independently from the context in which it exists, and regardless of its meaning. Basing my analysis on what is called post-classical narratology, I argue that the narrative voice in the war novels studied here serves different valuable functions that are not limited to enunciation. In some cases, the narrative voice speaks using the first-person subject or the feminine 'I' which forcibly enters the public space traditionally reserved for males in order to speak up in an armed conflict, to bear witness to her own trauma and the trauma of others, to render justice to the victims, and to write history. In some other cases, the narrative voice speaks from an omniscient position. While I acknowledge that the concept of omniscient narrator has raised some issues, it is however useful in a war narrative: the omniscient narrator monopolises the voice in a cacophonic crowded narrative space to spread a peaceful message and speak in the name of shared human values.

As for the narrative body, I argue that, just like the voice, the body contributes to the construction of war narratives. This is not to say that the narrative does not have a voice as an enunciating subject. It simply means that the real meaning of the war narrative goes through the body as if it is the body that is speaking to tell the war story. As such, the body displaces the voice to become the structure on which the narrative is built. It carries multiple meanings: it is the evil female body that brings destruction to the city and ignites the combats; it is the sick female body that refuses to abide by the social rules and engages, just as war-torn Lebanon, in a self-destructive behaviour; it is the magical female body that can only exist in the margins of society; it is finally the grotesque body that just like the war itself does not make much sense and functions according to surreal rules of time, space and reason.

In this book, I focus on ten novels: Georgia Makhlouf's *Les Absents*, Etel Adnan's *Sitt Marie Rose*, Andrée Chedid's *La Maison sans racines* and *Le Message*, Evelyne Accad's *Coquelicot du massacre*, Hyam Yared's *L'Armoire des ombres* and *La Malédiction*, Vénus Khoury-Ghata's *La Maîtresse du Notable*, *Vacarme pour une lune morte* and *Les Morts n'ont pas d'ombre*.

In general, Lebanese women's writings of French expression have been studied by scholars like miriam cooke, Michelle Hartman and Evelyne Accad. However, they were examined either from different angles such as motherhood, sexuality and gender tensions, linguistic identity, or inserted in survey studies of Lebanese literature or Arab literature that did not necessarily distinguish between the languages of production.

The originality of my book resides in its deliberate attention to a smaller corpus of French expression, and its offering of a new approach of examination, one that has been traditionally restricted – not without criticism – to Eurocentric texts. In fact, to my knowledge, this book is the first to apply post-classical narratology to non-Western literature of French expression, and to examine its intersection with trauma and gender studies.

In addition to providing analysis of relatively well-known authors such as Etel Adnan, Andrée Chedid and Evelyne Accad, my book offers an analysis of newly published novels by second-generation writers like Hyam Yared and Georgia Makhlouf, and of novels by first-generation writers that received very little to no attention such as Vénus Khoury-Ghata's *La Maîtresse du Notable*, *Vacarme pour une lune morte*, and *Les Morts n'ont pas d'ombre*.

Although the French language is the common denominator between the novels, I did not choose the texts simply because of their language of expression but rather for their remarkable literary value and their general address of the civil war in Lebanon. It is worth mentioning that in many of these novels, and unlike other francophone literary texts, the French language is not necessarily a point of contention.

Even though the language of this literary production is not the topic of study in this book, I still excluded novels in other languages, such as Arabic or English, in order to ensure the homogeneity of my project. Additionally, I adopted the method of close reading as it is required for the proper examination of the narratological voice and body and for the identification of linguistic details such as enunciating subject and gender agreements. Also, I adhere to Elizabeth Weed's defence of close reading in 'The Way We Read Now' where she argues that close reading is a valuable mechanism to fight against fetishism and other traps of capitalism (Weed 2012).

In order to avoid the traps of oversimplification and generalisation of surface reading, I implement the method of close reading to move the discussion beyond commodity fetishism. As Amal Amireh says '[t]he debate should go beyond "appreciative" criticism that condescendingly praises Arab women writers for "daring" to put pen to paper' (Amireh 1996). Aligning with Weed and Amireh's arguments, I provide a detailed analysis of the novels in question precisely to give each novel the level of analysis it deserves, and to avoid orientalist and reductive lenses of analysis.

As for the book's theoretical framework, I mostly refer to Western literary critics and critical theories primarily because of their establishment in the fields of narratology, trauma studies, women's gender and sexuality studies and francophone studies.

Finally, I rely on or refer to existing translations in English when they are available. For the novels, I provide both the original French and the English versions when available, otherwise, I offer my own translation.

Narratology: Classical and Post-classical

First, what is a narrative? Phelan defines a narrative as 'a rhetorical act: somebody tells somebody else on some occasion and for purpose(s) that something happened' (Phelan 2005: 18).[1] For Gerald Prince, a narrative is a 'representation of one (or more than one nonrandomly connected and noncontradictory) transformation of a state of affairs, one (or more than one) event which does not logically presuppose that state and/or does not logically entail its transformation' (Prince 2005: 373). A narrative is not a single linguistic sign or a phatic utterance or one argument or statement. A narrative, designed to be understood and not just recognised, is diverse in its possible forms 'oral, written, or sign language, still or moving pictures, gestures, or a combination' (Prince 2005: 373), dimensions and unlimited topics. A narrative can be true or false, factual or fictional, traditional or modern, spontaneous or deliberate (Prince 2005: 374). For Hervé Corvellec, '[s]chematically, a narrative is an account with a plot', characters, time and space in which the plot takes place so the audience can make sense of it (Corvellec 2011: 102–3). In short, a narrative is a story. It is the product of our human nature as we like to tell what happened. It is the story:

> at the heart of what it is to be psychosocial human being. We naturally try to make sense of things . . . Inevitably, owing to our social nature, our individual narratives are determined not only by how we think, our own memories of our experiences, but also by others, and by the social discourses that exist in society. Individuals do not have a single narrative; the narrative depends on the audience. (Hunt 2010: 97–8)

Second, what is narratology? It is the study of narrative which was defined by Tzvetan Todorov as 'la science du récit' or the science of narrative (Todorov 1969: 10). It examines 'what all narratives have in common – narratively speaking – and which allows them to be narratively different' (Prince 1982: 4–5).

According to Ansgar Nünning, narratology has evolved from crisis and bankruptcy to revival with a renewed interest in storytelling (Nünning 2003: 239). For Nünning, the term narratology can be understood broadly to include different narrative theories. More commonly, it is understood to be restricted to narrative theories from the sixties and the seventies, primarily from France. In 'A Feminist Approach to Narrative', Robyn Warhol argues that it is best to employ the term narrative studies because narratology 'still connotes to many a theoretical approach cut off from questions of history and context' (Warhol 2012: 9).

Today we cannot speak of narratology without considering all the new approaches that help revive the field. According to Nünning, we should speak of multiple narratologies since we are, as David Herman calls it, in the post-classical narratology era and no longer in the realm of classical structuralist narratology (qtd in Nünning 2003: 243). Post-classical narratology is defined as 'a broader reconfiguration of the narratological landscape. The root transformation can be described as a shift from text-centered and formal models to models that are jointly formal and functional – models attentive both to the text and to the context of stories' (qtd in Nünning 2003: 243).

According to Nünning, there are four key elements that distinguish structuralist classical narratology from new post-classical narratologies. First, post-classical narratologies were born from the theorists' focus on the relationship between text and context, a point that has been ignored by classical narratology. Second, classical narratology offers a dry analysis of a narrative as opposed to post-classical narratologies which lead the way to content analysis and synthesis. Third, classical narratology is only interested in the structure of a narrative, not the production of a moral or meaning. Post-classical narratology pays close attention to both. Fourth, post-classical narratologies focus on issues like history, gender and text interpretations which are ignored by classical narratology (Nünning 2003: 244–5). Nünning does acknowledge, however, that the divide between classical and post-classical narratologies is not always clear. Some concepts in post-classical narratologies obey a specific time period (since it relies on context). Also, other concepts belong to both narratologies, for instance the concept of the unreliable narrator which raises questions related to narrative structure, morality, context and interpretation (Nünning 2003: 245).

For Nünning, it is clear that classical narratology is eroding, and it is becoming more and more interdisciplinary. He divides post-classical narratologies into eight groups noting that the list is by no means exhaustive, and that some groups bleed into each other as they are not firmly segregated (Nünning 2003: 249–51).[2] Among these groups, we find feminist narratology, postcolonial narratology and postmodern narratology.

Feminist narratology is 'the oldest and most established of contextual approaches' of narratology (Sommer 2007: 65). Considered a post-classical narratology, feminist narratology examines questions related to gender and sexuality as important constructive elements of the narrative. It is concerned with 'the ways in which various narratological concepts, categories, methods and distinctions advance or obscure the exploration of gender and sexuality as signifying aspects of narrative' (Lanser 2013: 1). Additionally, it is 'the umbrella term which embraces the exploration of narrative from this [feminist] point of view' (Lanser 2013: 1).

Feminist narratology is attributed to the work of Susan Lanser who, in her 1986 essay 'Toward a Feminist Narratology', protested classical narratology's dismissal of key terms like gender and provided compelling reasons in favour of feminist narratology. On the surface, classical narratology and feminist criticism seem conflicting. Traditionally, classical narratology, which mostly relies on men's texts in its analysis, sees the narrative as a semiosis or to put it simply as a language structure. As such, it focuses on the technical aspect of a narrative and does not study categories like gender, sex, context or characters. Feminist criticism, according to Lanser, views narrative as a mimesis or a representation of the real world, and contrary to classical narratology, it examines categories like gender, sex, context and characters (Lanser 1986: 342–3).

Feminist narratology does not seek to threaten classical narratology or feminist criticism but to challenge them into recognising the dual nature of a narrative. For Lanser, a pure semiotic approach to a narrative runs the risk of isolating the texts from their contexts of production (Lanser 1986: 344); that is why she calls for a reflection on both mimetic and semiotic experiences in reading literature and a study of narrative 'in relation to a referential context that is simultaneously linguistic, literary, historical, biographical, social, and political' (Lanser 1986: 345).

For Lanser, this new kind of narratology should function just like speech act theory which 'understood that the minimal unit of discourse was not the sentence but the *production* of the sentence in a specific context' (Lanser 1986: 354); it should therefore examine categories like gender (as the marker of social identity), sex (as a biological designator) and sexuality (attraction towards a sexed or gendered subject) as they play a vital role in the construction of a narrative (Lanser 2013: 2).

In 1988, in response to Lanser's essay, hardcore formalists like Nilli Diengott in 'Narratology and Feminism' called for a turn away from the contamination of contextualised narratology and for a return to the pure form of narratology as an objective study of the narrative. Despite their calls, feminist narratology thrived to become a well-established field. Credit must be particularly rendered to Robyn R. Warhol's *Gendered Interventions* (1989), Susan Lanser's *Fictions of Authority* (1992) and Kathy Mezei's edited collection *Feminist Narratology and British Women Writers* (1996). Nevertheless, today feminist narratology faces legitimate criticism; some have argued that the field is locked into a restrictive binary opposition between male and female, that it assumes that women are a homogenous group with similar experiences and as such ignores the fluidity of gender, and that it remains a very Eurocentric field that focuses mostly on Western narratives. This criticism led to the call for a global feminist narratology, and to the rise of intersectional narratology and queer narratology (Lanser 2010; Lanser 2013). Additionally, some said that feminist narratology runs the risk of isolating theory from practice since it is only 'concerned with texts and how these might relate to their various contexts, whereas "feminism(s)" [is] a movement' which actually aims to modify the real context in which it exists (Page 2006: 10). In other words, some are wondering about the usefulness or limitations of feminist narratology and its relevance to the real world. For Ruth E. Page, 'the concept of feminist narratology is not without limitations. But this does not mean that it is of no use' (Page 2006: 11). It remains valid and valuable but indeed needs to work on quickly absorbing the new ramifications of feminism (Page 2006: 15).

As for postcolonial narratology, Monica Fludernik illustrates how postcolonial literary theory might be advantageous to structural narratology. She shows how the notions of identities and alterities valuable for postcolonial studies inform the narrative structure. In fact, they may lead to the development of narrative strategies and the enunciation of comments by the narrator that reveal a postcolonial agenda. For her, postcolonial narratology describes:

> how the choice of specific narrative techniques helps to transmit underlying orientalist or patriarchal structures and how the narrative, by its choice of focalization, plot structure, or use of free indirect discourse sometimes resists these structures, undermines or deconstructs them. Postcolonial narratology is concerned with experimental narrative techniques that correlate with the celebration of cultural hybridity or the symbolic liberation of the subaltern. (Fludernik 2005: 45)

Writing in 2002, Marion Gymnich supports Fludernik's approach to postcolonial narratology. She defines postcolonial narratology as the mechanism that examines the relationship between narrative structure and key concepts of postcolonial studies such as ethnicity, race, class and gender (qtd in Sommer 2007: 68). Fludernik and Sommer each argue that postcolonial narratology does not aim to examine narratology from a postcolonial point of view. Instead, it seeks to build bridges between the two fields in using narratology's heuristic potential to reveal postcolonial meanings (qtd in Sommer 2007: 69). Gerald Prince states that postcolonial narratology is 'sensitive to matters commonly, if not uncontroversially, associated with the postcolonial (e.g., hybridity, migrancy, otherness, fragmentation, diversity, power relations); it envisages their possible narratological correspondents; and it incorporates them' (Prince 2005: 373). Prince argues that narratology can be useful to postcolonial studies as it allows an examination of points of view, speed, mode of discourse, actantial roles and transformations in the narrative which all serve an ideology constructed and represented by the narrative (Prince 2005: 372). In fact, narratological concepts like space, time, characters, events, structure, narrative frequency, order and voice can all be revised from a postcolonial point of view.

Andrew Gibson advocates for postmodern narratology. According to him, classical narratology is filled with the fantasy of geometrical structure as if it is possible to geometrise a narrative and study it like an accurate science. Discussing the works of Genette, Barthes, Chatman and Booth, he shows how classical narratology has imagined the narrative space as a 'unitary, homogenous space' (Gibson 1996: 7). This tendency to geometric rigid thinking started in ancient Greece and spilled into contemporary Western culture. It is dangerous as it hardens space and freezes time; it also limits the source of knowledge to one (Gibson 1996: 14).

For Gibson, narrative space has often been disturbed by non-conventional interruptions that do not necessarily go into the classical narratology's descriptions. These disturbances are postmodern in nature as they break with the mainstream imperialistic discourse and offer a multi-spaced narrative which disrupts the singular space assumption under which classical narratology operates. In short, multiple spaces bring multiple knowledge. He says:

> Narrative space is now plastic and manipulable. It has become heterogenous, ambiguous, pluralized. Its inhabitants no longer appear to have an irrefuta-

ble or essential relation to any particular space. Rather, space opens up as a variable and finally indeterminate feature of any given narrative 'world'. (Gibson 1996: 12)

For Gibson, classical narratology seeks to create a rigid structure for a narrative. Citing Derrida's theory of structure, according to which structure implies the existence of centre, Gibson argues that the centre of classical narratology is immobile and the narrative in its entirety refers to it (space and time are fixed according to an exact science, all thoughts are linked in a particular order . . .) (Gibson 1996: 19). For Gibson, postmodern narratology wants to destroy this idea of a centre, of a rigid structure, unified space, frozen time and one source of knowledge.

It is important to note that feminist, postcolonial and postmodern narratologies are intertwined. As Sommer points out, many of the contextual narratologies overlap precisely because of the kinship between the various contexts (Sommer 2007). For Prince, 'many postcolonial texts are (post) modern or feminist too' and there are many links that are relevant to all three fields of postcolonialism, postmodernism and feminism, such as the communal representation of the narrative voice as an I/we (Prince 2005: 374), or the representation of the power struggle between a hegemonic domination and a suppression.

In this book, I read the corpus in question in light of contextualised narratology, particularly feminist, postcolonial and postmodern narratology as they help understand the narrative structure of war stories and interpret the interaction between the form and content.

I align my method with Lanser's conviction that a narrow and dry reading of a narrative may cause its alienation and that the context of production (in this case war) plays an important role in the narrative's construction and meaning. As such, I argue that concepts like voice, body, gender, otherness, fragmentation, hybridity, power struggles, space, time and knowledge, which are valuable to feminism, postcolonialism and postmodernism, participate in the construction of war narrative in supporting its structure and providing meaning. The narrative voice and body tell us about the war. Often alienated from the rest of the society, they reflect on the war in terms of gender, dominance and suppression. Existing in a non-traditional time and space, they speak up to bear witness and to offer an alternative reality to the mainstream imperialistic knowledge.

Narratology and Narrative Voice

Narratology has always been interested in the concept of the voice which is a complex and problematic category: 'As an entity attributed to (silent) written texts, the concept of voice inevitably raises questions of ontology and meta-phoricity which remain inseparable from its more technical delimitation as a textual function of effect' (Aczel 1998: 467). For Gibson, this is indeed odd for multiple reasons: how can we speak of voice in a written text? How can narratology examine the voice since it is the token of subjectivity and nar-ratology is all about studying a narrative as a science? (Gibson 1996: 143) Traditionally, the term 'voice' has been associated with Genette's work to imply an examination of who speaks. In fact, Genette studies the voice as an objective entity that utters the narrative. In *Narrative Discourse Revisited*, he argues that the choice of the narrative voice is irrelevant:

> [T]he writer, I imagine, one day *wants* to write this narrative in the first person and that narrative in the third person, for no reason at all, just for a change. Some writers are totally resistant to one or the other, for no reason at all, because it is what it is, because they are what they are: why do some writers use black ink and others blue ink? . . . In short, the most profound (the least conditional reason) here, as is often the case elsewhere, is 'because that's the way it is.' Everything else is motivation. (Genette 1988: 113)

Genette also maintains that every narrative is in the first person: 'in my view every narrative is, explicitly or not, "in the first person" since at any moment its narrator may use that pronoun to designate himself' (Genette 1988: 97).

Unlike Jakobson and Benveniste who consider the value of the enunciat-ing subject, Genette dismisses it and focuses more on the context in which the communication occurs. His views, along with the proclamation of the death of the author by Roland Barthes (1978), constitute in part classical narratol-ogy that focuses on the technicality of a narrative, and ignores the meanings attributed to the narrative voice.

While Genette distinguishes between different persons, levels and points of view of the narrative voice (the extradiegetic/intradiegetic narrator, the homodiegetic/heterodiegetic narrator with internal/external focalisation or focalisation zero), Seymour Chatman argues that the categorisation of the narrators (as the speaking narrative voice) is less important than the identification of 'the features that mark their degree of audibility' (Chatman 1978: 196). As such, Chatman makes the distinction between the most covert to the most overt narrator without focusing on the qualitative voice.

Classical narratology, in opposition to post-classical narratology, offers a scientific homogenous view of the narrative voice, and makes it the only source of knowledge void of all cultural implications. For Gibson, Genette 'simply ignored the extent to which voice is always overcoded' (Gibson 1996: 144). Richard Walsh argues in favour of multiple definitions of voice and narrative. Focusing primarily on Genette's structuralist theories, he states that a narrative voice is generally understood within the narrating instance, which means it is always assumed within a communicative model of narration (Walsh 2010: 35). In addition to this definition of the voice as a narrating instance, the voice is also or should be regarded as a 'represented idiom' (Walsh 2010: 48); it is a mimetic voice that speaks for the others and invites an 'evaluation of the character whose discourse it represents – the discursive and narrative subject' (Walsh 2010: 49). Walsh argues that both senses of the voice are not necessarily antagonistic, and they do not obscure each other: whereas one functions to highlight the job of narration, the other functions as a representation and 'contributes to the job of characterization' (Walsh 2010: 49).

From a feminist narratology point of view, the narrative voice is most definitely the carrier of meaning. For Lanser, the narrative voice is 'for the collectively and personally silenced . . . a trope of identity and power' as it has been traditionally assigned to educated white men (Lanser 1992: 3). Concerned with women finding their voices, she calls for a 'coming to voice' moment for women but also other silenced communities such as 'people of color, peoples struggling against colonial rule, gay men and lesbians' (Lanser 1992: 3).

Wondering what forms of voice have been available to women, Lanser examines the intersection between social identity and textual form and distinguishes between three voices: the authorial, the personal and the communal voice. Traditionally masculine, women's authorial voice is heterodiegetic, public and self-referential. In many ways, it defies men's hegemony and women's exploitation and goes against narrative and social conventions. The personal voice refers 'to narrators who are self-consciously telling their own histories' (Lanser 1992: 18). The personal voice, according to Lanser, might be less powerful than the authorial voice 'since authorial voice claims broad powers of knowledge and judgement, while a personal narrator claims only the validity of one's person right to interpret her experience' (Lanser 1992: 19). The communal voice is 'a spectrum of practices that articulate either a collective voice or a collective of voices that share narrative authority' (Lanser 1992: 21). Lanser is clear in saying that the communal voice is not simply the inclusive 'we'. It is instead 'a practice in which narrative authority is invested in a definable community and textually inscribed either through multiple, mutually authorizing voices or through the voice of a single individual who is manifestly authorized by a community' (Lanser 1992: 21). Additionally, in re-examining Genette's extradiegetic and intradiegetic narrators, Lanser distinguishes between the private voice 'narration directed toward a narratee who is a fictional character' (Lanser 1992: 15) and the public voice 'narration directed toward a narratee "outside" the fiction who is analogous to the historical reader' (Lanser 1992: 15). For her, this distinction between the public and the private is important in the study of women's texts:

> For women writers . . . the distinction between private and public contexts is crucial and a complicated one. Traditionally speaking, the sanctions against women's writing have taken the form not of prohibitions to write at all but of prohibitions to write for a public audience. (Lanser 1986: 352)

She also makes the distinction between a narrator who exclusively engages in acts of representation and a narrator who undertakes extrapresentational acts: the first 'simply predicate the words and actions of fictional characters' while the second engages with 'reflections, judgments, generalizations about the world "beyond" the fiction, direct addresses to the narratee, comments on the narrative process allusions to other writers and texts' (Lanser 1992: 16–17). The first narrator has a limited role while the second one is able to 'expand the sphere of fictional authority to "nonfictional" referents and allow the writer to engage, from "within" the fiction, in a culture's literary, social, and intellectual debates' (Lanser 1992: 17).

For Lanser, these distinctions are not just technical since they represent 'a particular kind of narrative consciousness and hence a particular nexus of powers, dangers, prohibitions and possibilities' (Lanser 1992: 15). In other words, these categories allow for the establishment of a female narrative voice that speaks from a position of power. Following these definitions, I adopt the post-classical interdisciplinary approach according to which a voice is simultaneously an enunciating subject and an idiom. It is the speaking narrator but also the carrier of meaning. It is the alienated voice that speaks up to destroy the hegemonic centre and to offer an alternative knowledge. It is the woman's voice that bears witness to trauma and records history; it is a humanist omniscient voice that seeks to advocate for shared human values; it is an authorial and personal voice that tells the stories of others as well as one's own. It is a communal voice as it involves the entire Lebanese community. It is a private voice that engages in conversations within the novel, but also, and most importantly, it is a public voice as it leaves the private space traditionally assigned to women and transgresses male space. It is finally a voice with extra representational acts as it goes beyond the structural limits of a narrative to engage the world outside.

The Narrative Body and the Body as Narrative

Traditionally, the body, unlike the voice, was not considered part of the narrative structure. Post-classical narratology changed this by paying attention to the plot's characters, to the way they occupy space and time, to their significance, complexity and stability of their identities (Prince 2005: 375). Post-classical narratology also allowed an examination

> of their perceptions, their utterances, thoughts, and feelings, their motivations, their interactions, and their position with respect to such commonly exploited semantic categories as goodness and badness, class and power, sex, gender, or sexuality . . . colonizing and colonized, race or ethnicity, otherness and hybridity, collaboration, (forced) assimilation, resistance, or ambivalence, and obviously, linguistic and narrative capacity (Prince 2005: 375–6)

In a way, through the study of the characters, post-classical narratology opened the door to study the body in all the features mentioned above as a participant in the narrative structure and meaning. Furthermore, the body has traditionally been perceived as only the identity carrier but recently there has been a push to recognise the body as diegetic and semiotic narrative tool. As Emily Heavy shows, in recent years more attention has been paid to the body as an active participant in the narrative particularly when the body is in crisis. In fact, 'stories always "come out of" bodies, and stories and storytelling are based on lived, embodied experience of narrators, and interpreted through the filter of the lived embodied experience of the audience' (Heavy 2015: 430). As Kristin M. Langellier and Eric E. Peterson say: 'some *body* performs narrative. Performing narrative requires bodily participation: hearing and voicing, gesturing, seeing and being seen, feeling and being touched by the storytelling' (Langellier and Peterson 2004: 8).

Heavy advocates for what she calls the 'narrative embodiedness' according to which the body is 'the source and topic of narrator's stories' (Heavy 2015: 432). We live in our bodies. We experience the world with our bodies, and we tell stories with our bodies and about our bodies. For Langellier and Peterson, and as Heavy states, the narrative embodiedness should include all forms of storytelling including the virtual forms. Heavy, however, limits her argument to face-to-face storytelling (Heavy 2015: 432).

In this book, I adopt the dual approach of the body of what I call the narrative body and the body as narrative, where I consider the body as the enunciating subject of the narrative but also the carrier of meaning. This is not to say that the narrative voice is absent as the narrative still requires a narrator. However, the war story is told by and through the body and its experiences rather than the voice.

I borrow Heavy's theory of narrative embodiedness and extend it to fictional bodies to examine Vénus Khoury-Ghata's *La Maîtresse du Notable*, *Vacarme pour une lune morte* and *Les Morts n'ont pas d'ombre*, and Hyam Yared's *La Malédiction* and *L'Armoire des ombres*. I primarily focus on women's bodies and argue that these novels tell war stories through images of bodies in crisis: evil bodies, ill and disabled bodies, magical bodies and grotesque bodies.

In discussing women's bodies, the word 'woman' frequently implies a problematic unity of gender and sex. Gender, according to Judith Butler, is the cultural meanings that are socially performed by the body. Sex, she argues, is the anatomical and biological aspects of the body (Butler 1998: 29). Gender is often thought to mimic the performance of the sexed body. However, this may not be true in some instances where the two categories of gender and sex do not necessarily overlap. As a result, a man or the masculine might be found in a female body or a woman or the feminine might reside in a male body (Butler 1998: 29). I acknowledge the differences between these two terms. However, in this book, when I use the term 'woman' I refer to the social performance of the female gender within the female sexed body. In other words, I assume a unification of female sex and female gender.

Narratology and Transnational Feminism

Transnational feminism was born in North American academe. According to M. Jacqui Alexander and Chandra Talpade Mohanty, it refers to sets of theories and practices in which questions related to sex, gender, economy, global movements of goods, people, values and power struggles are examined in their own geographical spaces rather than in a global and general context, within their cultural differences and marginality and away from the Eurocentric homogenous white feminism. It focuses on collective practices undertaken by women in different parts of the world in order to understand the genealogies of feminist political struggles (Alexander and Talpade Mohanty 1996).

The term 'transnational' came as a reaction against other terms such as 'international' and 'global'. For transnational feminists, the term 'international' focuses on nation-states borders and entities which leaves some women's voices out, and the term 'global' assumes a certain level of kinship or sisterhood across the world which ignores the experiences of third-world women and women of colour.

Transnational feminism encompasses women-of-colour feminism, third-world feminism, multicultural feminism and other forms of feminism (Nagar and Lock Swarr 2010: 3). Transnational feminism has multiple merits, one of which is challenging the North American academy. For Alexander and Talpade Mohanty, the US academy 'is a very particular location for the production of knowledge' (Alexander and Talpade Mohanty 2010: 26). With its increased corporatisation, it is becoming a space of conformity and hegemony where fields studying questions of sex, gender, race and ethnicity run the risk of co-optation. The originality of transnational feminism is that it allows one to question the source of knowledge and decentralise it. In fact, transnational feminism is not location-bound in a sense that it opens the doors for scholars and activists to examine sources of knowledge outside the centre whether the centre is US academy or North America or the global North.

However, transnational feminism faces some serious challenges. In 'Continuing Conversations. Critical Transnational Feminist Praxis Contributors', the contributors end the edited volume by acknowledging that transnational feminism has gained fame in the past decade and a half notably in the global North. However, this popularity caused its definition to become elastic:

> The transnational [became] a wide net that catches all, and, in doing so, [lost] the traction that is so important in understanding or illuminating the various investments, contradictions, and relations of power embedded in diverse feminist projects to which it is so intimately linked. In that light, the transnational is in danger of becoming an empty metaphor for academic feminist theories – signifying everything and nothing. (Bouchard et al. 2010: 207)

For Inderpal Grewl and Caren Kaplan, transnational feminism is an over-used expression; it has 'become so ubiquitous in cultural, literary and critical studies that much of its political valence seems to have become evacuated' (Grewl and Kaplan 2001: 664). For them, transnational feminism is often understood as designating postcolonialism, and as such it became the go-to tool by Western scholars in examining women's issues in the global South.

Rich Nagar and Amanda Lock Swarr discuss the contradictions within North American academia when it comes to transnational feminism, critical theories and activism. They show how academic work is by nature highly collaborative and yet academia celebrates, quantifies and rewards individual work, which means there is always a need to oppose other works to advance in a field. This false assumption of individual knowledge in academia generates various dichotomies: it restricts the collaborative works between colleagues, and it limits the space of knowledge to personal grounds; it creates a hierarchy in knowledge and fields based at times on popularity. As a result, transnational feminism is immediately invoked when discussing the subaltern with complete disregard to other fields (Nagar and Lock Swarr 2010: 2). Consequently, transnational feminism becomes the 'totemic modes of feminist inquiry' against heteronormative, patriarchal and capitalist contexts. It becomes the cartographic manner of examination with rigid boundaries expected in the neo-liberal homogenous academic or scholarly spaces (Bouchard et al. 2010: 207).

Since transnational feminism is the expected lens to examine Lebanese women's literature and because scholars like miriam cooke have already done some of the work, I opted for a more unique and different approach, and chose narratology as my main frame of work. Just like transnational feminism, narratology displaces the source of knowledge and while transnational feminism gives a voice to the others from outside the homogenic homogenous Eurocentric space, narratology zooms on the narrative as the first source of knowledge and allows for a close reading and detailed analysis of narrative voices.

When this approach is utilised in the context of non-mainstream literature like Lebanese women's literature of French expression, it opens the door for under-represented voices to emerge, to be understood and to be heard. Thus, narratology fills an existing gap in the study of Lebanese women's literature of French expression. So far, this literature has been examined under the scopes of transnational feminism and postcolonialism. Very frequently, it has been compared to literature in the region, and inserted in anthologies examining the works of other Arab or Middle Eastern women writers. This method while scientifically commendable does not do the Lebanese literature justice as it makes surface level links between women writers and promotes a fetishist and orientalist reading. Therefore, narratology destabilises the cartographic mode of examination mentioned earlier as it regards the text itself as the centre of knowledge. I adopt the post-classical narratology as my primary lens knowing that it was shaped by feminism (second wave and transnational), postcolonialism and postmodernism.

In examining Lebanese women's literature of French expression, I employ intersectional narratology, which is defined as 'a method that can accommodate the different directions and locations of a rich set of texts, contexts, and identities while framing global observations about the working of narrative in the world' (Keen 2015: 123). It is a narratology that 'seeks to understand why certain positions and concepts are privileged while others suffer from inattention or disparagement' (Keen 2015: 125), and that aims to show how a narrative can give a voice or silence individuals based on their social relations and contexts. As Keen argues, intersectional narratology seeks to uncover discriminatory representations in both narrative structure and meaning, to reveal feminist agenda in non-mainstream texts, to enable the discussion on the complex relationship between narrative form, context and reception of the creation, identity and meaning (Keen 2015: 125).

Lebanese Francophone Women Writers

Lebanese literary production is not restricted to francophone texts, and it includes writings in Arabic and English languages. Arabophone writers like Hanan Al-Shaykh and Hoda Barakat and anglophone writers like Rawi Hage and Rabih Alameddine, to name a few, have largely contributed to the field and enriched it. Today, their works are internationally known and have been translated into different languages.

In this book, I do not engage in the discussion surrounding the language of production primarily because I wanted to focus on war narratives of the same language and thus preserve the unity of the project. Additionally, it would have been impossible to study a francophone corpus in length and simultaneously engage in a comparative approach to include texts of other languages.

This is not to say that the question of language of production is not an interesting one. On the contrary, it is a question that certainly deserves our attention. The language of writing has multiple ramifications. One can say that it is a personal choice that it is intimately tied to the author's upbringing, life and context. While this may be true, there is no denying, however, that the choice of language conveys a political meaning. Due to this political dimension, some francophone writers have been accused of favouring the language of the former coloniser over their native language; they were criticised for writing in French rather than Arabic. Some were accused of contributing to an orientalist Western agenda that seeks to portray the East as stagnant, barbaric and incapable of change. To respond to this harsh criticism, many writers have claimed French as their own language. For some francophone writers, French is no longer exclusive to Metropolitan France, but is today – and to borrow Kateb Yacine's famous expression – a 'butin de guerre' or the spoil of war appropriated by the postcolonial subjects to use freely and as their own (Kilanga-Musinde et al. 2010: 263).

Furthermore, the choice of the language of war narratives raises other issues related to the expression of trauma. Are there differences between trauma and war writings in French, English and Arabic? If so, what are these differences? As a first immediate difference, one can potentially advance the theory that war narratives could be more authentic when written in the writer's native language. Native language reflects indigenous expressions, emotions and dialectal nuances that may not be available in a non-native language. Following this argument, it is possible to argue that a war narrative written in Arabic can potentially be more reflective of the Lebanese society and possibly more genuine in its depiction of Lebanese expressions than a francophone or anglophone text. However, this is not the position of francophone writers who debunked this theory claiming that they feel comfortable expressing themselves and faithfully representing their societies in what others consider to be a foreign language.

It is interesting to note that translation studies attempted to reduce the gap between different languages especially with the new development in translation methods. Lawrence Venuti (2013) tracks the change that happened in the translation studies field from the 1990s where translation was mostly focused on linguistics. Foreign elements were either neglected or assimilated into the translated text. According to Venuti, this is no longer the case as the new approach considers the source text and its context. Therefore, translation no longer aims to assimilate the original text but rather to recognise its cross-cultural differences in an ethical way. Despite this new approach, the question regarding the limitation of languages and translation in representing war and trauma remains a valid one.

As I begin to examine the history of the Lebanese francophone novel, it is important to note that Lebanon has always had a special connection with the French language. In 1943, after two decades of mandate, France left Lebanon, but this parting did not change the relationship Lebanon has with the French language, nor did it erase the consequences of centuries-long contact with France. Today, the Lebanese francophone literary field is a well-established one.[3]

By Lebanese francophone literature, I mean the literature produced by

Lebanese writers of French expression. It is important to note that I acknowledge the debate that surrounds the terms francophone and francophonie (particularly regarding its colonial heritage).[4] However, I do not engage this discussion in the scope of this book. Furthermore, and as we will see below, the language of expression of the women writers examined in this book is not necessarily a topic of contention.[5]

Zahida Darwiche Jabbour (2007) traces the history of francophone literature in the Near East beginning with the early twentieth century. Between 1900 and 1920 Lebanese and Syrian writers used the French language to express their nationalism and attachment to their land.[6] Under the French Mandate and particularly the years between 1920 and 1946, the political environment changed, which led to two distinctions: one between Lebanese and Syrian writers, and another between Arabic and French writings. Under the Ottoman Empire, Lebanon was part of Greater Syria. On 1 September 1920, the State of Greater Lebanon was created under the French Mandate for Syria and Lebanon, which influenced literature and gave birth to Lebanese voices writing for an independent Lebanon. Some rejected the Arabic language as the exclusive language of Islam and others rejected the French language, seen as an expression of allegiance to the colonial powers and a rejection of the Arab identity.[7] Thus, depending on the writer, the French language became 'either a possible expression of hegemonic power or path toward liberation' (Touya De Marenne 2011: 6).[8]

Early in the twenties, the Lebanese novel of French expression saw a shy beginning with Farajallah Haïk's *Larmes et soupirs* (1927) and *Le Paradis de Satan* (1928). The success started however in the forties with Haïk's *Barjoute* (1940). According to Darwiche Jabbour, Haïk's writings occupied almost exclusively the literary scene for three decades.

After independence on 22 November 1943, Arabic became the official language in Lebanon, but French remained the language of education. Miriam cooke (1996) claims that the French language remained available in Lebanon due to the Christian pro-French majority as well as the lack of serious resistance and advocacy for the Arabic language.[9] As a result, Lebanon continued to have an easy affiliation with the language and people who spoke and wrote in it did so by choice. For cooke, these choices are either passive or active. By passive choice, she means 'as one that is made by another: for example, parents who send their sons and daughters to *lycées*, assuming that such an education is a surer provider of status' (cooke 1996: 142). By active choice, she means the choice made by the subject. As a result of these choices, by the time they graduated from high school, the Lebanese were fluent in two languages and comfortable in two cultures.

The sixties witnessed the rise of new Lebanese writers of French expression. Unlike their predecessors from the early twentieth century, they neither glorified France nor denied their Lebanese identity. Just like the Lebanese writers of Arabic expression, these writers addressed similar issues (particularly of identity) utilising the French language. They embraced their bilingualism and saw it as a source of wealth rather than conflict. Vénus Khoury-Ghata is one famous example of this acceptance of language hybridity. She says that she writes Arabic in French; she integrates the Arabic language in the French language: the form of the sentence is French, but the content is Arabic: '[m]es dialogues sont de l'arabe écrit en français. J'ai intégré la langue arabe dans la langue française: la forme de la phrase est française mais le contenu est arabe' (qtd in Darwiche Jabbour 2007: 89). More recently, Vénus Khoury-Ghata claimed, in defending French against the English invasion and distortion in text messaging, that French does not belong to the French people alone but to all those who write in it and enrich it by bringing in what their own languages have to offer. For her, the French language belongs to all the francophones who use the language in their work, who sweat and suffer with the language, who adopted its spirit, its fervours:

> La langue française, en effet, n'appartient pas aux seuls Français mais à tous ceux qui l'écrivent, l'enrichissent en lui offrant les apports de leur langue, la défendent contre l'anglais qui envahit tous les espaces; elle appartient aux francophones qui en ont fait leur outil de travail, ont sué et souffert avec elle, adopté son esprit, ses ferveurs . . . (Khoury-Ghata 2013: 59)

In the war period (1975–90), Lebanese francophone writing, particularly women's writing, bloomed. Some have argued that Lebanese women writers unanimously condemned the violence and the eruption of the war, called for the immediate restoration of peace, wrote against religious conservatism and patriarchal values, and called for more women's rights.

miriam cooke, who does not necessarily distinguish writers by their language of expression, calls these writers 'Beirut Decentrists', and defines them as a group of women writers who lived in Beirut and experienced the war:

> They are decentred in a double sense: physically, they were scattered all over a self-destructing city; intellectually, they moved in separate spheres. They wrote alone and for themselves. They would not conceive of their writings as related to those of others, yet their marginal perspective that gave insight into the holistic aspect of the war united them and allowed them discursively to undermine and restructure society around the image of a new center. (cooke 1987: 4)

For cooke, these middle-class, educated women, who wrote in different languages (Arabic, French and English), did not consciously form a unified group; they all wrote about the war and its impact on civilians, particularly on women. They also wrote on exile, Lebanese identity and responsibility in war. Their writings, according to cooke, redefined the canon of modern Middle Eastern literature (cooke 1987: 4). Additionally,

> [b]y the early 1980s, the Decentrists had discursively transformed the meaning of women's passive waiting in war-torn Lebanon into survival and resistance. With the memory of Algerian women's unacknowledged participation still vivid, they inscribed their activism into the war story. (Biddle et al. 1995: 417)

Darwiche Jabbour, who only focuses on Lebanese literature of French expression, argues that francophone women writers did not necessarily constitute a unified voice. Some like Vénus Khoury-Ghata, Evelyne Accad, Andrée Chedid and Dominique Eddé wrote from a humanist point of view to condemn the war while others like Etel Adnan, Lina Murr-Nehmé and Désirée Aziz, who are known for their political views, showed some bias in their writings. For example, Etel Adnan, known for her leftist pro-Palestinian position, defended the Palestinian presence in Lebanon and wrote against the armed activities of the Christian militias. On the other hand, Lina Murr-Nehmé and Désirée Aziz adopted a different position and wrote in defence of a Lebanese Christian identity.

Political affiliations clearly informed and influenced women's writings, but despite these differences, Darwich Jabbour argues, there is still a common core to these Lebanese francophone women's writings: most of the Lebanese women writers of French expression addressed the war and its consequences; most of them spoke of the internal segregation and sectarianism; most of them presented the readers with protagonists who are taken hostage by the war and are called to bear witness to trauma; most of them avoided explicitly naming those who are responsible for the war. Frequently, the war was portrayed as a background noise or as the consequence of an invisible force or as a shared Lebanese responsibility; most of them criticised the sectarian system and the patriarchal values; most of them referred to Beirut as the space of all actions; most of them addressed the complex issue of the Lebanese identity; finally, most of them called for a secular Arab identity that respects minorities' rights and freedom.

This common core also applies to the post-war periods (1990 until the present day) or the writings of what Felix Lang calls the second-generation authors. He distinguishes between two generations of authors (male/female of Arabic, French and English expressions). The first generation, he says, is the generation that experienced the war as adults and began publishing in the early 1980s. The second generation includes authors who grew up during the conflict and appeared on the literary scene from the late 1990s onward (Lang 2015: 4).

To adopt Lang's distinction, the Lebanese francophone women writers examined in this book are of first and second generation. While Andrée Chedid, Etel Adnan, Vénus Khoury-Ghata and Evelyne Accad are of first generation, Hyam Yared and Georgia Makhlouf belong to the second. It is also possible to say that they also share some commonalities. Aside from French as the language of expression, these Lebanese francophone women authors called for the cessation of violence and wrote to advocate for peace, to criticise the religious patriarchal system in place and to defend women's rights.

Arab and Lebanese Feminism

Chandra Talpade Mohanty argues that women are always assumed to be a category of analysis, which implies 'that all women, across classes and cultures, are somehow socially constituted as a homogeneous group identified prior to the process of analysis' (Talpade Mohanty 2003: 22). She adds that women are put together due to their 'sameness' and on the basis of their shared oppression, which in many ways not only eliminates their individualities but also undermines historical specificities proper to different groups; it also objectifies them:

> What is problematic about this kind of use of 'women' as a group, as a stable category of analysis, is that it assumes an ahistorical, universal unity between women based on a generalized notion of their subordination . . . Because women are thus constituted as a coherent group, sexual difference becomes coterminous with female subordination, and power is automatically defined in binary terms: people who have it (read: men) and people who do not (read: women). Men exploit, women are exploited. Such simplistic formulations are historically reductive; they are also ineffectual in designing strategies to combat oppressions. All they do is reinforce binary divisions between men and women. (Talpade Mohanty 2003: 31)

I start this section on the premise that Arab women do not constitute a homogenous group and there is not one history of Arab feminism. As a matter of fact, Arab feminism developed differently in each Arab country and in many ways it accompanied the rise of national consciousness. However, there are shared experiences across the borders, and my references to 'Arab women', 'Arab feminism' or 'Lebanese women' are not by any means intended to suggest a monolithic reading of these different entities.

They instead serve two purposes: on the one hand, they highlight the shared history in the Arab World, and on the other, they provide the opportunity for a brief examination of feminism in the Arab World with a focus on Lebanon.

Margot Badran and miriam cooke (1990) trace the history of feminism in the Arab World. The meaning of feminism appeared as early as 1909 when Malak Hifni Nasif (1886–1918) published under a pen name a book called *Al-Nisaiyat*. The term *al-nisaiyat* is an adjective that translates into 'by or about women'; it does not necessarily mean feminist. However, according to Badran and cooke, it carries the connotation, especially considering the book *Al-Nisaiyat* addressed issues relevant to women such as education, job opportunities and religious criticism (Badran and cooke 1990: xxv). The book's impact on men and women was immediate. In 1923, the Egyptian Feminist Union, who wrote primarily in French, used the term *nisai* as the equivalent of 'feminist'. As Badran and cooke mention, the distinction in French between 'feminine' and 'féministe' is clear. However, this distinction is not necessarily available in Arabic and the term for feminist in Arabic remains ambiguous even today. Michelle Hartman points out that indeed this issue remains unresolved and Arabic words like 'nisai' and 'unthawi' are often used to reflect the English meanings of feminine, feminist, female, and woman (Hartman 2002: 10).[10]

Regardless of the term used in Arabic, Arab women have had an apparent feminist agenda as early as the 1860s. The historical evolution of Arab feminism can be divided into three waves: the first period from the 1860s to the early 1920s where feminism evolved in private spaces;[11] the second period from the 1920s to the end of the 1960s, when the Arab World witnessed the public development of women's movements; and the third period from the 1970s to the present day with the emergence of feminist voices from Egypt, Lebanon, Syria and Iraq.

In the first period from the 1860s to the early 1920s, the Arab World, which includes North Africa, the Levant and the Arabian Peninsula, was under the Ottoman rule. After the First World War, the region was divided mostly between French and British colonial powers which impacted the Levant and North Africa differently. In the Levant or the Mashriq, there was a call for a secular form of governance with respect of minority rights. Arabic remained the main language of expression but French and English, which replaced Turkish, were spoken among the aristocracy and upper classes. In North Africa or the Maghreb, French and Italian replaced Arabic in government, in schools and in the streets. In many cases, the colonial laws were imposed to replace the local Islamic laws.

Girls' education varied depending on the country but overall, it began mid-nineteenth century (particularly in Egypt and Lebanon) with foreign missionaries. The upper classes used the services of European governesses to teach French and English, and male tutors to teach Arabic, Turkish and Persian. As Badran and cooke claim, girls' education forced a review of traditional patriarchal values particularly regarding the segregation of sexes and the veil (Badran and cooke 1990: xxxiv). In Lebanon, advocacy for girls' education can be found in 1847 writings of Butrus al-Bustāni (1819–83), one of the most influential male figures of the *Nahda* or the Arab renaissance. He was followed by other men writers such as Jurji Niqula Baz (1881–1959) who was labelled the 'Supporter of Women' for his work on women's biographies, and Amin al-Rihani (1876–1940). The only female voice recorded during this time was Madame Mansur Shakkur, who, in an 1874 article published in the journal *Al-Jinan*, calls for women to seek education and higher positions in society (Zeidan 1995: 24).

It is also possible to add the names of Zaynab Fawwaz (1860–1914), who wrote poetry and prose and advocated for the liberation of women, and of Julia Tomeh Dimishqiyyeh who defended women's rights. She was Christian but married a Muslim, which was revolutionary at that time. In 1921, she published her magazine *The New Woman*, which addressed various women's issues (Rustum Shehadeh 1999: 37–8).

Girls' education led to the rise of Arab feminism in a pre-colonial context, which was followed by the rise of Arab consciousness and nationalism. Arab women who first became aware of women's rights also became aware of their national rights. Women's unions and movements were born and became involved in nationalist feminist agendas. In 1914, they established *the Yaqzat al-Fatat al-Arabiyyah* or the Awakening of the Arab Girl, which was mostly a cultural movement but addressed national liberation from the Turks and foreign powers (Rustum Shehadeh 1999: 39). In 1919, women held the first conference at the Syrian Protestant College which is today the American University of Beirut. In 1924, *Al-Nahda al-Nisaiyyah fi Bayrut* or the Women's Renaissance in Beirut was created. It called for equality of the sexes. *Al-Ittihad al-Nisa'i fi Suriya wa Lubnan* or Women's Union in Syria and Lebanon was founded soon after. It was one of the most influential organisations until the 1950s (Rustum Shehadeh 1999: 39–40). In 1944, Arab women created the Arab Feminist Union (Rustum Shehadeh 1999: xxxv), and in the 1980s they created the Arab Women's Solidarity Association (AWSA) under the presidency of Nawal el-Saadawi (1931–2021) in Cairo.

In the literary context, no woman's work was published before the nineteenth century, but women orally transmitted stories; they were also considered to be the guardians of sacred texts. With education spreading, women benefited from the *Nahda* of the Mashriq. Literary salons were held,[12] and in 1914 Huda Shaarawi (1879–1947) founded the Intellectual Association of Egyptian Women. Early in the twentieth century, Arab women's writings started spreading even into male spaces (such as the famous exchange between the Lebanese writers May Ziyada 1886–1941 and Gibran Khalil Gibran 1883–1931). However, overall, male writers and readers ignored women's texts. It is only in the 1960s and 1970s that Arab women writers reached a wider audience. In Lebanon in 1958, Laila Baalbaki published the novel *I Live Ana Ahya*, which was an autobiographical narrative against traditional practices.[13] She was followed by fellow Lebanese writers like Andrée Chedid (1920–2011), Emily Nasrallah (1931–2018) and Nadia Tuéni (1935–83), who wrote about their lives and personal spaces. The 1970s and 1980s saw the birth of bold Arab women writings, such as Nawal el-Saadawi's fiction, which openly criticised male oppression, patriarchal values and some religious traditions. The 1980s and 1990s were marked by multiple conflicts in the region, including and not limited to the Israeli–Palestinian conflict, the Lebanese civil war and the Algerian civil war, the collapse of the Soviet Union, the Cold War and the first Gulf War . . . Arab women writers, such as Assia Djebar (1936–2015), Hanan al-Shaykh (b. 1945) and Hoda Barakat (b. 1952), addressed these issues in different ways and different languages.

Some have argued that since the 1950s Arab feminism has not evolved. In some cases, it has retreated into the private space; in others, it was limited to advocating for better working conditions for the traditional roles of educators or care givers (see Rustum Shehadeh 1999: 40). However, with the Arab Spring, Arab feminism was rejuvenated as women not only were very visible in the public sphere and participated in the revolution but also made their demands heard.[14] The Arab Spring did not take place in Lebanon but in some neighbouring countries. Nevertheless, Lebanon was impacted by it and Lebanese feminism continues to make headway as a result. In 2011–12, feminist groups in Lebanon organised campaigns against sexual harassment and racism against migrant domestic workers. In summer 2015, Lebanon faced an unprecedented garbage crisis. Due to corruption and short-term planning, the government mishandled public funds allocated to waste management which led garbage to pile up in the streets. Environmental activists started the You Stink movement and were joined by feminist activists. Both groups opposed political corruption, capitalism, sectarianism and the government's complete disregard for people's lives. Alliances were formed as activists recognised that sectarianism and patriarchy combined with racism violently threaten the environment, women's rights and nonconforming marginalised sexual identities. A 'Feminist Bloc' was formed and it included feminist groups like Sawt al Niswa (Voice of Women), and feminist student clubs from different public and private university campuses. They were joined by anti-racism movements and leftist groups (Kaedbey and Naber 2019: 459). In the Lebanese October Revolution of 2019, Lebanese women were on the front line of the protests. The revolution started when the government suggested adding a $6 tax on free internet services and applications like WhatsApp. Protests erupted and Lebanese women largely participated to demand the end of corruption, sectarianism, toxic masculinity and patriarchy.

It is important to point out that Badran and cooke (1990) adopt a general definition of feminism as the voice and activism of Arab women from the late 1800s. It includes one or more elements of the following: 'awareness by women that as women they are systematically placed in disadvantaged position; some form of rejection of enforced behaviours and thought; and attempts to interpret their own experiences and then to improve their position or lives as women' (Badran and cooke 1990: xxvi–xxvii). Badran and cooke add that it is important to distinguish between different forms of feminism in the Arab World: feminism of women and feminism of men, Muslim feminism, Arab feminism and Western feminism.[15] For the feminism advocated by men, some pinpoint its origin with the publication in 1899 of the book *The Liberation of the Woman* by the Egyptian male lawyer Qasim Amin (1863–1908).[16] According to Badran and cooke, male-driven feminism was influenced by colonial powers where women in general were much more present in the public eye. As for women's feminism, it started initially within the upper-class community and expanded downwards. Muslim feminism was born from women's advocacy against some practices and traditions they considered unfair and non-Islamic. They called for an abandonment of these practices and for a return to religious texts.

For Joseph T. Zeidan, in the context of Lebanon, we should distinguish between feminism of the Christian communities and feminism of the Muslim communities. Zeidan argues that '[C]hristian women did not have to struggle against the veil or total sexual segregation except in extreme cases, although they faced many other obstacles characteristic of the patriarchal society in which they also found themselves' (Zeidan 1995: 25).

For Badran and cooke, Arab feminism has always been and continues to be misunderstood. Some men and women have interpreted feminism as a purely Western construct that aims to destroy the fabric of the Arab society and to promote anti-Islamic values. Some consider it an imported elitist concept that is disconnected from the majority's needs. Others have criticised the movement of Muslim feminism and argued that Islam and feminism are an oxymoron by nature (Badran and cooke 1990: xliv).

Clearly, there is not one definition of feminism; feminism is a plurality. In this book, and just like Badran and cooke, I employ a general definition of feminism as the expression of women's resistance against men's oppression, activism and advocacy for women's rights. I hesitate to call the women writers addressed in this book feminist. Although they produce a feminist discourse, they do not necessarily claim to be feminist.

The Civil War in Lebanon: History and War Memories

In the years that followed Lebanon's independence in 1943, the country flourished. It was compared to Europe and referred to as both the Paris and the Switzerland of the Middle East. However, the events in the region, particularly the Arab–Israeli conflict and the influx of Palestinian refugees to Lebanon in 1948 and 1967, took their toll on Lebanon. They polarised public opinion between those who supported the Palestinian refugees, and those who wanted Lebanon to remain impartial to the neighbouring conflicts. Many feared the growing presence of armed Palestinians in Lebanon and started arming themselves. They also feared the rise of conservative Islam and saw pan-Arabism as a threat to Lebanon's independence and religious minorities. Others were sympathetic with the Palestinian armed presence in Lebanon and saw in the Palestinian cause a fair fight against imperialism and neo-colonialism. Eventually, and as cooke puts it, hatred, anger and fear exploded and penetrated every aspect of Lebanese lives. The war was economic because 'of the rapidly growing belt of [Palestinian] refugees from the Israeli-threatened South'; it was religious because of the vast dissatisfaction of the various religious communities with their political representation; it was political as it was a power struggle between the left and the right, the far left and the far right; it was internal as it divided Lebanese against each other, but it was also international as it engaged multiple non-Lebanese agents such as the Palestinians, the Syrians, the Israelis, the Americans, the Iranians . . . (cooke 1987: 4). For Rustum Shehadeh, 'there was never "a Lebanese conflict", but a complex variegation of conflicts. The Lebanese did not go to war to change their political system; they joined a war fought on their land by the Arab states, Israel, and the superpowers to defend certain policies and ideologies' (Rustum Shehadeh 1999: 11).

Palestinian refugees became politically and militarily organised in Lebanon. Before 1975, there were multiple confrontations between the Palestinian Liberation Organization (PLO) and the Lebanese Army. In fact, the Palestinian refugee camps had gradually been transformed into territories of armed militia to the point that they created a state within a state. It has been estimated that they had over 20,000 fighters. They ignored the warnings of the Lebanese authorities and continued their armed strikes against Lebanese civilians and Israel from Lebanese soil which eventually led to the Israeli invasion of Lebanon in 1982 (Rustum Shehadeh 1999: 16).

On 13 April 1975, members of the Democratic Front for the Liberation of Palestine fired on right-wing Christian members as they were leaving church in Ain-al-Rummaneh (a suburb of Beirut). The right-wing Christian militia retaliated, fired on a bus heading to a refugee camp and killed twenty-nine passengers. Soon after, violence broke in different parts of the country.

According to the International Center for Transitional Justice in its report 'Failing to Deal with the Past. What Cost to Lebanon?' published in January 2014:

> [I]t is estimated that some 2.7 percent of the population was killed as a result of violence, 4 percent wounded (the overwhelming majority being civilians), 30 percent displaced, and about 33 percent have emigrated. Further, 0.36 percent of the population was permanently disabled, and 0.75 percent forcibly disappeared. Serious human rights violations have included systematic and mass displacement, wide-scale killing, rape, torture, arbitrary detention, and enforced disappearance. (ICTJ 2014: 1)

Despite the war, many Lebanese demonstrated the desire for peace and unity. When the news of the bus incident broke in 1975, many Lebanese from different religious backgrounds opposed the quick rise of violence. The Lebanese Council of Women met with the prime minister and made a public appeal for an immediate cessation of violence. They organised meetings in various parts of Lebanon to raise awareness about the war (Rustum Shehadeh 1999: 26). During the Israeli siege of Beirut in 1982, many Lebanese from West Beirut (which is predominantly Muslim) found shelter in East Beirut (predominantly Christian), and a spontaneous sit-in was held at the American University of Beirut against the siege; it lasted twenty-three days. Different women's organisations formed and called for peace, security and stability. In May 1984, Imane Khalifeh, a member of the Institute for Women's Studies in the Arab World, organised a march for peace in Beirut, precisely at the National Museum which was the frontier between East-West Beirut. The march was to unite the Lebanese and rally them against the war. The march was cancelled due to intensive shelling. Forty years later, Offre-Joie, an apolitical and non-confessional non-governmental Lebanese agency organised a march at the same place under the slogans 'Yakfi' or 'Bikaffi', which translates from Arabic into 'Enough' (Boustani 2016: 255–6).

Lebanese women's movements were not limited to national soil. Some were international like Suad Salloum's three-day sit-in in November 1984 at the United Nations Headquarters in New York. It is important to acknowledge, however, that not all women's movements called for peace and unity. Some supported the Palestinian cause and called women to continue to resist against the Israeli occupation. Some glorified martyrdom in the name of the religion, and some carried suicide missions (Rustum Shehadeh 1999: 27). According to Rustum Shehadeh, '[t]here were those who confronted the war by becoming actively involved either in politics and dissemination of ideology or actually carrying guns and joining the fighting themselves' (Rustum Shehadeh 1999: 5).[17]

The war lasted fifteen years (1975–90). It ended with the signing of the Taif Agreement in 1989, which is a national accord document that redistributed political powers between different religious communities. It was also followed by the General Amnesty Law passed by the Parliament on 26 August 1991. The law 'which pardoned all political crimes committed prior to March 28, 1991 . . . undermined accountability for past grave violations' (ICTJ 2014: 9–10). According to the International Center for Transitional Justice in its report on Lebanon, '[t]he amnesty protected perpetrators of egregious violations of inalienable and non-derogable human rights and established discriminatory and unequal legal protection based on status – as violations against "ordinary" citizens could not be prosecuted' (ICTJ 2014: 10).

Today there are no national agreements on the facts of the war. Events are still disputed and narrated differently depending on who one is talking to. The Lebanese authorities have not done much to investigate what happened. A few measures of reparations such as compensation and rehabilitation have been implemented but they are far from being on a national scale. No formal apology, expression of guilt or acknowledgement of responsibility has been voiced. As a result, Lebanon does not have an accurate number but only an estimate of the dead, missing, displaced, injured and handicapped (ICTJ 2014: 15). Only recently, in 2018, Lebanon's Parliament passed a bill to address the issue of the missing and disappeared. According to Lynn Maalouf, Amnesty International's Middle East Research Director:

> This law, which was initially presented by civil society organizations following two years of consultations, is a major step towards the creation of a national commission. With a mandate to investigate individual cases, locate and exhume mass graves and enable a tracing process which will finally provide closure to the families. This would be the first time Lebanon acknowledges and addresses in a meaningful manner one of the most painful legacies of the conflict, which affected all communities across the country. Appointing appropriately qualified members of the national commission should be the immediate next step. (Amnesty International 2018)

With the relentless work of non-governmental agencies and activists, some facts about the war are slowly emerging, such as the discovery of mass graves (Waddell 2019), the documenting of rape cases during the war (Hayek 2019) and the unveiling of child trafficking from Lebanon to Europe and the United States (El-Hage 2019). However, despite these efforts, Lebanon continues to struggle with the memory of the war. Between the state-sponsored amnesia, the continuous disagreement on a unified historical narrative, the trauma and the pain of remembrance, and the fear of returning to war, little has been written or officially recognised. As Sune Haugbolle argues, memory is a taboo in Lebanese society, especially since '[t]hose responsible for the war – for massacres, theft, war crimes, and displacement of civilians

– became responsible for rebuilding the country. Naturally, these people have had no great desire to shed further light on the past' (Haugbolle 2005: 192).

T. G. Ashplant et al. (2000) study the formation of collective war memories. They argue that war memories can be constructed from the top to the bottom of society where the nation state imposes a specific national narrative using a pre-existing repertoire which would allow it to reimagine a war narrative that ensures its hegemony and silences sectional narratives. This scenario is particularly true in the case of civil war where sectional discourses are suppressed in the name of national commemorative narrative. Also, war memories are formed from the bottom up. Civil society plays a role in creating the war narrative. Oral history, individual stories and some cultural practices of mourning all contribute into the formation of collective war memories. In fact, war memories always start with individuals like veterans or civilians, and they transition from the personal/private to the public with a large influence from the local pre-existing culture. Collective war memories are therefore not necessarily (or should not be exclusively) the property of the nation state but 'the product of individuals and social groups who come together, not at the behest of the state or any of its subsidiary organizations, but because they have to speak out' (qtd in Ashplant et al. 2000: 9).

Some individual memories become public, which means they benefit from an official national consensus and circulate in the public domain. Some memories never make the transition: they are either suppressed by the state or are never shared out of fear or shame. Some memories are only remembered in private, which creates a disconnect with the collective war memories:

> The weaker and more marginalized have less access to the agencies of either state or civil societies, and less capacity to influence prevailing narratives or project their own narratives into wider arenas. This is apparent in relation to both race . . . and class. Such differential access to power is also very marked as regards gender. In the context of national imaginaries, dominant memory is often centered around the idealized figure of the masculine soldier. This may have the effect that the meanings and memories of others who have sacrificed and suffered – above all women – are relegated to the margins. (Ashplant et al. 2000: 21)

In addition to how it is generated, collective war memory can influence history, history as a 'non-psychological past that is defined and determined by the systematic research of academic historians' and as the 'reevaluation of the past, particularly in its written form – narrative and reinterpretable' (Hunt 2010: 97–8). For Maurice Halbwachs, history is an objective discourse, as opposed to collective memory which is always subjective. It is subjective because it begins with the individual and is socially constructed: '[w]hile the collective memory endures and draws strength from its base in a coherent body of people, it is individual as group members who remember' (Halbwachs 1992: 48). Pierre Nora states that memory and history are 'far from being synonymous, [they] appear now to be in fundamental opposition' (Nora 1989: 8). Memory is the living past as opposed to history which is the attempt to reconstruct the past (Hunt 2010: 101).

> Memory is a perpetually actual phenomenon, a bond tying us to the eternal present; history is a representation of the past. Memory, insofar as it is affective and magical, only accommodates those facts that suit it; it nourishes recollections that may be out of focus or telescopic, global or detached, particular or symbolic – responsive to each avenue of conveyance or phenomenal screen, to every censorship or projection. History, because it is an intellectual and secular production, calls for analysis and criticism. (Nora 1989: 8–9)

> History is perpetually suspicious of memory, and its true mission is to suppress and destroy it. At the horizon of historical societies, at the limits of the completely historicized world, there would occur a permanent secularization. History's goal and ambition it not to exalt but to annihilate what has in reality taken place. A generalized critical history would no doubt preserve some museums, some medallions and monuments – that is to say the materials necessary for its work – but it would empty them of what, to us, would make them *lieux de mémoire*. (Nora 1989: 9)

In Lebanon's history, particularly the period of the civil war, there are no collective war memories but rather competing sectional memories. They are sectional as they belong to different religious and political groups; they are competing to transition into the public sphere and to dominate the public discourse. Some collective war memories are shared; this is true in the case of many civilians. However, these memories (of stories about shelters, water and electricity outages, lack of access to healthcare, etc.) remain mostly private. Also, because they are a shared experience, they are dismissed by most Lebanese, who consider them trivial. They are often accompanied by the attitude 'Everybody lived the war, so what?' Furthermore, some of these private memories were not shared because they dealt with issues like sexual trauma. Many accounts of rape have never been shared nor recorded, deemed too painful and shameful to become public. Additionally, a lot of Lebanese tend to falsely believe that the militias had a code of honour that respected women and children and kept the war between men. Consequently, most Lebanese are either surprised by the topic or deny that it even took place during the civil war.

Regarding sectional memories, they are apparent in current political practices: from the renaming of boulevards, avenues and streets after deceased fighters (particularly Hezbollah), to the renaming of the international airport of Beirut after the assassinated Prime Minister Rafik Hariri, to the addition of national holidays to commemorate 'martyrs' of certain political groups, to the creation of war museums like the Hezbollah Museum of Resistance or the Independence Museum (sponsored by the Kataeb Party). All these practices lead to the erosion of collective war memories which potentially could give birth to a national identity; they also obstruct history as an objective discourse. To give an example, Lebanon celebrated Martyrs' Day, which commemorated the execution of Syrian and Lebanese nationalists in Damascus and Beirut on 6 May 1916 by Jamal Pasha, the Ottoman ruler of Greater Syria. They were killed in what is today known as Martyrs' Square in Beirut, and their sacrifice led in many ways to the independence of Lebanon. This national day that had the potential to unify all Lebanese has been replaced by Liberation Day, which marks the withdrawal of the Israeli armies from Southern Lebanon on 25 May 2000. This day has its own value for it is the day when Lebanon became whole again. However, it is problematic and politised because it was pushed for by Hezbollah, which seeks to glorify and amplify its own war memories in the public eye.

Additionally, and as mentioned before, Lebanon does not have a written history as an objective narrative of the war. History books stop at 1975 and the curriculum in both public and private schools does not address the civil war (Blaik Hourani 2017: 256). New generations are raised having vaguely heard about the war without knowing its facts. As such, they cannot draw lessons from what happened and continue to support warlords and corrupt political parties. Aside from the welcome efforts of the Center of Lebanese Studies at the Lebanese American University and the Moise A. Khayrallah Center for Lebanese Diaspora Studies at the North Carolina State University, Lebanese universities do not necessarily provide 'Lebanese Studies' or 'war memories studies' an appropriate space in their curriculums, which means that the Lebanese civil war continues to be ignored even within an academic setting. As a result, each Lebanese political and religious group has its own ghosts to mourn. These ghosts are never seen as part of a unifying national sacrifice but rather as the price of belonging to the group in question.

Michael Rothberg asks whether collective memory functions as a real-estate development, according to which space becomes scarce. He says: '[m] any people assume that the public sphere in which collective memories are articulated is a scarce resource and that the interaction of different collective memories within that sphere takes the form of a zero-sum struggle for preeminence' (Rothberg 2009: 3). Against this framework, Rothberg advances the theory that collective memory is not competitive but rather multidirectional: 'as subject to ongoing negotiation, cross-referencing, and borrowing; as productive and not privative' (Rothberg 2009: 3). While I agree with Rothberg that different memories of war can negotiate meanings and inform each other, I stand with the idea that in the case of Lebanon sectional war memories are competing against each other as, in many cases, they seek to annihilate each other and to dominate the public sphere and the state discourse. This attitude of all or nothing leaves no room for negotiation. If a memory borrows meaning or content from a competing other, it is simply to completely deny it or destroy it.

Finally, one can say that it is against the competition of sectional war memories and in the name of a unified national narrative that Lebanese francophone women authors wrote. They wrote to combat the state-sponsored amnesia and amnesty, the bullying of sectional war memories, the hegemonic control of war narrative by a small group and the attempt to drown civilians' shared war memories. They wrote to bear witness to what happened in

Lebanon during the civil war and in the years that followed, to raise the awareness of the young generation of the dangers of wars and to, in many ways, fill the rapidly growing void created by history books. Literature became, therefore, the space where the real is represented and remembered.[18] Lebanese francophone women authors mostly wrote fictional war stories that would help Lebanese society remember its own past. For '[w]ithout memory we do not exist. Where there is no remembered past there is no present, because the present cannot be interpreted without knowledge of the past' (Hunt 2010: 100).

Structure and Chapter Summaries

This book contains a general introduction, four chapters and a conclusion; its scope is multigenerational as it examines the works of six Lebanese women writing in French during different times.

Chapter 1: The Feminine 'I'

I purposely title this chapter the feminine 'I' and not the feminist 'I'. As mentioned earlier, many of these women authors wrote from a feminist point of view but did not necessarily claim to be feminist. As such, I hesitate to label the narrators as feminist. Instead, I chose the word feminine to emphasise the appropriation of a traditionally assigned male space by a female voice. This clearly does not exclude a feminist agenda.

In this chapter, I examine two novels, *Les Absents* (2014) by Georgia Makhlouf and *Sitt Marie Rose* (1977) by Etel Adnan, where I discuss the narrative voice and the way by which the female narrator bears witness to trauma. In the Arab World, social norms and religious traditions dictate prudery for both genders but more so for women. Women's bodies and voices are traditionally assigned to the private domain, and for a long time it was shameful for a woman to speak up in public spaces. Assia Djebar speaks of the *hochma* or the shame of speaking up using the first-person subject. Women who said 'I' were considered witches, impure, immodest, obscene and public (Djebar 1999: 106). Badran and cooke state that '[w]omen's voices were even considered by some to be *awra* (something shameful) to be hidden [such as private body parts]' (Badran and cooke 1990: xxx). This attitude towards women claiming their voices and speaking up using the first-person subject explains why the Layla Baalbaki's 1958 novel *Ana Ahya* (*I Live*) was so revolutionary for its time. The feminine 'I' that appropriates the voice goes against the mainstream and destroys the patriarchal representation of women.

Les Absents and *Sitt Marie Rose* place the feminine voice in front and centre of the novels. Reading these novels from the angles of trauma studies, postcolonial and feminist narratologies, I examine the intersection between trauma, gender and postcolonialism, go against classical narratology and argue that the feminine 'I' is not placed there innocently or randomly but rather serves multiple purposes. In addition to giving a voice to a woman narrator in a violent male space, it allows women narrators to bear witness to the war, to tell their stories and the stories of others, to render justice to the victims, to fight against the state-sponsored amnesia and to write history. In *Les Absents*, the unnamed narrator shares her trauma with the reader, opens her phone book and tells us about the people in her life. Many disappeared because of the war in Lebanon, but also because of her exile to France. Trauma, in its amnesiac, collective and unspeakable characteristics, becomes the language by which the feminine 'I' bears witness to her own trauma but also to the trauma of others. Trauma thus creates a testimonial space for the narrator, who at times falls silent or cannot remember the details of what happened. Silence, in addition to repetition, become meaningful spaces where the narrator speaks and where trauma expresses itself.

The novel of *Sitt Marie Rose* is divided into two sections. In the first section, the female narrator tells us about the pre-war period in Lebanon, which was marked with the rise of toxic violent masculinity as a result of the colonial education. When the war erupts, the feminine 'I', who is a film maker, finds herself confined to the private space and limited in her reporting duties. In the second section, the unnamed female narrator shares the narrative scenes with different narrative voices including the voice of Marie Rose and the militia men. They all speak using the first-person subject. Marie Rose, just like the unnamed female narrator, attempts to speak up to rectify history in the minds of colonialist militiamen. She transgresses the boundaries set by patriarchal religious traditions and intrudes on the male space to express herself. She pays the price of her transgressions and dies. Both her and the unnamed female narrator fail in their missions as historians.

Chapter 2: The Humanist Voice of the Omniscient Narrator

In Chapter 2, I continue to examine the narrative voice from a post-classical narratology point of view and argue that the omniscient narrator available in Andrée Chedid's *La Maisan sans racines* (1985) and *Le Message* (2000), and Evelyne Accad's *Coquelicot du massacre* (1988), allows a humanist reading of the war novels in question as it stands at equal distance from all protagonists and shows multiple perspectives including the ones of the fighters.

I acknowledge that the notion of omniscient narrator has been problematic and has raised many questions. After a lengthy examination of the definition (Roland Barthes, Gérard Genette and others) and a comparison of the technical benefits between omniscient narration and first-person narration, I argue that the omniscient narrator is a postmodern bold voice that speaks with authority about the complexity of Lebanon; it is a 'licensed trespasser' (to use Eugene Goodheart's (2004) comparison borrowed from the narrator of George Eliot's *Adam Bede*) that provides a sense of unity to a very divided world.

La Maison sans racines is the story of a reunion on ancestral land between a grandmother (Kalya) and her granddaughter (Sybil). While Kalya is retrieving her childhood memories, Sybil is visiting for the first time, but the war erupts and ends their joyous visit. The narrative alternates between the peaceful past and the violent present, between Kalya's memories of her own grandmother and Sybil's experiences in Lebanon. The narrative structure is intricate. Divided into three periods of time, July–August of 1932, July–August of 1975, and one morning in August 1975, the novel allows the development of three different stories located in different times and spaces. The first story is situated one morning in August 1975 where Kalya witnesses the shooting of two young women who organised a march for peace. The second story takes place in 1932 and focuses on Kalya's childhood in Lebanon. The third story takes place between July and August 1975, and shows the family's arrival in Lebanon and the events that led to the outbreak of the civil war. It is interesting to note that Kalya's childhood stories from 1932 are told by a first-person narrator or the feminine 'I', and the two other stories from 1975 are told by an omniscient narrator.

Inspired by the Bosnian war, *Le Message* tells the story of Marie and her lover Steph. The time and the place are never mentioned, and the war suddenly becomes universal; the events could be happening in any country at any time. The narrative is told by an omniscient narrator (with some interruptions told in free-indirect speech style that could possibly be attributed to the writer).

Coquelicot du massacre by Evelyne Accad focuses on the lives of three women during the civil war in Lebanon: Nour, Hayat and Najmé. Nour and her son Raja are crossing Beirut looking for a safe haven; Hayat is a poet and a university professor who is in love with a Muslim man named Adnan; Najmé is a young college student who is addicted to drugs. Structurally, the narrative and story-time are fragmented and cycle between the three stories. All stories are told by an omniscient narrator with a few exceptions narrated by the feminine 'I' which appears abruptly in Hayat's poems and Najmé's writings.

In addition to the traditional technical benefits of omniscient narrative, I argue that in the case of war stories, the omniscient narrator roams freely between the protagonists and provides a humanist reading of the events. Additionally, in a cacophonic world where people are not listening to each other, the omniscient narrator acts as an amplified voice that on the one hand highlights the disappearance of the feminine 'I' or the impossibility for the individual (particularly women) to speak up and on the other hand hijacks the voice to silence the canons and to talk of peace and love.

Chapter 3: The Evil, Sick and Disabled Female Body

Chapter 3 marks a shift in my analysis as I focus on the female body. I argue that the female body, just like the voice, contributes to the construction of war narratives. Referencing the works of Simone de Beauvoir, Michel Foucault, Julia Kristeva, Susan Bordo, Susan Brownmiller, Edward Said, Frantz Fanon, Mary Douglas, among others, I examine Vénus Khoury-Ghata's *La Maîtresse du Notable* (1992) and Hyam Yared's *La Malédiction* (2012).

La Maîtresse du Notable tells the story of Flora, a Polish woman, living in an unnamed war-torn city. Married to a Christian man, she has three children, one of whom is the narrator. Flora lives at the borders between the Muslim and the Christian sectors and has many neighbours. When she is pregnant with her third child, Flora sees her ex-lover the Muslim Notable out of her window. Shortly after, she gives birth and leaves with him. The fragile peace between the sectors is broken and violence erupts again. Flora, who is a silent protagonist, is considered the source of all the city's ailments. Her body is the source of the war: it is the white body that scares the natives; it is the generative body that produces hybrid monsters and it is the Western body that settles in the East.

La Malédiction (2012) is about an abusive mother–daughter relationship. It tells the story of Hala, a teenager growing up during the civil war in Lebanon. Hala attends a strict Catholic school and has a controlling mother. For comfort, Hala overeats and engages in a lesbian relationship with her schoolmate Fadia. When she turns eighteen, Hala is pushed into marriage and has two daughters. Her husband, equally controlled by his mother, dies from the fictional disease of erosion. Hala's mother-in-law sues her over the custody of the girls. She considers Hala unfit to be a mother. Hala returns to her overeating habits. The more oppressed she is, the more she eats and vomits. Aware that she is going to lose her daughters, she kills them and commits suicide. Throughout her life, Hala struggles with her femininity and tries hard to conform to social norms. Her body, which functions as a metaphor of Lebanon, is at war with itself: it attempts to find consoling solutions, only these solutions are self-destructive. They rendered her ill to the point of disability and death.

Chapter 4: The Magical Body and the Grotesque Body

I continue with the examination of the representation of the female body as a mechanism through which the war story is told, and I focus on the grotesque female body in Hyam Yared and Vénus Khoury-Ghata's writings. According to Mary Russo (1994), the grotesque female body, which is always in excess, manifests itself under two forms: the uncanny and the carnivalesque. Following Russo's distinctions, I examine magical realism as it appears in Hyam Yared's *L'Armoire des ombres* (2006) and grotesque realism or the carnivalesque in Vénus Khoury-Gahta's *Vacarme pour une lune morte* (1983) and *Les Morts n'ont pas d'ombre* (1984).

Regarding magical realism, I study the history of the genre and its definition according to the works of Tzvetan Todorov, Wendy Faris and others. I argue that the postmodern genre of magical realism allows the writer to represent the war from the alternative space of magic, a space traditionally dedicated to the post-colonial marginalised voices who wish to speak against mainstream imperialistic powers.

Hyam Yared's *L'Armoire des ombres* tells a story of a divorced woman who, desperate to pay her rent, auditions for the leading role in a play. Encouraged by her best friend Yolla, she goes to the theatre and is asked to leave her shadow behind. Stunned by this unusual request, she eventually does and moves onto the stage. Not given a scenario, the unnamed narrator must improvise. She finds a wardrobe that is full of shadows; she puts them on one by one and plays their roles. They are all the roles of abused women. She plays Greta the prostitute, Léna the lesbian bartender and Mona the battered wife. Eventually, the reader comes to realise that she is all these women and that she is telling their war and post-war stories.

As for grotesque realism, I review Mikhail Bakhtin's works, particularly his study of François Rabelais's *Gargantua and Pantagruel* and identify the elements of grotesque realism as they appear in Vénus Khoury-Ghata's *Vacarme pour une lune morte* and its sequel *Les Morts n'ont pas d'ombre*. These novels put forward the carnivalesque upside-down world of Nabilie (which is Liban/Lebanon spelled backwards), where logical rules that govern space, time, life and death are suspended. They tell the story of the Alpha family, their numerous neighbours, friends and enemies and the ongoing illogical war between these different parties. I argue that Vénus Khoury-Ghata, just like Rabelais, creates this vulgar upside-down universe to represent the madness happening in violent Lebanon. She creates her own rules of time, space and values to reflect the chaotic world of war, a world that cannot be understood with reason nor logic.

Notes

1 For a criticism of Phelan's definition of narrative, see Nielsen 2010.
2 The groups are: (1) The contextualist, thematic and ideological approaches such as feminist narratology and post-colonial narratology; (2) The transgeneric and transmedial applications and elaborations of narratology, which include narratology and genre theory, drama, poetry and film studies, among others; (3) Pragmatic and rhetorical kinds of narratology such as ethics and narratology; (4) Cognitive and reception-theory-oriented, kinds of meta-narratology such as psychoanalytic narrative theory; (5) Postmodern and poststructuralist deconstructions of

(classical) narratology; (6) Linguistic approaches/contributions to narratology; (7) Philosophical narrative theories; (8) Other interdisciplinary narrative theories such as artificial intelligence, anthropology, oral history, etc.

3   It is interesting to note that while the field itself is recognised, and while Lebanon recognises major Lebanese francophone writers like Amin Maalouf, Alexandre Najjar, Vénus Khoury-Ghata, Andrée Chedid and others, the study of Lebanese francophone literature remains slim in Lebanese public and private universities. In a recent study published in 2013, Carla Sarhan shows how Lebanese universities still tend to focus heavily on French literature. Francophone literature has been allocated a small limited space so far due to many factors including the lack of specialists, but also a colonialist approach to education and literature (Sarhan 2013: 161–84).

4   The word 'Francophonie' made its first appearance in the 1880s. It was coined by the geographer Onésime Reclus, who used it to refer to France's colonial empire. The term remains problematic today. While some scholars and writers see it only as synonymous to 'of French expression', others argue that it has a colonial connotation. On 15 March 2007, the French newspaper *Le Monde* published a manifesto *Pour une littérature-monde en français* written by Michel Le Bris, Jean Rouaud and Alain Mabanckou and signed by forty-four writers; it argues against the distinction between French and francophone writers, and defends the creation of a world literature in French. Despite the problematic aspect of the term 'Francophonie', the term continues to be used and the field of Francophone Studies, which is a well-established field, especially in North American institutions, has not been renamed. For more information on Francophone Literature, see: Le Bris et al. 2007; Moura 2007; Bruyère 2012; Migraine-George 2013; Clavaron 2018.

5   For more on the relationship between Lebanese women authors and the French language, see Hartman 2014.

6   According to Sélim Abou, the French language allowed for national sentiments to be expressed in the most direct way. French became the main weapon of resistance for the liberation of the Arab Near-East: '[c]'est dans la langue française que le sentiment national allait trouver son expression la plus directe. C'est la la langue française qui, vers la fin du XIXe siècle, devient, sous la plume d'écrivains libanais, l'arme principale de lutte pour la libération du Proche-Orient arabe' (Abou 1962: 433).

7   According to Darwiche Jabbour, a quick reading of the journal *La Revue phénicienne* founded in 1919 immediately reveals this distinction between Syrian

Lebanese writers and this irrational fear of Arabic-Islamic hegemony. The reading of the poetry produced by the movement called 'Libanisme Phénicien' and founded by Charles Corm reveals the rejection of Greater Syria, the declaration of allegiance to France and the French language and the open hostility towards Arabic (Darwiche Jabbour 2007: 86–7).

8   This is, for instance, true in Algeria where the French language is much more problematic. See writings by Assia Djebar or Leila Sebbar.

9   miriam cooke acknowledges that some writers criticised the preference of French and English languages over Arabic. One of these writers was Layla Baalbaki who protested this bourgeois choice of the colonial language (cooke 1996: 142).

10 Hartman adds that the appropriate term for feminism in the Arab World as well as the applicability of Western feminism in the Arab World have been greatly discussed by important Arab writers and critics such as Nasr Hamid Abu Zayd, Emily Nasrallah, Mumammad Banis, Hisham Sharabi, Mai Ghoussoub and Khalida Said. Their works were featured in the special issue on the Arab woman in the journal *Mawaqif* (Hartman 2002: 10).

11 Badran makes the distinction between visible and invisible feminisms. Invisible feminism started in the private spaces of mostly upper-class women (particularly in Egypt in the 1920s) and allowed for feminism to grow without being perceived as threat to the public space. It became more visible in the 1950s and the 1970s and as such became the subject of male suppression (qtd in Badran and cooke 1990: xxvi). See Badran 1993: 129–48.

12 Badran and cooke give the example of Eugenie Le Brun Rushdi. She was a French woman who married an upper-class Muslim Egyptian and converted to Islam. She held literary salons for women to meet (Badran and cooke 1990: xxxviii). Rustum Shehadeh gives the example of Fatmeh al-Rifai who held a famous literary salon known as the Rifai Symposium in 1927 (Rustum Shehadeh 1999: 38).

13 For more information on Layla Baalbaki, see Accad 1993: 224–53.

14 For more information on Arab feminism and the Arab Spring, see cooke 2016: 31–44.

15 For a general introduction and overview of feminism (Western and across the world), see Walters 2005. For a criticism of Western feminism for its relationship with 'Third World Feminism', see Talpade Mohanty 2003: 17–24.

16 Badran and cooke provide other examples of men's pro-feminist writings. In addition to Amin's *The Liberation of the Woman*, they mention the Egyptian Murqus Fahmi's *Woman of the East* published in 1894, the Tunisian Tahir

al-Haddad's *Our Women in Islamic Law and Society* published in 1929, the Egyptian intellectual Ahmad Lutfi al-Sayyid founder of *Al-Jarida* newspaper and the Iraqi poet Jamil al-Zahawi. In general, these men advocated for better education and visibility for women in the Arab World and criticised social practices that restrict women such as veiling (Badran and cooke 1990: xxvii).

17 For more information on Lebanese women combatants, see Eggert 2018: 1–31.

18 In a 2016 interview conducted by Zéna Zalzal about the novel *Tout est halluciné*, Hyam Yared says that the Lebanese are still stuck in the civil war and that we are all comatose (Zalzal 2016).

PART I
THE NARRATIVE VOICE

I

The Feminine 'I'

In this chapter, I examine the novels *Les Absents* by Georgia Makhlouf and *Sitt Marie Rose* by Etel Adnan. These war stories are told by a feminine 'I' who, against the structuralist claim according to which the choice of the narrative voice does not matter, plays multiple important roles. Speaking from a gendered position, the 'I' appropriates the narrative space traditionally occupied by men's voices, to bear witness to her own trauma and to the trauma of others, to preserve the victims' memories, and to write the war history. In *Les Absents*, the witnessing 'I' tells her story of war and exile and shows the reader the many aspects of trauma: trauma is amnesiac, individual and collective and unspeakable. It is also a nagging repetition of thoughts and themes. Trauma becomes the language by which the 'I' bears witness.

In *Sitt Marie Rose*, the 'I' attempts to record history as it unfolds but fails. Her narrative space is drastically reduced with the emergence of other voices all speaking with the first-person pronoun. They are the voices of the militia men and of the activist they have kidnapped, Marie-Rose. Just like the unnamed narrator, Marie-Rose challenges the men's historical views, and tries to tell her version of history. She ends up dead.

Before we proceed to the examination of the 'I' as the witness of trauma in *Les Absents* and the witness of history in *Sitt Marie Rose*, it is important to ask first what the functions are of the 'I' as narrator.

'I' as narrator

The literary choice of the first-person pronoun as narrator is significant. From a linguistic point of view and as suggested by Roman Jakobson, the pronouns 'I' and 'you' are both codes and messages. They are codes as they clearly carry their own definitions; they are messages as they vary in the context in which they are enunciated (Jakobson 1963: 176–9). To say it differently, the pronoun 'I' will always mean the reference to the self. However, this speaking self varies depending on the context. The same logic applies to the 'you' pronoun but not necessarily to the 'he/she/it' pronouns. Furthermore, the first and the second person pronouns 'I/you' exist in a bilateral relationship where the 'I' assumes the role of the enunciating subject and the 'you' assumes the role of the recipient. These pronouns cannot exist outside this relationship of enunciator–recipient. The third-person pronoun, however, breaks away from this existential condition as it can be used in the absence of the subject. For Émile Benveniste, the concept of personhood is exclusive to the pronouns 'I/you'; it lacks, however, in the case of the third-person pronoun (Benveniste 1966: 251). One can also add that the pronouns 'I/you' allow the individualisation and the appropriation of language in a specific space. The 'I' exists and is speaking now as opposed to the 'he/she/it' that is (or can be) completely absent from the time and space of the enunciation.

Jakobson's and Benveniste's theoretical points are important when transplanted in the context of war narratives; one can argue that the feminine 'I' speaks for an audience, for a reading 'you'. The narrative engages the reader who becomes subsequently and simultaneously the witness to the events. The feminine 'I' is also a person who is available at the time and place of the war (where the enunciation is taking place). The presence of a 'seeing I, a seeing *eye*' (Stanley 1992: 21) as opposed to an omniscient narrator, is important as it gives the testimony a sense of immediacy and veracity. Lastly, the feminine 'I' enables women to speak and to appropriate the language in war-torn male spaces.

It is important, however, to acknowledge that 'I' as narrator raises real issues, such as the identity of the speaker. Who is the speaking 'I'? Is it the real author or is it a fictional voice? Is the text autobiographical or fictional?[1] Following Philippe Lejeune's argument in *Le Pacte autobiographique* (1975), one could be tempted to say that the 'I' is the marker of an autobiography. However, this is not always true especially with the rise of the autofiction genre.[2] The other issue raised is related to the reliability of the narrator: to what extent can the reader believe the speaking 'I'? Is the narrator truthful? What if the narrator suffers from mental illness and is imaging the events? Finally, the last issue is related to memory: can the narrator really remember all these details or is he or she filling the memory gaps for the sake of the narrative?

These questions are not necessarily new to the field and have been amply addressed particularly in relation to Rousseau's *Confessions*.[3] In the cases of *Sitt Marie Rose* and *Les Absents*, the problem is not so much in the veracity of the witnessing or the reliability of the narrators but rather in their identities. At times, it is difficult to distinguish between the feminine 'I' (who is fictional) and the writer's voice. In *Sitt Marie Rose*, some passages clearly reflect Adnan's sociopolitical views, and one can safely assume that it is indeed the writer speaking through the narrator. As for *Les Absents*, Muriel Maalouf interviews Georgia Makhlouf in June 2014 on Radio France International and asks her if the novel is autobiographical. Makhlouf says no but acknowledges that it borrows from aspects of her real life. She adds that a big portion of the narrative is fictional, and the characters are themselves fictional even though they borrow from real people in her life. She admits combining many real individuals into a single fictional character:

> [le roman] est très impurement autobiographique. C'est-à-dire il est évident qu'il emprunte une trame qui est celle de ma vie mais il est comme tout roman d'ailleurs qui puise dans l'autobiographie. Mais il y a une grande part de fiction, une grande part de construction narrative. Je veux dire que les personnages sont vraiment des constructions même combien ils s'ils s'inspirent de personnages réels. Parfois plusieurs personnages réels ont servi à construire un personnage fictif. (Maalouf 2014)[4]

Les Absents by Georgia Makhlouf

Published in Paris in 2014 with Rivages, *Les Absents* is Makhlouf's first novel; it tells the story of an unnamed female narrator, her adolescent life in a war-torn Lebanon and her exile to France. The novel, which won the 9th Prix Léopold Sedar Senghor for a first francophone novel, is structurally interesting and different from other francophone novels. It opens on a prologue followed by two phone books. The first phone book is called 'Le Carnet de Beyrouth' and has twenty entries with the stories of twenty people. The second phone book is called 'Le Carnet de Paris' and has fifteen entries.

The narrator tells her story using the feminine 'I'. She does not tell the events in chronological order; instead, she follows alphabetical order, just like in a phone book. According to the writer in the interview mentioned above, the alphabetical order better reflects the functioning of a real memory that does not follow a linear time.

In the 'Carnet de Beyrouth', the narrator tells us about her adolescent life and early adulthood, her family, her sisters, her cousins, her grandmother, her neighbours, her housekeepers, her seamstress, her friends and classmates, her love relationships and her college experience. All these stories take place during the Lebanese civil war, and at times they appear like a background noise and others come to take a more central space in the story. In the 'Carnet de Paris', she tells us about her transition from Lebanon to France, her college experience, her romantic relationships, her struggle to obtain stay and work permits, her marriage and its failure, her children, her friends, her colleagues and her jobs. In this second part, the civil war is never totally absent; it remains omnipresent in the narrative. In addition to the shadowing war, the narrator experiences exile and betrayal.

Facing this hardship, the feminine 'I' feels the imperative to speak and to tell her stories which are intertwined with the stories of others. She bears witness to her own trauma but also to the trauma of others. How does she speak of trauma or in what way does she represent trauma? In order to answer this question, we should start with the definition of trauma. It is important to note that the point of this study is not to diagnose the narrator – who remains a fictional protagonist – with trauma, but rather to show how the narrator depicts trauma in the narrative and how trauma as inscribed in the narrative is the language that bears witness to life and death.

What is Trauma?

There are multiple definitions and approaches to trauma, and there is a necessary conflation between the definition of trauma, the effects of trauma and the representation of trauma. The field of trauma studies has expanded to include literary, social, historical, cultural theorists and clinical practitioners who do not necessarily agree on the matter. The boundaries of the field are unclear as they keep shifting based on the discipline discussing trauma, and they are still evolving following the movements of new ideas and discoveries. Despite its vagueness, one can say that all disciplines agree (to a certain extent) that trauma questions the relationship 'between the everyday and the extreme, between the individual identity and collective experience, between history and the present, between experience and representation, between facts and memory, and between the "clinical" and the "cultural"' (Casper and Wertheimer 2016: 4). Also, they all agree that trauma should not be taken for granted and should always be examined ethically (Casper and Wertheimer 2016: 5).[5]

For Cathy Caruth – the first to use the expression of 'trauma theory' (Radstone 2010: 10) – trauma is defined as 'an overwhelming experience of sudden or catastrophic events in which the response to the events occurs in the often delayed, uncontrolled repetitive appearance of hallucinations and other intrusive phenomena' (Caruth 1996: 11–12). Focusing primarily on Freud's works, Caruth considers trauma to be both amnesiac and unrepresentable. She argues that the pain is so intense that the mind does not process it as it should. As a result, the victim may not even remember the traumatic event. The trauma thus remains unclaimed as it cannot be expressed through literal language. This is indeed problematic because if trauma is unspeakable, if trauma cannot be told in a narrative, how can one represent trauma? For Caruth, it is done through an imaginative or a performative language that refers to trauma without necessarily acknowledging it as such; trauma is therefore represented indirectly in creative writing (such as literature), dreams or repetitive behaviours.

Trauma is also incomprehensible. In fact, trauma narratives not only represent violence but also convey the incomprehensibility of the event. For Caruth, what haunts the victims 'is not only the reality of the violent event but also the reality of the way that its violence has not yet been fully known' (Caruth 1996: 6). The story of trauma becomes thus a delayed impact, a 'belated experience' (Caruth 1996: 7) that does not necessarily tell the story of escaping death but rather its endless impact on one's life. It becomes an oscillation between what Caruth calls the crisis of death and the crisis of life.

Caruth examines Freud's usage of the epic poem *Gerusalemme Liberata* by Tasso where Tancred kills his beloved Clorinda not knowing it was her as she was disguised in the enemy's armour. After the burial, he goes into a magical forest where he fights the Crusaders and slashes a tree with his sword. Blood comes out from that tree along with Clorinda's voice. Her soul has been imprisoned in this tree and Tancred had killed Clorinda once again (Caruth 1996: 2).

For Caruth, if Freud refers to literature to analyse a traumatic experience, it is because literature has the distinctive ability to juxtapose the known and the unknown, the act of witnessing trauma, the language of witnessing trauma and psychoanalysis (Caruth 1996: 3). She continues to say:

> So trauma is not locatable in the simple violent or original event in an individual's past, but rather in the way that its very unassimilated nature – the way it was precisely *not known* in the first instance – returns to haunt the survivor later on.
>
> What the parable of the wound and the voice thus tells us, and what is at the heart of Freud's writing on trauma, both in what it says and in the stories it unwittingly tells, is that trauma seems to be much more than a pathology, or the simple illness of a wounded psyche: it is always the story of a wound that cries out, that addresses us in the attempt to tell us of a reality or truth that is not otherwise available. This truth, in its delayed appearance and its belated address, cannot be linked only to what is known, but also to what remains unknown in our very actions and our language. (Caruth 1996: 4)

Caruth acknowledges that this approach to trauma has been criticised. Some accuse it of being too Eurocentric as it glorifies the West through stories of Crusaders and wars; others point the omission of Clorinda's voice (the woman's voice) in expressing trauma. For Caruth, these comments reflect the ambiguity of the speaking voice and raise the following questions: Who is allowed to speak of trauma? Who is not allowed to speak and who is heard? She goes back to Freud's reference to the epic poem to show that the voice expressing trauma carries in fact multiple meanings. It simultaneously represents the 'fatalism of repetition' and 'the surprise of traumatic experience' (Caruth 1996: 119). In other words, the narrative represents the trauma itself but also figuratively tells us something: it is the story of a traumatic event from which the voice of a woman has been omitted, and for Caruth this omission is precisely what makes her voice heard. The poem's focus on someone else's trauma allows the voice to be heard even when the trauma narrative remains silence. For Caruth, it is easy to say that the language of the poem did not represent the woman's voice. However, the silence of the language is precisely what makes her voice available. She concludes by saying that when reading trauma stories, one must ask '[W]ho speaks from the site of trauma?' (Caruth 1996: 120).

To answer this question, Caruth argues against the assumption that trauma is individualised. For her, trauma is an individual experience but also a collective one. As such, the witnessing voice of trauma oscillates between the self and the others, between the individual and the collective:

> Although isolating, traumatic experience can never with certainty be reduced to, or framed within, the boundaries of an individual life. The annihilation of experience at the core of what we think of as personal trauma is never wholly extricable from larger social and political modes of denial. In this sense, I would suggest the 'individual' and the 'collective' cannot be extricated from each other, in the destruction of experience, which can never be grounded in the unity of a single position or voice. (Caruth 1996: 121)

In *Literature in the Ashes of History* (2013), Caruth gives us two examples regarding the performative role of language in expressing trauma; she studies Freud's *Beyond the Pleasure Principle* and his two encounters with First World War veterans and with a child playing a game.

The veterans of the First World War had repetitive nightmares of the battlefield. For Freud, dreams tend to represent wishes and desires and yet in this case they were horrifying. They were also surprising, as if they were seen for the first time. In order to explain this compulsory repetition of trauma, Freud defines consciousness as a form of awareness of the world, a world that is experienced in an expected order. This consciousness has a protective attribute. It seeks to protect the organism in which it resides from hostility. Trauma is a breach to this order. Based on her readings of Freud, Caruth defines trauma as 'an encounter that is not directly perceived as a threat to the life of the organism but that occurs, rather as a break in the mind's experience of time' (Caruth 2013: 5). It is a form of breach that is caused not by the threat or injury itself but rather by the lack of the organism's preparedness to absorb the stimulus. The veterans' dreams, thus, reflect the anxiety and the fear that should have been available when the event occurred, and repetition becomes a form of protective compensation for the lack of preparedness. This repetition occurs during the dream itself but also at the waking where the veteran remembers the missed encounter with death as well as his survival. The repetition of trauma becomes the creative language by which trauma is expressed but also the witness to life and death.

Regarding the child's game, Caruth tells us of an encounter between Freud and a child playing a game, where he would throw a wooden spool on a string then retrieve it while saying the German words 'fort' and 'da' ('gone' and 'here'). It seems that the game re-enacts the departure and return of the boy's mother into the room.[6] For Caruth, the repetitive game is not only the story of departure and return but also of pain and loss through the pleasure of creation. It is a language of creativity that bears witness to the past by departing from it but that also bears witness to the possibility of life as it does not focus on the past alone but also, through repetition, looks to the future.

Caruth argues that this story has been ignored by contemporary trauma studies which tends to focus on history and memory. For her, in order to fully understand Freud's theory on trauma, we should juxtapose both languages of the veterans' nightmares and the child's game to understand that trauma is the unexpected encounter with an event that the mind misses but then repeatedly attempts to grasp. The story of trauma carries both the drive for death (near-death experience) but also the drive for life (the survival). Both are expressed in a creative language that expresses either loss for a child or fear in the battlefield for veterans.[7]

The Feminine 'I' Witness of Trauma in Les Absents

Reading Caruth is vital for us to understand the novel *Les Absents* where trauma, in its amnesiac, collective and unspeakable traits, becomes the language by which the feminine 'I' bears witness to life and death.

Trauma is amnesiac: this is not to say that the subject will never remember the traumatic event. If or when remembrance occurs, it will be delayed in comparison to the time in which the traumatic event occurred. As such, life goes on carrying the unknown of the past which may become known in the present through different remembrance practices. In *Les Absents*, time has elapsed between the events of the war and exile and the acknowledgement of the values of the phone numbers. One can safely assume that the numbers were written down on various social occasions. It is only when the narrator revisits the phone books that she remembers the stories associated with these entries. The phone books or 'les carnets' function as a tangible reminder of a past that has not been properly processed. They become the site of memory or 'lieu de mémoire' to borrow Pierre Nora's expression (Nora 1989: 7);[8] the return to this site triggers the remembrance of the traumatic event right at the opening of the phone book and the reading of the numbers.

The slow work of memory in remembering trauma is available to the reader in the prologue as the narrator tells us about her phone books, and how they represent different aspects of her life. She confesses to a practice that is more or less a common one: she writes phone numbers and addresses using a pencil which allows her to either easily erase or modify the entry. She says that erasing could be difficult especially when it is the result of a break-up, deception, error of judgement or a naïve hope: '[e]ffacer peut-être une opération douloureuse, le résultat d'une rupture, d'une déception, d'une erreur d'évaluation, d'un espoir naïf et déplacé' (Makhlouf 2014: 9). She admits erasing phone numbers of people she does not see or call anymore, of people who made her angry or hurt her, of people she precisely does not want to call, of people who were never meant to be in her life, and of people she forgot about and quickly and insignificantly passed through her life. She stops to say that she does not erase the numbers of the absents, the people who once mattered in her life but left for lack of love, selfishness, cowardness and sometimes for no reason.

There is an abrupt linguistic shift in the narrative as if the narrator is suddenly confronting the source of her pain. In discussing the various entries, she uses the two terms of numbers and names. However, when she gets to the names or numbers associated with people with whom she experienced or witnessed trauma, she says: '[e]t puis il y a les absents' (Makhlouf 2014: 10) / 'And then there were the absents.' She defines her absents as the people that are no longer here but continue to live in her flawed memory, in certain gestures, in unexpected emotions that submerge her at times, in sadness that catches up with her, and in miniscule faithfulness to shared moments:

Ce sont ceux de personnes qui ont compté, mais qui sont sorties de ma vie, par désamour, par égoïsme, par lâcheté, et parfois sans raison . . . Ce sont aussi ceux des personnes qui ne sont plus mais qui continuent de vivre dans les failles de ma mémoire, dans certains de mes gestes, dans des émotions inattendues qui parfois me submergent, dans des chagrins qui me rattrapent, dans des minuscules fidélités à des moments partagés. (Makhlouf 2014: 11)

The narrator admits not erasing these unused numbers and not wanting to forget about them: 'des morts dont je ne veux pas être consolée' (Makhlouf 2014: 11). These numbers jolt the narrator's memory and push her to remember what happened. She then proceeds to explain her relationship to these numbers and the people behind them. It is interesting to note that the narrative does not contain many dialogues and is almost entirely (aside from a few exceptions) narrated in indirect speech by the feminine 'I'. One could potentially argue that the feminine 'I' monopolises the voice and speaks only of her trauma. However, and following Caruth's analysis of Tasso's poem, the voices of the others and their traumas are present by their precise omission. In other words, the silence of the normative language in expressing the others' voices is in fact a representation of their trauma and of their death (whether literal or figurative). The feminine 'I' is alive, and is able to tell what happened to the self but also to the others. She is the voice that memorialises those who are gone, while also recognising her own life.

This is true in the story of Alice, who is the narrator's cousin, childhood friend and playmate. Despite her parents' divorce, Alice is described as a child full of life and laughter. Sadly, she dies from a bomb. In the narrative, her voice is heard one time (through direct speech) when she tells the narrator about her father's intention to remarry. Although Alice's voice is absent in print, it is not unavailable, and her trauma has not gone unwitnessed. This void is in itself a representation of Alice's trauma witnessed by a feminine 'I'. Additionally, Alice's trauma is represented in the narrator's change of tone and choice of words.

Regarding the tone, the feminine 'I' shifts from describing a lovely picture of children at play to the bomb shelling of Alice's village. This shift not only speaks of Alice's trauma but also echoes the unannounced shelling of the civilians in the village.

Regarding the choice of words, in describing Alice's death, the narrator uses the verb 'effacer' or erase, and it is the same verb she uses in the prologue when discussing unused phone numbers. For the narrator, 'effacer' or erasing should apply to numbers and should be the result of a break-up, a deception, an error of judgment or a hope that is short-lived (Makhlouf 2014: 9). Human life should not be erased and certainly not by a bomb. Life decided otherwise; it treated Alice as a number and erased her. The narrator defies this cruel twist of events and says that she knows Alice's phone number by heart (15) as if she is telling life that she will never erase it from her phone book or her memory.

The feminine 'I' concludes this entry on Alice by a surprising reference to the Life Savers candy. She says that these candies, which look like colourful lifebuoys, may have melted on their tongues but never managed to save anyone from drowning: 'Les bouées de sauvetage colorées avaient fondu sous nos langues mais n'avaient sauvé personne du naufrage' (Makhlouf 2014: 19). This image of playful children sharing candy brings Alice momentarily to life only to be contrasted with the unforeseen reality of her death. This back-and-forth movement between life and death brings to mind Freud's encounter with the child playing 'gone' and 'here'. The narrator's language and tone mimic this movement of 'gone' and 'here': she memorialises her cousin, all while she acknowledges her own survival; she brings her back to life through playful language only to abruptly mention her death.

Alice's story also tells us that trauma is simultaneously individual and collective. It is a shared experience between the survivors. The collective aspect of trauma appears first in the title '[l]es absents'. The novel is not just about one singular absence but rather many. It is interesting to note that the narrator (or one should say in this case the writer via the narrator) did not use a possessive pronoun to refer to the absents but rather a definite article.

In fact, the definite article allows the narrator to create some distance not between her and the characters she tells us about but between these characters and the official authorities in Lebanon. For the narrator, the 'absents' and despite their physical disappearance are clearly heavily present in the novel. However, they remain unclaimed absences in Lebanon; despite their differences in sex, age, skin colour, ethnicity, citizenship, religion, socio-economic and educational backgrounds, they are shared absences across the Lebanese communities, but absences for which no one has claimed responsibility.

Collectivity of trauma also manifests itself through the narrative voice. In fact, the anonymity of the feminine 'I' implies that she could be anyone's mother, sister, aunt, friend. While it is true that she speaks from a gendered position as a woman, she does not speak for herself alone or for her family but rather for everyone she knows. This is particularly true when she shifts from the feminine 'I' to the 'we' pronoun, which allows her to include the reader and to speak for the entire country. To give a few examples, she says: 'nous sommes habités par nos disparus . . . Car nos vies sont en fragments . . .' (Makhlouf 2014: 11) / 'we are inhabited by our missing persons . . . because our lives are fragmented'.

Also, she slips into the 'we' ('nous/on') when making political comments. It is possible to argue that she uses the group power as a shield to hide her opinion, but this is not necessarily true as she does not distance herself from the group. Instead, she positions herself as part of the group and speaking from within it. For example, in describing the never-ending war, she alternates between the feminine 'I' and the 'we' pronoun. She uses the 'we' pronoun to represent the civilians of which she is a part. She says: '[d]ans ce paysage continuellement recomposé, nous étions des novices, nous devions sans cesse réapprendre le mode d'emploi de guerre qui changeait de langue et de terrain et nous commettions encore beaucoup d'erreurs qui coûtaient la vie à certains' (Makhlouf 2014: 84) / 'in this scenery that is continuously recomposed, we were novices, we were supposed to repeatedly relearn the user's manual of the war which kept changing its language and its terrain, and we made a lot of mistakes which cost the lives of some'.

Another example would be when she describes the status of Palestinian refugees living in poverty in Lebanon. She says: '[o]n envisageait différentes solutions pour « faire face » à ce problème . . . on ne savait pas trop comment s'y prendre pour opérer ces déplacements . . .' (Makhlouf 2014: 53–4) / 'we considered different solutions to face the problem . . . we did not know how to manage these displacements'. The 'on' pronoun can reflect either a specific group (and be translated as the 'we' pronoun) or an unspecific group (and be translated as 'one' or 'they'). In the example provided, it is safe to assume that the *on* pronoun is the equivalent of 'we' and not 'they', precisely because of the sense of community the narrator is trying to cultivate throughout the novel.

Trauma is also unspeakable, and this is reflected in the narrator's inability to tell Saydé's story. She begins the entry by admitting that she cannot speak of her: '[d]'elle, je ne peux pas parler' (Makhlouf 2014: 177). She repeatedly says that she does not know how to speak of her: '[d]'elle, je ne sais pas parler' (118). She even confesses not remembering what happened as her memory has been hit by amnesia: '[u]ne zone de ma mémoire dont le contour reste flou est frappée d'amnésie que je sais fragile et vers laquelle je ne cherche que rarement à m'aventurer' (117). She tells the reader of her special bond with Saydé, of when she taught her how to read and write, of their times spent together after school, but her memory gets foggy when she gets to the traumatic event: '[m]a mémoire d'elle est trouée . . .' (122).

Despite its unspeakable trait, trauma is represented in the text through the narrator's nightmare of Saydé:

> [I]l m'arrive encore de me réveiller en sursaut la nuit parce que je la vois à côté de moi. Elle m'apporte une limonade ou une tisane, elle dit mon nom douce-ment et il y a dans sa voix un mélange de tendresse et de reproche parce que je ne suis pas raisonnable, j'ai encore lu beaucoup trop sous mes couvertures, ou je n'ai pas pris mes médicaments et j'ai le front brûlant. Et elle est là à côté de mon lit, mais elle n'a plus d'yeux, ses yeux sont des orbites vides, elle ne me regarde plus . . . et j'ai peur, je suis en nage, je crie . . . (Makhlouf 2014; 118)/

> It happens that I still wake up startled at night as I see her next to me. She brings me a lemonade or herbal tea; she says my name softly and in her voice is a mixture of tenderness and reproach. I read for too long under my covers or I did not take my medications and my forehead is burning. And she is here next to my bed, but she does not have eyes, the eyes are empty sockets she is no longer looking at me . . . and I am afraid, I am soaked, I scream . . .

In describing her nightmare, the narrator uses the present tense as if Saydé is alive for the duration of the nightmare. She also describes her as a ghostly appearance rather than a nightmare, as if Saydé really comes back from the dead to bring her a drink and to speak to her softly. Just like the veterans of the First World War who were examined by Freud, the narrator acts surprised as she is waking up, as if she is seeing what happened to Saydé for the first time.

The narrator remains faithful to Saydé's memory and even though time has elapsed, she still cannot speak of her: '[j]e n'ai moi-même jamais raconté. D'elle je ne veux ni ne peux parler' (Makhlouf 2014: 132) / 'I myself never told. I do not want to, and I cannot speak about her.' It is actually the narrator's father who describes Saydé's death: 'la bouche de mon père qui racontait de façon quasi obsessionnelle et à toutes sortes de visiteurs, d'amis et de vagues connaissances le sac de notre appartement et la mort de Saydé . . .' (130) / 'my father's mouth that told almost in an obsessional way to all visitors, friends and vague acquaintances, the sacking of our apartment and the death of Saydé'.

Clearly, the narrator disapproves. Multiple times, she asks him to stop telling the story especially that every time he did, he exaggerated certain elements and emphasised Saydé's nudity and bruises (Makhlouf 2014: 131). For the narrator, her father betrays Saydé's memory; he dishonours her to seek his visitors' sympathy and attention.

Saydé's trauma as witnessed by the feminine 'I' is represented in the father's normative language but also in the novel's performative language, through the narrator's nightmare and its repetition. In other words, and just like Caruth claims in the case of Freud's examination of First World War veterans, the compulsive repetition of the nightmare becomes the imaginative language by which the narrator bears witness to both her trauma and Saydé's. Repetition is therefore simultaneously a symptom of trauma, but also the language that records Saydé's death and the narrator's survival.

Beyond the narrator's nightmare, repetition as the language of trauma is available in the novel's structure and redundancy of certain themes. Regarding the structure, and just like the *Arabian Nights* where Scheherazade continuously chains stories and postpones their endings in order to avoid her own death (Faris 1982: 811–30), the narrator proceeds alphabetically and tells us thirty-five stories. She could go on and on for as long as there are names to enter in a phone book. The possibility of adding more names is suggested at the end of the novel when the narrator receives a phone call from Lebanon. In the conversation, the interlocutor says that once wars are started, they never finish. They only change their faces: '[l]es guerres une fois commencées ne finissent jamais. Elles prennent seulement d'autres visages' (Makhlouf 2014: 301). This endless (or potentially endless) repetition of the act of narration is in its own right a performative language of trauma by which the feminine 'I' (and just like Scheherazade) speaks of her survival and bears witness to the death of others.

Regarding the themes repeated in the novel, they are: death and violence, guilt and shame, deception and betrayal and exile. It is not surprising to see death and violence as a repeated topic in both phone books. Death comes literally but also figuratively as the end of relationships; it also comes as the result of war but also of natural causes. The narrator loses many people in her life to death: her cousins Alice (Makhlouf 2014: 15–19) and Elias (39–48) were killed in the war; she also loses contact with people who meant much to her like her sister Dina (29–38). The narrator blames the war for these losses. She says that during the war, families are dislocated; social codes are shattered; violence becomes routine; lying, deception and betrayal become common: '[l] es familles se disloquaient . . . [l]es codes sociaux se fissuraient . . . [l]a violence devenait routine' (163).

The shadow of death and violence follow her to France. It is present in the apartment she shares with Simon: '[c]'était au 88 de la rue Oberkampf . . . Je ne parlais pas allemand, mais je l'entendais en allemand, avec l'accent militaire. Je voyais sa couleur kaki et bruits de bottes. La guerre, partout, me poursuivait' (Makhlouf 2014: 182) / 'It was on 88 street Oberkampf . . . I did not speak German but I heard it in German, with the military accent. I saw this kaki colour and boots' noise.'[9] It comes as an unpleasant surprise when she takes her son to the pediatrician. Dr Benjamin Olmert has been to Lebanon not as a pediatrician but as a soldier during the 1982 Israeli invasion. Multiple times, he tells the narrator while performing circumcision on her son: '[q]uel beau pays!' (260) / 'what a beautiful country', as if he had been there as a tourist. It is also present when she runs into her Lebanese friend Salwa in Paris. Salwa is a left-wing activist who is writing on the Lebanese detained in the Syrian jails. Salwa not only reminds the narrator of what is going on in Lebanon, but also represents an extension of the war to the French soil. Salwa mysteriously dies in a car accident (272). Death also takes the narrator by surprise when her friend Eléonore dies by suicide (209), and when the Armenian restaurant owner named Jean tells her about his family's survival of the genocide (238).

Shame and guilt also repeatedly surface in the novel and function simultaneously as the symptom of trauma but also as its language of expression. For Ruth Leys,[10] in *From Guilt to Shame: Auschwitz and After*, shame and guilt have different meanings as they are the result of two different approaches to trauma: the mimetic theory and the antimimetic theory. In the mimetic theory, Leys says:

> The mimetic theory explains the tendency of traumatized people to compulsively repeat their violent experiences in nightmares and repetitive forms of acting out by comparing the traumatic repetition to hypnotic imitation. Trauma is therefore interpreted as an experience of hypnotic imitation and identification that disables the victim's perceptual and cognitive apparatus to such an extent that the experience never becomes part of the ordinary memory system. This means that the amnesia held to be typical of psychical shock is explained as kind of posthypnotic forgetting. (Leys 2007: 8)

Basing her analysis on Primo Levi's *The Drowned and the Saved*, Leys argues that the mimetic theory gives birth to guilt since the victim involuntarily identifies with the aggressor, and subsequently feels a sense of responsibility.

As for the antimimetic theory, it regards trauma as a 'purely external event coming to a sovereign if passive victim' (Leys 2000: 10). The victim becomes the spectator to trauma which creates a distance between the real self and the traumatised self. For Leys, the antimimetic theory safeguards the victim's agency, and places the responsibility entirely on the aggressor. It also leads to shame defined as 'an experience of consciousness of the self when the individual becomes aware of being exposed to the diminishing or disapproving gaze of another' (Leys 2007: 11).[11]

Depending on the phone entry, the narrator oscillates between feelings of shame and guilt. She feels guilty towards Fairuz, the little Palestinian refugee she invites home. Through Fairuz's eyes, the narrator becomes aware of her wealth and feels bitter and uncomfortable (Makhlouf 2014: 59). When Fairuz's camp is bombed, the narrator tries to find her but fails. She is left wondering whether Fairuz enjoyed their time together or whether the visit made her more aware of her own poverty. The narrator's guilt is apparent in her feelings of responsibility towards Fairuz, as if her parents' nice apartment, her refrigerator full of food, and her closet full of clothes and shoes are an indication of a status earned unfairly during the war and at the expense of those who are struggling.

This sentiment of responsibility is also available when she tells the stories of Jamilé and Angela. Jamilé is the nanny and housekeeper. She dies in her room bleeding silently from her leg. Afraid to bother the family, she does not seek their help (Makhlouf 2014: 81). Angela is the narrator's neighbour in France. She works in a hair salon but is also a sex worker. She projects a happy and frivolous image, but one day the narrator hears her sob; her father has died. As Angela tells the narrator about her father, the narrator becomes aware of the living conditions in the Soviet Union. She immediately feels guilty. Just like an aggressor, the narrator feels she became insensitive to human misery. She says: '[l]a guerre ne nous avait pas seulement coupés du monde, elle nous avait rendus sourds et aveugles' (188) / 'the war not only cut us off from the rest of the world, but also made us deaf and blind'.

Repeatedly in the narrative, the narrator expresses her shame which is particularly apparent in Saydé's story. When the narrator finds Saydé's dead body, she becomes dissociated from her own. She falls ill and is hospitalised. The narrator vaguely remembers the hospital room, the strong scents of chlorine, excrement, vomit and ether. She remembers biting her fingers until blood comes out and her inability to talk, to scream and to eat (Makhlouf 2014: 128–9). The narrator's shame is represented in this distance she creates between the feminine 'I' narrating the self and the narrator's body that falls sick. It is also present when the narrator's father speaks about Saydé's death and naked body. In her own way and despite her shame, the narrator attempts to preserve Saydé's dignity from voyeurism. Her father, on the other hand, tells the story to gain listeners' sympathy.

Betrayal and deception are also recurrent themes in the narrative. Jenny Edkins argues that trauma involves a betrayal of trust, especially when it comes from a source that is meant to protect us:

> This can be devastating because who we are, or who we think we may be, depends very closely on the social context in which we place and find ourselves. Our existence relies not only on our personal survival as individual beings but also, in a very profound sense, on the continuance of the social order that gives our existence meaning and dignity: family, friends, political community, beliefs. If that order betrays us in some way, we may survive in the sense of continuing to live as physical beings, but the meaning of our existence is changed. (Edkins 2003: 4)

Betrayal thus redefines one's position in society, and it functions as a two-way street: the survivor feels guilt and shame for having survived the trauma as if he or she has betrayed those who are gone; the survivor experiences betrayal by those who are perpetuating the trauma. By leaving Lebanon, the narrator feels as if she betrayed her own people. This is particularly true in the description of her journey to Cyprus on Vlado's yacht (Makhlouf 2014: 149–56) and of the free legal aid she obtains from Jacques Aubert, the French attorney who helps her legalise her stay in France (191–6). The same fate that led so many to death led her to safety. At the same time, the narrator feels betrayed by so many starting with her own compatriots like Kamal Takieddine, a militia man who pretends to give her access to a landline and attempts to rape her (93), and Gebran who pretends to be her friend and uses her to get closer to her friend Soraya (76). The topic of betrayal is not restricted to the war and is also available in the French phone book, for instance in the entry about Clémence. Clémence is the narrator's close friend. She deceives the narrator and engages in a sexual relationship with her husband Paul (197–8).

Finally, the last topic repeated throughout the novel is exile. Defined by Edward W. Said as an 'unhealable rift forced between a human being and a native place, between the self and its true home' (Said 2002: 173), the feeling of exile as a 'crippling sorrow' (Said 2002: 173) is present in both phone books. It appears in the narrator's childhood when she compares herself to her French classmate Blandine. The narrator is jealous of Blandine, who is described as a superiorly intelligent, popular, beautiful blond girl. She tries to become her friend and be like her; she quickly realises that she will never be French and that she can only be an eternal travesty: 'jamais je ne deviendrais une vraie Française, que je devrais me contenter d'un éternel simulacre' (Makhlouf 2014: 22). Exile appears after Saydé's death when the narrator feels disconnected from everything and everyone: '[c]'est ce jour-là, ce jour de honte et d'épouvante, que je suis devenue exilée, même s'il m'a fallu encore du temps pour m'arracher à ce pays . . .' (132) / 'it is on this day, this day of shame and fear, that I became an exile even though it still took me some time to leave this country . . .'

The narrator's acknowledgement of her Frenchlessness and of her exile in Lebanon get aggravated when she realises that she does not belong in France either despite her education and knowledge of the French language and culture. This shows in her encounter with the Parisian college student Irène. Just like Blandine, Irène is described as superior to the narrator. She is highly intelligent, does not take notes in class, and speaks to the professors as an equal. She is also a free spirit, a rebel who is not afraid of openly talking about her sexuality (Makhlouf 2014: 228–9). She tells the narrator all sorts of things, and the narrator admits wanting to tell her about the unpredicted hardship of her Parisian exile, about being in a city that she thought was hers just because she spoke its language and read its literature, and yet constantly reminded her of her precarious status of a stranger: '[j]'avais en moi aussi soif de me confier, de raconter les duretés imprévisibles de cet exil parisien . . . dans une ville que j'avais crue mienne parce que j'en parlais la langue et en lisais la littérature, mais qui me renvoyait sans cesse à mon statut précaire d'étrangère . . .' (231).

The narrator concludes the novel on the topic of exile. She tells the reader of how she became a French mother to two successful French children, how she made sure that her children followed their father's French traditions, how she integrated her husband's family but also how she feels absent from herself and how she does not see herself in the mirror anymore (Makhlouf 2014: 297–8).

The redundancy of certain topics along with the cyclic narrative structure and the narrator's repeated nightmare participate in the expression of trauma and become part of the language by which the feminine 'I' bears witness. Trauma is amnesiac and yet the narrator is able to retrieve some memories in visiting the site of trauma. Trauma is individual and collective; certain memories belong to the narrator alone while others are part of the entire nation. Trauma is unspeakable but it still finds a way to speak through the narrator's performative language.

At the end of the novel, the narrator acknowledges that her 'absents' became heavy. She told their stories and preserved their memories. In return, they consumed her: 'je n'étais plus vivante qu'à moitié. J'étais habitée par des morts, des disparus, des fantômes, des absents, j'étais une maison hantée. Il fallait que je me secoue . . .' (Makhlouf 2014: 300) / 'I was only half alive. I was inhabited by the dead, the missing, the ghosts, the absents; I was a haunted house. I should shake myself . . .'

Life forced upon her the burden of witnessing. With all what she has been through she wonders whether she still belongs in Lebanon or whether, just like a dried river that can no longer run to its sea, she can no longer remain faithful to a country that asked and took so much of her. When the narrator's phone rings and shows her daughter's number, she does not feel like answering. However, when it rings again with a Lebanese number, she answers hastily. The narrator may still be experiencing exile and doubting her belonging to Lebanon, but the last phone call suggests that her relationship to Lebanon is not completely severed. The stories will continue to flow.

The Historian Feminine 'I' in *Sitt Marie Rose*[12]

The novel *Sitt Marie Rose* is based on the true story of Marie Rose Boulos, a feminist Syrian social worker who assisted Palestinian refugees in Lebanon and worked in a school for children with special needs (Mejcher-Atassi 2006: 203). Killed by the Christian militia, her story shook the public opinion. In the novel, Marie Rose Boulos becomes Sitt Marie Rose, the principal of a school for the deaf-mute.[13]

The novel is divided into two sections: 'Temps I Un million d'oiseaux'/ Time I A Million Birds and 'Temps 2: Marie-Rose' / Time II Marie-Rose. The first section is narrated by a first-person pronoun while the second section, divided into three subsections, alternates between the seven voices of Marie Rose, the Christian combatants (Mounir, Tony, Fouad), the priest (Bouna Lias), the deaf-mute children and the narrator of Temps I.

The fragmentation of the narrative and the sudden shift in the narrative voices highlight the gradual disappearance of the feminine 'I' in both sections. In fact, the sounds of the war and the rise of male voices drown the feminine 'I' (Foster 1995: 61). According to Amal Amireh, the feminine 'I' in Temps I is unable to assert herself. She witnesses history without being able to change its course.[14] As a result, she leaves the scene submerged by the other narrative voices of Temps 2 (Amireh 2005: 257).

'Temps I Un Million d'Oiseaux' / 'Time I A Million Birds'

In the first pages of the novel, we do not know the narrator's gender but it is clear that he or she holds a secondary status compared to Mounir: 'Mounir me téléphone. Il compte faire un film et me demande de lui écrire le scénario. Il veut que . . .' (Adnan 2010: 9) / 'Mounir is on the phone. He is planning to make a film and wants me to write the scenario. He wants . . .' (Adnan 1982:

1) Mounir is the subject of all the actions while the narrator is the object. In fact, the narrator has the limited role of reporting conversations to the reader:

> Mounir commente de vive voix. Par terre sont assises sa femme, ses deux belles-sœurs et l'une de leurs amies. Il y a un public de femmes dans l'une des plus belles maisons de Beyrouth. Tony est d'ailleurs le cousin d'une des filles présentes et elle prend le tout avec un air plutôt dépité. Les « hommes » ont refusé de l'emmener avec eux à la chasse, en Turquie. Ils n'avaient pas voulu s'encombrer. (Adnan 2010: 9–10) /

> Mounir comments in a loud voice. His wife, two sisters-in-law and one of their friends are seated on the floor. He has an audience of women in one of Beirut's most beautiful houses. One of the girls present is Tony's cousin, and she takes it all with a rather spiteful air. The 'men' refused to take her hunting in Turkey. They did not want to be bothered. (Adnan 1982: 2)

Unlike the men, women have no names. The narrator portrays them as a cohesive group with no distinctive individuality. Geographically, they are removed from the male space: they are sitting on the floor inferior to men and they were not allowed to accompany them hunting in the desert. They lack agency and access to the source of information which are both seen as male spaces (Ofeish and Ghandour 2001: 131).

As the narrative progresses, Mounir's privileged status is asserted:

> Mounir explique avec beaucoup de douceur . . . « Vous n'avez rien vu, dit Mounir. Je ne peux pas vous raconter ce que c'est le désert. Il faut voir! Seulement vous, les femmes, vous ne le verrez jamais. Il faut prendre des pistes, il faut même s'orienter avec une carte et une boussole pour vraiment le voir. Vous, vous ne pourrez jamais. » (Adnan 2010: 11–12) /

> Mounir explains with a certain modesty . . . 'You didn't see anything, really,' Mounir says, 'I can't tell you what the desert is. You have to see it. Only, you women, you'll never see it. You have to strike out on your own, find your own trail with nothing but a map and a compass to really see it. You, you'll never be able to do that.' (Adnan 1982: 3–4)

According to Lisa Suhair Majaj, Mounir acts as if his masculinity is the centre of power, privilege and knowledge (Suhair Majaj 2002: 213). For

Mounir, the desert is a masculine space, and women lack what it takes to access it. As such, they are excluded from the source of information. The narrator interrupts Mounir to say: 'C'est vrai. "Nous les femmes" nous étions heureuses de pouvoir au moins voir ce bout de cinéma coloré et imparfait donnant pendant une vingtaine de minutes une sorte de prestige à ces hommes que nous voyions tous les jours' (Adnan 2010: 12) / 'It's true. "We women" were happy with this little bit of imperfect, colored cinema, which gave, for twenty minutes, a kind of additional prestige to these men we see every day' (Adnan 1982: 4).

By associating herself with the group of women, the narrator reveals her gender to the reader. However, unlike the group, the narrator is not content to be a passive viewer. She seems unimpressed by the movie and very much aware of this gendered division of spaces. This awareness is visually indicated to the reader with the use of quotation marks to say 'we women'.

Additionally, and again unlike the other women, the feminine 'I' has agency since Mounir asks her to write a script for his movie on the Syrian workers in Lebanon. However, this agency remains limited since Mounir insists that it is his movie: 'Je veux faire un film avec toi. Mais ça sera mon film. Je veux le faire avec toi' (Adnan 2010: 12) / 'I want to make a film with you. But it will be my film. I just want to make it with you' (Adnan 1982: 4).

In order to respond to Mounir's request, the feminine 'I' tries to interview the Syrian workers to document their lives in Beirut. Her motivation is different from Mounir's. Aware of the importance of providing space of expression to the most vulnerable, the feminine 'I' attempts to document history but fails for two reasons: first, the workers refuse to speak to her. They see her womanhood and Lebaneseness as an infrangible barrier. They prefer to stay quiet and keep their jobs: '[j]'essaie de les faire parler. Ils refusent' (Adnan 2010: 18) / 'I try to get them talking. They refuse' (Adnan 1982: 19). Secondly, the war erupts on 13 April 1975. The space of the feminine 'I' is drastically reduced. She feels like a prison is closing up on everyone: 'sensation que la prison se referme sur chacun de nous' (Adnan 2010: 22) / '[e]veryone feels a prison closing in . . .' (Adnan 1982: 14); and that time is distorted, passes by quickly and differently 'que les minutes semblent plus avoir soixante secondes mais bien moins. Elles filent plus vite. Le mécanisme du temps s'est détraqué' (Adnan 2010: 23) / '[m]inutes seem to have fewer than sixty seconds. They go faster. The mechanism of time is out of order' (Adnan 1982: 15).

The feminine 'I' feels trapped in deformed spatial and temporal dimensions. This is visually reflected in the numbering of the novel's sections. In the French version published in 1977, 'Time 1' has a roman number as opposite to 'Time 2' that has an Arabic number, a way to suggest a breach in time from the pre-war to the war periods. It is interesting to note that the English version published in 1982 does not carry this difference as both numbers are roman. Nevertheless, in the French version one can say that the distortion of time is not just the narrator's impression. It also seeps into the narrative itself.

Despite these obstacles, the feminine 'I' continues to attempt to report history as it is unfolding before her eyes. She adopts the tone of a war reporter and reads the list of the latest incidents, which include the death of Lebanese civilians from different regions and religions, the death of three Syrian workers, the bombing of the establishment, the recovering of mutilated unidentified bodies . . . (Adnan 2010: 30–1 / Adnan 1982: 22–3). Visually, these incidents interrupt the narrative; they are enumerated under bold bullet points on a separate page in the French version and after a large space in the English version. Also, they are told by a passive voice, and the sentences are brief and factual as they include precise time and location.

Nevertheless, the feminine 'I' fails in her mission to record history since she admits to Mounir her inability to finish the movie. She tells Mounir she wants to address the death of the Syrian workers in the movie. He refuses and claims it would be too political: '[c]'est trop violent. Trop politisé. Et puis moi, pour defender mon point de vue, je veux que l'un d'eux revienne à son village' (Adnan 2010: 33) / 'It's too violent. It's too political. And anyway, to defend my point of view, I want one of them to get back to his village' (Adnan 1982: 24). Mounir sounds disconnected from reality, almost delusional in his response. He does not want to address the issue of war ravaging Lebanon and prefers to focus on the struggle and success of migrant workers in Lebanon as if Lebanon continues to be a desired luring space to foreigners. To this the feminine 'I' says: '[j]e crois, Mounir, que je ne peux vraiment pas faire ce film avec toi' (Adnan 2010: 33) / 'I think Mounir that I really can't make this film with you' (Adnan 1982: 24). Mounir dismissively responds: 'Ne t'en fais pas. Tony, Fouad, Pierre, et moi, nous allons en discuter. Je trouverai bien quelque'un. Toi, viens dîner à la maison ce soir' (Adnan 2010: 33) / 'Don't worry about it. Tony, Fouad, Pierre and I will discuss it. I'll find someone. You come to the house for dinner tonight' (Adnan 1982: 24).

For Amireh, the feminine 'I' tries multiple times to assert herself but is repeatedly met with male obstacles. She becomes aware of her inability to assert herself and to bear witness to the vulnerability of others. Following this failure, the feminine 'I' suddenly disappears to be replaced by multiple narrative voices in Temps 2. All these narrative voices speak in the first-person pronoun (Amireh 2005: 256). The feminine 'I' of Temps I falls silent.

'Temps 2 Sitt Marie-Rose' / 'Time II Marie-Rose'

In 'Temps 2', the narrative is fragmented, and it alternates between multiple 'I's. This narrative strategy allows the reader to directly access the protagonists' intimate thoughts, to note for instance Tony's deep hatred of Marie-Rose, or Bouna Lias's religious justification of violence, or the children's fear. Marie-Rose's feminine 'I' speaks from her own site of trauma as she is being kidnapped and tortured. She refuses to become a story told by her male aggressors. She speaks as a subject with agency, asserts and inserts herself in the narrative. She rejects all forms of imprisonment from the physical walls that hold her hostage, to the patriarchal conservative values, to the point of views of male narrators.

She expresses pity for her male aggressors and humanises them in describing them as the victims of colonial education.[15] For Suhair Majaj, this postcolonial identity is what generates violence (Suhair Majaj 2002: 211). In fact, from the beginning of the narrative, the male group (in 'Temps I', comprised of Mounir, Tony and Fouad, with Pierre added in 'Temps 2', which suggests the group is growing) presents itself as modernised and European. In describing his trip to Syria, Mounir speaks snobbishly as if he was a Western tourist visiting the Arab World for the first time: 'quand nous sommes arrivéz chez eux nous étions les premiers Européens qu'ils avaient jamais vus. Pardon, je veux dire, Libanais' (Adnan 2010: 13) / '[b]ut when we arrived, we were the first Europeans they had ever seen. Excuse me, I meant Lebanese' (Adnan 1982: 5).

The feminine 'I' in Temps I is quick to point out that Mounir chooses to ignore the shared history and culture with the Syrians. He acts arrogantly and speaks as if he were a colonial conqueror arriving for the first time in a foreign land. Ironically, Mounir finds this image of the superior colonial conqueror to be flattering, especially when he admits seeing himself as European. Frantz Fanon discusses at length the issue of postcolonial identity particularly in the chapter on 'Mésaventures de la Conscience Nationale' (Fanon 1961) / 'The Pitfalls of National Consciousness' (Fanon 1963). He argues that during colonisation, the educated national middle class serves as a mediator between the colonised masses and the colonial authorities. After independence, this educated national middle class thinks it can replace the colonisers, and becomes the new dominant national bourgeoisie: '[d]ans son narcissisme volontariste, la bourgeoisie nationale s'est facilement convaincue qu'elle pouvait avantageusement remplacer la bourgeoisie métropolitaine' (Fanon 1961: 146) / 'In its narcissism, the national middle class is easily convinced that it can advantageously replace the middle class of the mother country' (Fanon 1963: 149).

This emerging national bourgeoisie follows its own interests and gradually forgets about national interests. It is aided by the Western bourgeoisies 'qui se présentent en touristes amoureux d'exotisme, de chasse, de casinos' (Fanon 1961: 149) / 'who come to it as tourists avid for the exotic, for big game hunting, and for casinos' (Fanon 1963: 153).

The national bourgeoisie identifies with the Western bourgeoisies. It exploits the country the same way the colonisers did, appoints one political party to govern, neglects to cultivate a national consciousness among the people, and subsequently fails in its mission to form a nation. All of this eventually leads to the rise of ultra-nationalism, chauvinism, racism and religious conservatism.

According to Marie-Rose (who also speaks and records history using the feminine 'I'), this occurred in Lebanon when the educated Christian middle class appropriated colonial traits particularly through colonial education. Here is how she describes her aggressors:

Ils étaient ces jeunes garçons, férus des Croisades. Lui [Mounir] s'identifiait à Fréderic Barberousse parce qu'il était légèrement roux. Il regrettait amèrement, comme si c'était récent, que Salahaddine el Ayoubi eut conquis Jérusalem. Il en souffrait. Les Croisades les exaltaient tous. Ces prêtres français dirigeaient chaque année une procession où les élèves des Écoles chréti-

ennes étaient habillés d'une tunique blanche sur laquelle était cousue devant
et derrière, une croix carrée en étoffe rouge. (Adnan 2010: 57) /

These young boys were exalted by the Crusades. Mounir identified with
Frederick Barbarossa because he was himself slightly red-haired. He bitterly
regretted, as though it had happened recently, that Saladin had conquered
Jerusalem. It caused him actual pain. The Crusades excited all of them. Every
year, those French priests led a procession in which all the students of the
Christian schools dressed in white tunics with square red crosses sewn front
and back. (Adnan 1982: 47)

Colonial education explains why Mounir prefers everything that is
European: he listens to Chopin's music, and mocks Marie Rose for preferring
Arabic music, particularly Oum Koulsoum (Adnan 2010: 56 / Adnan 1982:
46). He falls in love with Marie Rose because of her blue eyes; he says she
resembles the modern girls in the movies, and, because of this, she is worthy of
him (Adnan 2010: 44 / Adnan 1982: 34).

For Kaja Silverman, the colonised subject wishes to identify with the
coloniser (Silverman 1989: 3) and Mounir, as a postcolonial subject, identifies
with the West from a religious point of view. He considers the West to be
Christian just like himself. Sonja Mejcher-Atassi calls Mounir an orientalist
(Mejcher-Atassi 2006: 205). Mounir sees Syria as an exotic place, frozen in
time, unchangeable and faithful to itself (which is akin with Edward Said's
definition of orientalism). It is the 'Other' that is simultaneously fascinating
and terrifying.

Furthermore, the aggressors' identity issue appears clearly in Mounir's
wishes to produce a film on Syrian workers in Lebanon: 'comme les films
qui montrent les ouvriers algériens à Paris' (Adnan 2010: 14) / 'like those
that show the Algerian workers in Paris' (Adnan 1982: 6). For Suhair Majaj,
'[t]heir cameras act as emblems of representational power, enabling them to
refute the identity of "native" and to claim instead the identity of tourist, mili-
tarist, photographer, voyeur' (Suhair Majaj 2002: 214).

The immediate link between the colonial education of the Christian
bourgeoisie and the eruption of violence appears in the beginning of the novel
where the feminine 'I' tells us about Mounir and his group's fascination with
hunting: 'Tony tire. Un oiseau tombe. Pierre tire. Un oiseau tombe. Mounir

tire. Un oiseau tombe. Fouad tire. Un oiseau tombe. Tous les visages sont épanouis. Sauf celui de Fouad. Fouad est le tueur parfait' (Adnan 2010: 10) / 'Tony shoots. A bird falls. Pierre shoots. A bird falls. Mounir shoots. A bird falls. Fouad shoots. A bird falls. All their faces glow. Except Fouad's. Fouad is the perfect killer' (Adnan 1982: 2); 'Fouad chasse comme un obsédé. Il préfère chasser que baiser. Il déteste l'expression "faire l'amour"' (Adnan 2010: 10) / 'Fouad hunts as though obsessed. He prefers killing to kissing. He hates the expression "to make love"' (Adnan 1982: 2).

For Gérard Mendel, and as referenced by Accad (1990: 69), violence is a language to be interpreted either as sign of human suffering and or as emblem of monstrosity (Mendel 1980: 37). These young men's attraction to violence appears in their body and verbal languages. Not only do they like hunting and killing innocent creatures, but they also take pride in these actions to the point of making a movie about them. They feel superior to the others, whether the others are women, Syrians or Palestinians. Fouad says, 'Je suis le pouvoir absolu. Je suis l'efficacité absolue. J'ai réduit toutes les vérités à la notion de vie et de mort' (Adnan 2010: 47) / 'I am absolute power. I am absolute efficiency. I've reduced all truths to a formula of life and death' (Adnan 1982: 37). Just like a coloniser, he holds the power of life and death over the colonised.

Colonial education of the Christian bourgeoisie allows Mounir, Fouad, Tony and even Bouna Lias to justify their criminal acts. They are truly convinced that their enemies must die for Lebanon to exist and advance. For Fouad, 'c'est la violence qui accélère le progrès des peuples' (Adnan 2010: 65) / 'It's violence that accelerates the progress of a people' (Adnan 1982: 55). Ofeish and Ghandour note that the group 'create[s] self-righteous categories that divide people and issues, creating oppositions between themselves and others (the "enemy"), right and wrong, good and bad, civilized and less civilized, who should live and who should die' (Ofeish and Ghandour 2001: 129). The group also acts as a homosocial unified entity with shared ideology, which explains why Marie-Rose refers to it as 'chabab' or young men in Arabic.[16]

Educated in the same way and sharing the same beliefs, the 'chabab' behave as one body, and Marie-Rose is perceived as a threat to their self-imposed social order. She is a figure of transgression; she embodies everything that the 'chabab' despises: she is in a position of leadership in a school for children abled differently; she is a divorced mother of three; she is a Christian

Lebanese in a relationship with a Muslim Palestinian; she lives in the Muslim sector and sympathises with the Palestinian cause. Marie-Rose's transgressions are reflected in her life choices and in the narrative through the interjection and interruption of male narrations and voices by the feminine 'I'. The feminine 'I' speaks from a male space, transgresses the walls of her imprisonment to voice out her opinion on colonial education, politics and religion (Amireh 2005: 260–1). For the 'chabab', Marie-Rose's transgressions should be punished.

For Tony, Marie-Rose deserves what is happening to her as she dared intrude on male public spaces. In comparing Marie-Rose to his sister, Tony says:

> Si elle avait été ma sœur voici longtemps que je l'aurais tuée. Ma sœur est très bien. C'est une autre chose. Elle ne sort jamais sans être accompagnée de ma mère. Quand on lui parle elle baisse les yeux. Mais quand des putains se mêlent de la guerre, il y a de quoi être dégoûté (Adnan 2010: 69) / If she were my sister, I would have killed her long ago. My own sister is very nice. That's something else. She never goes out except with our mother. When you speak to her she lowers her eyes. But when whores get mixed up in war, now that's something to be disgusted about. (Adnan 1982: 60)

For him, Marie-Rose should die because she threatens everything he stands for: 'Elle est chrétienne, elle est passée au camp musulman. Elle est libanaise, elle est passée au camp palestinien' (Adnan 2010: 46) / 'She's Christian and she went over to the Moslem camp. She's Lebanese and she went over to the Palestinian camp' (Adnan 1982: 36). While Marie-Rose believes in the possibility of coexistence, Tony believes that Muslims are a threat to his Christianity: 'Je m'appelle Tony et je ne m'appellerai jamais Mohammad . . . Cette femme, c'est une chienne. Mounir n'a pas à la regarder comme on regarde un être ordinaire' (Adnan 2010: 46) / 'My name is Tony and it will never be Mohammed . . . This woman is a bitch. Mounir should not regard her as an ordinary person' (Adnan 1982: 36). For him, Marie-Rose is not an ordinary human being. The fact that she transgresses the social order in which he believes dehumanises her in his eyes. She is an animal who deserves to die.

For Fouad, Marie-Rose is a traitor which is why the deaf-mute children should witness her punishment; they should understand what awaits those who infringe the established order (Adnan 2010: 70 / Adnan 1982: 61). For Bouna Lias, Marie-Rose is a child who lost faith and one should only hope that she will find her way back to Christianity (Adnan 2010: 71 / Adnan 1982: 63).

In addition to being transgressional, and according to Suhair Majaj, Marie-Rose is also a confrontational figure. When talking to Mounir, she challenges him and changes her status from the accused to the accuser (Suhair Majaj 2002: 222). Suhair Majaj adds that Marie Rose's transgression is not only religious and social, but also spatial. When the news of her kidnapping spreads throughout the city, many start praying: 'Ya Allah faites qu'elle revienne, disaient les uns, et les autres: Ô Sainte Vierge nous t'allumerions cent bougies si tu nous la ramenais saine et sauve' (Adnan 1977: 80) / 'Allah bring her back some said while others said "Blessed Virgin, we'll light a hundred candles for you if you just send her back to us safe and sound"' (Adnan 1982: 72). Marie-Rose's voice is heard beyond the walls of her prison. Her voice defies the rules of nature and reaches the minds of the deaf-mute children who can feel her fear.

At the end of the novel, Marie-Rose is killed. Her death is told from different points of view, including hers. For Bounas Lias, she dies for Christianity to be safe from women like her. For the 'chabab', she dies because she is a 'monstre femelle' (Adnan 2010: 98) / 'a female monster' (Adnan 1982: 92) who despite her arrest continued to defy male authority. For the deaf-mute children, she dies, and they can never tell her story. For the feminine 'I', Marie-Rose is the ultimate victim of conservative, tribal and patriarchal values. She represents all the strong independent women who were killed by men throughout time and space.

Both feminine 'I's fall silent. Marie-Rose is dead, and the unnamed feminine 'I' has nothing to report anymore. The gradual disappearance of the feminine 'I' reflects the limitations women face in violent patriarchal societies. The feminine 'I' of Temps I attempts to document the lives and deaths of Syrian workers in Lebanon but fails. The men-led war limits her in time and space; it limits her in her own narrative. She is almost forced out of the narrative and replaced by other voices, and yet she continues to try to document the war by bearing witness to Marie-Rose's trauma. She says, '[j]e veux parler de la lumière de cette journée . . . Je veux dire à jamais que . . .' (Adnan 2010:

104) / 'I want to talk about the light on this day ... I want to say forever and ever ...' (Adnan 1982: 98). She tells us about the day Marie-Rose died, and even points out the killers: '[r]egardez-les!' (Adnan 2010: 106) / 'Look at them!' (Adnan 1982: 100). This was the last attempt of the feminine 'I' to speak. She feels liberated from the cage but she quickly discovers the truth of her limitations: 'une limite fondamentale, une sorte de paroi intérieure de l'esprit' (Adnan 2010: 105) / 'a fundamental limit, a kind of inner wall to the mind' (Adnan 1982: 99). She falls back on the ground with nothing more to add. Marie-Rose's feminine 'I' tries to resist physical and mental violence. She rejects her objectification and asserts herself in male spaces and male narratives. She pays dearly for her transgressions. Meanwhile the male voices continue to rise and rage, and the deaf-mute children, in the absence of their voice, can only dance.

Without any doubt, one can say that the feminine 'I' plays important roles in war narratives. Just like Marie-Rose, the feminine 'I' represents transgression in space, time and in the narrative itself. She embodies women's agency and voice in traditionally male-dominated spaces. In *Les Absents*, the feminine 'I' bears witness to individual and collective trauma and preserves the memory of war victims. Her trauma speaks in multiple ways and becomes the language by which the feminine 'I' tells stories of death and survival. In *Sitt Marie Rose*, the feminine 'I' (of Temps I and of Marie-Rose) attempts to record history as it unfolds before her eyes but cannot go beyond the patriarchal limitations. The feminine 'I' falls silent; she either fails in her recording mission or dies.

Notes

1 As mentioned in the introduction, many Lebanese women wrote against the patriarchal society and war. Many of them wrote using the first person not only to represent the self but also the others. In examining women representations in Maghrebi novels, Hafid Gafaïti argues that the use of the first-person pronoun does not only respond to this personal urge to speak up but also to this need to speak in the name of oppressed women, of ancestors and sisters: 'Le "je" s'écrit au point de vue d'une femme à la recherche d'elle-même dans une société où l'affirmation de soi est faite en relation avec le sort des autres femmes ... Dans cette mesure, le "je" est porteur d'une expression et d'un message qui ne sont pas seulement personnels mais collectifs' (Gafaïti 1996: 168). Although speaking

about Maghrebi novels, Gafaïti's point can be easily transferred to the Lebanese context.

2 There are multiple definitions to the genre of autofiction. In general, it is defined as a genre where the writer employs the first-person pronoun in a fictional context; it is a genre that combines reality and fiction. Catherine Viollet traces the history of this hybrid genre. Born after the Holocaust and the rise of post-modernism, it combines the truthfulness of the information and the freedom of writing (Viollet 2007: 9). For Jean-Louis Jeanelle, it is a narrative that is strictly autobiographical because of the overlapping between the persons of the writer, narrator and protagonist. However, the organisation of the narrative and the style are fictional: 'récit dont la matière est strictement autobiographique, ainsi que l'atteste en théorie l'identité nominale entre auteur, narrateur et personnage, mais dont la manière, c'est-à-dire l'organisation narrative et le travail du style, est de nature romanesque' (Jeanelle 2007: 20). This genre encounters many issues including the tracing of the boundaries between the autobiographical genre and the fictional genre: when does a text stop being autobiographical to become fictional?

3 Brissette 2002: 181–96; Duffy 1994: 8–11; Lejeune 1975; Nalbantian 2003; Reisert 2000: 305–30; Starobinski 1970; Starobinski 1971; Taylor 1992; Trilling 1972; Velguth 1985: 811–19.

4 Additionally, in a private message exchanged on Facebook on 11 May 2019, I asked the writer if the novel *Les Absents* is autobiographical. She said that it is a collective autobiography. She added that what interests her in writing is the mix of reality and fiction, to start with real facts and build protagonists and situations from there: 'c'est une autobiographie collective. Dans l'écriture, ce qui m'intéresse est le mélange de réalité fiction. Partir de données réelles, construire des personnages et des situations à partir de là' (Makhlouf 2019).

5 On ethics and trauma, see Hunt 2010: 28–50.

6 According to Caruth, the child's game refers also to real death that enters the child's life and that is recognised in a footnote in Freud's writing. The mother, who is also Freud's daughter Sophie, dies toward the end of the writing of *Beyond the Pleasure Principle* (Caruth 2013: 16).

7 The understanding of the value of language in bearing witness to trauma came to Caruth not in her readings of Freud's theory but in her own encounter with a child in Atlanta who had witnessed urban violence. Gregory lost his best friend Khalil in a shooting. When interviewed, Gregory told heart-warming stories of his friend using a playful language all while shifting between past and present

tenses. The interview reflected the continuity of their bond despite death. For Caruth this creative language in speaking of the dead and this need to repeatedly speak of the dead remind us of the child's game of 'gone' and 'here' since Gregory's language, in recalling trauma, swings between the act of memorialisation of the friend and the act of self-recognition. Gregory uses 'a creative act, an act that bears witness to the dead precisely in the process of turning away. It is indeed a new language of departure, parting words that bind the living child to the dead one even as he takes leave from him, that binds him to his dead friend even in the very act of letting go' (Caruth 2013: 14).

8 According to Pierre Nora:

> Our interest in *lieux de mémoire* where memory crystallizes and secretes itself has occurred at a particular historical moment, a turning point where consciousness of a break with the past is bound up with the sense that memory has been torn – but torn in such a way as to pose the problem of the embodiment of memory in certain sites where a sense of historical continuity persists. There are *lieux de mémoire*, because there are no longer *milieu de mémoire*, real environment of memory. (Nora 1989: 7)

9 Georgia Makhlouf explains this point during her interview with Muriel Maalouf on Radio France Internationale (Maalouf 2014).

10 Caruth's understanding of trauma and its relationship to language is well received by the humanities particularly by the post-structuralists and postmodernists. However, Ruth Leys (2000) claims that Caruth selectively cited passages from Freud's *Moses and Monotheism* and misinterpreted them in order to advance her own theory. Leys adds that US-based theorists (including Caruth) conflate the mimetic theory and the antimimetic theory of trauma, and that trauma studies have been 'balancing uneasily or veering uncontrollably between the antithetical poles or theories' (Leys 2007: 8).

In *Trauma, A Genealogy*, Leys dedicates the last chapter to Caruth's work: 'The Pathos of the Literal: Trauma and the Crisis of Representation'. Leys starts by recognising Caruth's merit for incorporating neurobiology in her work, particularly the work of Bessel van der Kolk from whom she retains that trauma escapes representation. In fact, the ordinary mechanism of consciousness is suspended, and trauma is instead literally registered without the victim's knowledge only to return either as nightmares or repetitive behaviour. For Leys, Caruth draws on the work of der Kolk and Paul Man and argues that trauma is so intense that it escapes language as no words are available to describe it; and yet the materiality of the event requires the usage of a signifier, of language. Language thus holds a performative role by which the victim, unable to necessarily represent or speak of the trauma, 'obsessively "performs", reenacts, or reexperiences it in the form of flashbacks, dreams, and related symptoms' (Leys 2000: 267). For Leys, Caruth's theory of linguistic failure in representing trauma is a redundancy inherited from Holocaust theorists, but it has been widely approved by academia.

Additionally, she assesses Caruth's analysis of Freud. Caruth examines Freud's two approaches of trauma: the model of castration trauma and the model of traumatic neurosis. Caruth, like many theorists, rejects the castration model, and replaces it with the concept of latency according to which trauma is a delayed reaction deferred in time. As such, for Caruth, trauma is defined in terms of temporal cause and effect, as a linear trajectory of what happened in the past and what will reappear in the present and the future. For Leys, Caruth oversimplifies Freud's theory and only uses one aspect of Freud's definition of trauma which includes time and literal memory. She accuses her of purposely ignoring Freud's other approach of trauma as mimesis in order to push her own arguments. Leys says: 'Caruth is attempting not to provide a genealogy of the concept of psychic trauma but to use the notion of trauma as a *critical concept* in order to support her performative theory of language. For her project to succeed it is crucial for her to make the case for the literal in Freud . . .' (Leys 2000: 275).

Leys adds that while Caruth believes in the intergenerational transmission of trauma, she does not discuss Freud's theory on the inheritance of acquired characters in the transmission of trauma across generations, nor Freud's adherence to Lamarck's theory. This omission raises an ethical question for Leys who accuses Caruth of purposely omitting this examination to advance her own idea. She goes even further and accuses her of inappropriately citing Freud to ensure the success of her performative theory of trauma. In examining Freud's *Moses and Monotheism*, Caruth argues that Freud himself experienced trauma while writing this text (as he began writing it in 1934 and was forced under the Nazi persecution in 1938 to leave Vienna for England). She says that trauma in Freud's text is performative; it is revealed to the reader even though there are no words to express it. According to Leys, in quoting Freud, Caruth purposely removed sentences that contradict her point and in which Freud admits his own trauma: '[Caruth] proceeds as if she cannot afford to quote everything Freud wrote, because the words she omits contradicts her argument' (Leys 2000: 289).

11 For Leys, trauma studies should acknowledge the existence of both approaches to trauma since trauma itself is experienced through this 'continuous tension or

oscillation between the two paradigms' (Leys 2000: 10). She attributes the rise of the antimimetic theory of trauma to its ideological and political implications based on which the subject remains sovereign and autonomous (Radstone 2007: 15).

12 I published part of this study in French in the Italian journal *Trasparenze*: 'La Multiplicité des Voix Narratives ou le Jeu Narratif dans *Sitt Marie Rose*', *Trasparenze*, 3 (2018), pp. 39–52.

13 'Sitt' is an Arabic word and an honorary title usually attributed to married woman. It is the equivalent of 'Madame' in French.

14 History as reported by the feminine 'I' is still contested by many Lebanese scholars. For instance, Evelyne Accad argues that Etel Adnan romanticises the Palestinian cause: '[w]hile Adnan describes the Christian militias and some of the priests, in their travesty of Christianity, in the darkest terms, she glorifies the Palestinian cause' (Accad 1990: 73). She adds: 'Adnan, while correct in her criticism of the perversion of Christianity, romanticizes to the extent of falsifying the Palestinian cause' (73).

15 For more on colonial education (with a focus on Algeria), see Harrison 2019.

16 For a definition on homosociality, see Kosofsky Sedwick 1985. Fedwa Malti-Douglas (1991) makes the distinction between homosociality and homosexuality. She says: '*Homosocial* must be distinguished from *homosexual* and by no means implies a sexual relationship, but rather a social relationship between two individuals of the same gender' (Malti-Douglas 1991: 15). She warns against the Western tendency to interpret homosociality as homosexuality.

It is interesting to note that the homosocial group of militia men in *Sitt Marie Rose* acts as a unified group with one political agenda; it also exhibits intense hatred towards strong women particularly Marie-Rose. According to miriam cooke (1997), men's hatred could be explained by examining Klaus Theweleit's approach to masculinity in times of war. As Theweleit states, military groups provide an alternative womb for real men to be born. Women, but more precisely mothers' bodies, become irrelevant and unnecessary. Real men are born in the military field by fighting and killing (Theweleit 1987: 87–9; qtd in cooke 1997: 275). As such, it is possible to say that 'el-chabab' in *Sitt Marie Rose* act as a homosocial group with strong non-sexual male ties. They consider the militia as the birthplace of the real masculinity, and Marie-Rose is simultaneously unnecessary to them but also a threat to their gestational alternative womb. For this reasons, Marie-Rose becomes disposable.

2

The Humanist Voice of the
Omniscient Narrator

In this chapter, I examine the omniscience as a narrative technique employed in Andrée Chedid's *La Maison sans racines* and *Le Message* and Evelyne Accad's *Coquelicot du massacre*. My claim is that these women writers tell war stories through the voice of a humanist omniscient narrator who attempts to illustrate the goodness in all human beings and to emphasise their commonalities. The omniscient narrator's humanity is reflected through a technical ability to show multiple points of view including the views of the combatants during the civil war.

I should point out that the notion of omniscient narrator has in fact raised a lot of questions. How does one label a novel told by an omniscient narrator? Are there minimal requirements? And what if the omniscient narrator only has limited omniscience? (Dawson 2013: 32–3). These questions are mostly motivated by the fear of turning the omniscient narrator into a 'dumping-ground filled with a wide range of distinct narrative techniques' (Martin 1986: 146; Dawson 2013: 33). These concerns are certainly legitimate. However, as Meir Sternberg argues, theorists should be more concerned with the where, the how and the why all this privileging has happened. He says:

> [t]he question for the theorist, any narrative theorist, is rather where, how, why all this privileging has happened – or, as in some literary and most life story, hasn't. Under what (mental, cultural, artistic) auspices has omniscient discourse operated? Along what lines? In what variants, or packages, or cross-links? By what rationales? And with what difference from non-omniscient

insets (e.g., figural, monologue, dialogue, tale within tale) or strategies (e.g., restricted telling, factual or fictional?). (Sternberg 2007: 720)

As such, and in keeping with Sternberg's questions, I will examine the where, the how and the why the omniscient narrator appears in these novels. I will start by reviewing the definition of the omniscient narrator as it is essential to properly understand its role in war narratives. I will then move to examine the reasons that may explain the writers' decision to use the omniscient narrator and the limitations imposed by that decision. Finally, I will examine the role of the omniscient voice and its effects in *La Maison sans racines*, *Le Message* and *Coquelicot du massacre*.

What is the Omniscient Narrator?

Paul Dawson argues that the omniscient narrator is probably the most contested narrative voice in the literary field since so much has been written either against or in defense of the omniscient narrator (Dawson 2013: 14).

For a structuralist theorist like Barthes, the omniscient narrator is an:

apparently impersonal, consciousness that tells the story from an all-encompassing point of view, that of God: the narrator stands at the same time inside his characters (since he knows all that happens in them) and outside them (since he never identifies with one more than the others). (Barthes 1975a: 261)

For Genette however, omniscient narration or omniscience is:

[i]n pure fiction . . . literally, absurd (the author has nothing to 'know', since he invents everything), and we would be better off replacing it with *completeness of information* – which when supplied to a reader, makes him 'omniscient'. The instrument of this possible selection is a *situated focus*, a sort of information-conveying pipe that allows passage only of information that is authorized by the situation . . . (Genette 1983: 74)

In his essay 'Omniscience', Jonathan Culler agrees with Genette. He says, 'I *have* reached the conclusion that it is not a useful concept for the study of narration, that it conflates and confuses several different factors that should be separated if they are to be well understood – that it obfuscates the various phenomena that provoke us to posit the idea' (Culler 2004: 22). Culler, in fact, takes issue with the analogy between the omniscient narrator and God and argues that it is impossible for the novelist and the omniscient narrator to know everything like God. He asks what if one does not believe in God and adds that omniscience is incompatible with free will. For Culler, imagining that the narrator has agency is a false debate. In a way, he sides with Genette and argues that the narrative voice is simply the author's artistic choice to achieve a literary effect.

Barbara K. Olson responds to Culler in her essay 'Who Thinks This Book?' and argues that he takes the author/God analogy too seriously:

> Culler's own resistance also seems to me more theological than literary. For instance, while he decides not to call omniscience 'obscene', it is nearly so to him, smacking of arrogance and a Bush-like imperialism. He has a particular view of God – or a particular view of what others must be referring to when they use 'God' or godlike analogy. (Olson 2006: 341)

For Olson, discussing God's existence is unnecessary in narratology, and even if God does not exist one should not stop trying to understand narratology.

The American novelist Richard Russo defines the omniscient narrator as the voice that

> looks at characters from the outside but can 'see' inside, directly into thoughts and feelings. It transcends time and space. The omniscient narrator can be in as many places as he or she needs to be and possesses knowledge of all moments – past, present, and future – and is free to reveal it. (Russo 2001: 11)

He argues that using the omniscient narrator helps balance the story by giving equal time to each character, suggesting their equal importance as characters (Russo 2001: 10).

Russo reviews the reasons why omniscience has been rejected as a writing technique: for some, the omniscient narrator tells a lot and does not show, and it provides an outside point of view rather than one from inside the characters. For others, the technique feels old-fashioned; it is an arrogant technique by which the writer plays God and claims to know everything. For each of these arguments, Russo offers a counter-argument in defense of the omniscient narrator: he argues that telling is as valid a narrative technique as showing, and that a writer is above all a storyteller and not story-shower. Regarding the point of view, Russo says that sometimes there is nothing to gain from being inside a character and it is best to be outside. He acknowledges the fact that omniscience may be old-fashioned and continues to say, '[w]ell, gentle reader, who gives a damn?' (Russo 2001: 16). He considers arrogance part of the equation: '[w]e aren't writers to be timid. If playing God scares you, there are other professions. And who says authors shouldn't intrude into fiction? What they shouldn't do . . . is intrude clumsily or stupidly or unwittingly' (16). Russo concludes his essay by saying that:

> Omniscience not only invents a world; it tells how that world works or how we should feel about the way it works . . . Omniscience is permission to speak and to speak with authority we know we really don't have, about a world that in our century (any century?) is too complex to know. (Russo 2001: 17)

For Eugene Goodheart, the omniscient narrator is a 'licensed trespasser' that 'may be a necessity in a world riven by opposing perspectives, that a respect for a variety of perspectives that exist in the world depends upon it' (Goodheart 2004: 2). Goodheart starts by examining Bakhtin and Sartre's arguments against the omniscient narrator. For Bakhtin, he says, 'omniscience is the tyranny of the monologic to which he opposes the dialogic. The novelist, [in Bakhtin's view], refuses or should refuse authority to the voice of any single character, including the narrator' (1). As such, the novel should allow a harmonious polyphony. As for Sartre, atheistic hostility is the main motivation behind the rejection of the omniscient narrator. However, for Goodheart,

> [t]hose who win theoretical or cultural battles are not always in the right. The case against omniscience is vulnerable in its systematic claim – that is, when it develops from a genuine insight into a theory that betrays its own ambition to omniscience. The 'all-knowing narrator' has its uses, which the theory and its maker (whether Jameson or Sartre or Bakhtin) ignore. (Goodheart 2004: 2)

As for Dawson, the omniscient narrator is 'an all-knowing authorial narrator who addresses the reader directly, offers intrusive commentary on the events being narrated, ranges freely across space and time, provides access to the consciousness of characters, and generally asserts palpable presence within the fictional' (Dawson 2013: 1).

The omniscient form, as Dawson points out, is considered a relic of the nineteenth century, and it was abandoned in favour of other narrative forms particularly the first-person narrator. Dawson argues that it has been abandoned for many reasons: it is considered morally suspect, and the omniscient narrator came to be associated with an all-knowing God that leaves no agency for the characters in the novel, nor for the reader.[1] It is a pretentious voice that has unlimited knowledge that can be anywhere at any time; it is also a voice that has frequently been confused with either the voice of the author or the voice of third-person narrative mode.

However, the omniscient narrator made its comeback in the late twentieth and early twenty-first centuries to help face the decline of the novel. Many reasons contributed to the decline of the novel: the increase in sales of other genres such as memoires and personal essays, the commercial aspect of some publishing houses amplified with the availability of large bookstores and online booksellers, the competition of television and cinema and the broader challenges that traditional print faces versus the digital world. For Dawson, this decline translated into the loss of the literary voice and its representation in the real cultural world, which subsequently led to the revival of the omniscient narrator.

Dawson, however, notes a change in the omniscient narrator's attributes which shifted from the classic narrator with universal moral authority that cannot be questioned to a postmodern omniscient narrator. For Dawson, '[t]he commonly accepted features of post-modern fiction include self-reflexivity, parody, irony, playfulness, pastiche, nonlinearity and general tendency for formal experimentation . . .' (Dawson 2013: 65). He also adds that postmodern implies:

> [M]etafictional subversions of the relation between fiction and history (Hutcheon); fiction in which the generic dominant is a narrative foregrounding of ontological questions – as opposed to the epistemological dominant of modernism (McHale, *Postmodernist Fiction*); a tendency to favor diegesis over mimesis (Lodge, 'Mimesis'); and in a critique of formalist approaches,

the global expansion of English language fiction in the wake of colonialism (Berube). (Dawson 2013: 65)

As such, Dawson defines postmodernism 'as an aesthetic move beyond the "exhaustion" of modernist experimentation without returning to traditional realism, and a cultural response to a perceived crisis of authority for the novel · as a mode of public discourse, dramatised in the phrase "the death of the novel"' (Dawson 2013: 65–6).

Dawson's postmodern omniscient narrator is thus an intrusive and sometimes self-reflective narrative voice that engages the narratee and allows him or her to know the story-world and to question the grand narratives. By extension, the omniscient narrator is also pushing the reader to think about the novel and its cultural insights. After examining the texts of several anglophone writers, Dawson makes the distinction between what he calls the ironic-moralist omniscient narrator, the literary historian, the pyrotechnic storyteller, the social commentator, the self-reflective omniscient narrator with free indirect discourse (FID)[2] and the omniscient narrator in the context of different voices particularly the first-person narrator.

He defines the ironic-moralist omniscient narrator as the narrator who directly addresses the reader while self-consciously struggling with the legacy of the moral authority of classic omniscience. The literary historian is the narrator 'who asserts the historiographic value of imaginatively reconstructing history in fictional form, both drawing upon and challenging the authority of scholarly approaches to the archive' (Dawson 2013: 22); the pyrotechnic storyteller is the intrusive omniscient narrator that manifests himself or herself through stylistic expressions and precise language. The pyrotechnic storyteller is a 'personalised' narrator that engages the reader; the social commentator is the 'narrator whose "omniscience" operates in the hyperbolic sense of displaying polymathic knowledge' (22); the double-voiced omniscient narrator who accesses his or her characters through the usage of the FID and finally the first-person omniscience which is considered a 'parodic critic of the claims for authority made by classic omniscience' (23).

In conclusion, to all these different observations on the omniscient narrator's definition and attributes, one can say that an omniscient narrator is above all a conventionally recognised narrative voice. It is a voice that tells the story of others from a God-like 'all-encompassing point of view' (Barthes 1975a: 261). It is a voice that can see inside characters' heads and knows their thoughts. It is not restricted in time nor space. It is a bold voice that speaks with authority about the complexity of the world and it is a 'licensed trespasser' (to use Goodheart's comparison borrowed from the narrator of George Eliot's *Adam Bede)* that is necessary in a divided world. Finally, it is an intrusive self-reflective voice that encourages the characters and, by extension, the reader to challenge the historical narrative of the time.

Furthermore, the omniscient narrator has specific characteristics that distinguish it from the first-person narrator. On the one hand, the writer does not need to worry about developing the person of the omniscient narrator nor providing details on its progression in time and space. Philippe Lejeune argues that narrative told by a first-person narrator is bound to encounter the problem of identity, 'on rencontre fatalement le problème de l'identité' (Lejeune 1980: 35), which is not the case of the omniscient narrator.

On the other hand, the first-person narrator has a limited point of view, which, as an enunciating subject, is restricted to him or her. To understand the narrative, the reader must follow the thoughts of the first-person narrator, to penetrate their consciousness, and to follow their judgement and reasoning. For John Morreall, '[t]he events in the story are "filtered through" the consciousness of this character, and so the reader is entitled to ask anything in the story, "How did this character know or think that?"' (Morreall 1994: 432). In fact, the reader has the same limited point of view as the first-person narrator, who cannot access the consciousness of another character (unless they have a superpower that allows them to read the other characters' minds). The omniscient narrator does not suffer from this limitation since in theory they have unlimited access to information. Furthermore, as Alain Roger argues, the frequent use of the first-person pronoun might bore and tire the reader. Additionally, it may lead to inconsistencies in the narrative: '[l]a litanie du Je, outre qu'elle risque de lasser le lecteur, menace d'inconsistance, voire d'irréalité, les autres personnages, qui paraissent dotés d'une existence seconde, évanescente, et comme suspendue au bon vouloir, au bon regard du narrateur' (Roger 1984: 49).

This multilayered definition of the omniscient narrator and the exposé of its technical benefits, particularly in comparison to the first-person narrator, makes one wonder whether these are the reasons behind the choice of omniscience in *La Maison sans racines*, *Le Message* and *Coquelicot du massacre*. This brings us to the second part of the chapter where I examine the possible reasons for which the writers have chosen the omniscient narrator.

Why the Omniscient Narrator?

As pointed out earlier in the introduction, for Genette, the choice of the narrative voice is entirely aleatory (Genette 1988: 113). As a reminder, for classical narratology, the choice of the narrative voice carries no real meaning aside from the technical points it brings into the narrative (such as frequency, duration, level, point of view, among other things). It is the postclassical narratology that assigned meaning to the choice. For instance, feminist, postcolonial and postmodern narratologies assigned meaning and value to the first-person narrator. I would like to advance the theory that the choice of omniscience is not as aleatory as Genette suggested, particularly in the case of war stories. I argue that it is a deliberate choice that allows writers such as Chedid and Accad to benefit from the omniscient narrator's technical aspects, and to monopolise the voice or assign it to a God-like humanist voice in a chaotic and polyphonic country.

Several arguments could be advanced to support this claim: Women's texts are often quickly labelled feminist; they are assumed to be presenting a feminist political agenda in the way they speak of women as subjects and the way they represent them in opposition to men. While the label itself is not problematic, it comes, however, with certain risks.

Michelle Hartman (2002) discusses the danger of quickly labelling women's texts feminist. According to her, this label may contribute into the marginalisation of women writers who will only be assessed and saluted for their works as women writers rather than simply writers. Additionally, in the Arab World, there is a rejection of the feminist label because many consider it to be the carrier of a Eurocentric meaning:

> This can be understood as challenging the marginalization of women writers. One distinct concern expressed by many writers is that their works are not taken seriously and on the same level as men, leaving them isolated in a 'ghetto' of women writers. Any subsequent success would then always

imply a qualification – she is a good writer – for a woman. Moreover, the rejection of these labels is also a commitment to guarding against these issues in the Arab world being subsumed into a feminist agenda, defined by white, European and North American women and thus far removed from the situations of Lebanese and Arab women. The influence and relevance of many feminist ideas and movement are acknowledged by Arab critics, however, the importance of highlighting local issues is also a prominent focus for many. (Harman 2002: 11)

Talpade Mohanty shows how the danger of marginalisation could immediately result from mainstream Western feminism. Western feminism, although far from being monolithic, tends to view third-world women as a homogenous group and ignores the particularities of each region and culture, and, as such unfortunately, reproduces a colonial discourse. As such, '[t]hird-World feminisms run the risk of marginalization or ghettoization from both mainstream (right and left) and Western feminist discourses' (Talpade Mohanty 2003: 17).

For Anastasia Valassopoulos, there is also a risk of 'inevitable ranking of works in terms of how well they perform as "feminist" or "nationalist" texts' (Valassopoulos 2007: 9). Finally, for Elise Salem Manganaro, '[a]ttempts have been made to link the feminist with the pacifist, to read women's narratives in opposition to male discourse, and to identify supporting passages from fiction that obviously present an alternative to a seemingly male-driven war' (Salem Manganaro 1995–6: 169). For Manganaro, this is a false assumption and a very reductive view of this literature which in a way contributes to the perpetuating of the maternal stereotypes.

These risks are true in general to any woman's text whether it is written with a first- or third-person narrator (or omniscient narrator). However, an argument could be made that the first-person narrator or a feminine 'I' may aggravate these risks of marginalisation, dismissal, ghettoisation and assumption of pacifism. The consequences of these risks may be even higher in war stories since they amplify social and gender divisions, or as Lanser claims, 'personal narration offers no gender-neutral mask or distancing "third person", no refuge in a generic voice that may pass as masculine' (Lanser 1992: 19). Lanser also points out another risk: '[a] female personal narrator risks the reader's resistance if the act of telling, the story she tells, or the self she constructs through telling it transgresses the limits of acceptability feminine' (Lanser 1992: 19).

Could these be the reasons why Chedid and Accad utilised an omniscient narrator? While this reasoning holds, it remains broad with a lot of variables. As such, the answer to the question may be found in the writers' personal views on the matter. In the 1982 special issue of *Magazine Littéraire*, prepared by Xavière Gauthier and Anne Rivière on women writers and their works, Chedid argues that she has been writing for a long time and that she does not consider her womanhood the starting point of her writing: '[s]ur le plan de la recherche ça m'a beaucoup intéressée, mais dans mon écriture ça n'a rien changé. J'écris depuis très longtemps et je ne pars pas de l'a priori que je suis une femme . . .' (Gauthier and Rivière 1982: 36). In another interview with Bettina L. Knapp, Chedid protests the categorisation and labelling of her writings. She says, '[c]'est peut-être pour cela, pour sortir des catégories et des étiquettes que j'ai éprouvé le besoin de passer d'une forme à l'autre, poésie, nouvelles, romans, contes pour enfants, théâtre. Une sorte de rébellion perpétuelle (peut-être encore trop juvénile!) contre toute tentative d'encadrement!' (Knapp and Chedid 1984: 520). Chedid thus rejects the confinement in one literary form and alternates between poetry, novella, novels, children's tales and theatre.

In the same interview, Chedid adds that she prefers to distance herself from the protagonists and as such declines to share personal experiences:

> Quant aux personnages, j'ai besoin de leur présence pour m'attacher moi-même à ce que je suis en train d'écrire. Besoin de les aimer ou le contraire; besoin de les questionner et qu'ils ne surprennent. Découvrir l'aventure d'un livre avec leur appui. On a souvent parlé de l'autonomie des person-nages entraînant l'auteur dans leur sillage; bien que viscéralement atta-chés à l'écrivain, il est vrai que ces personnages vivent de leur vie propre. L'autobiographie ne m'ayant jamais tenté, il ne s'agit jamais pour ma part d'expériences personnelles, de souvenirs précis. (Knapp and Chedid 1984: 517)

Furthermore, and as many critics have already pointed out, Chedid's works are heavily marked by her quest of brotherhood. For Renée Linkhorn, it is hard to use terms like femininity or feminism to describe Chedid as a writer, for one term is insipid while the other has a militant echo to it, and both are far removed from the way the writer speaks of the true nature of a woman: 'mièvrerie du premier, échos militants éveillés par le second, et qui sont bien éloignés de ce qui, pour l'auteur, incarne la véritable nature de la femme' (Linkhorn 1985: 560). Linkhorn argues that the term 'féminitude' works better as it reflects Chedid's constant search for fraternity and her examination of women in their own cultural environment and as part of a larger community, in solidarity with their societies rather than on their margins (Linkhorn 1985: 560).

Georgia Makhlouf reminds the reader that Chedid is called 'l'auteur de la fraternité', or the writer of brotherhood (Makhlouf et al. 2013: 116). As for Accad, Chedid writes so the humanity (a feminine word that includes both man and woman) retrieves its lost self and achieves reconciliation: 'pour que l'humanité (mot féminin qui signifie donc le côté femme/homme et le sens complet de ce qu'Andrée Chedid nous dit) retrouve son visage perdu et atteigne la reconciliation' (Accad et al. 2013: 170).

Accad admits sharing Chedid's views of the world and her positive approach to hybridity which generates cosmopolitanism, richness, tolerance and openness: 'Je partage la vision d'Andrée Chedid qui insiste sur ce qu'il y a de positif dans le mélange, qu'elle appelle hybridation, soulignant le cosmopolitisme, l'enrichissement, la tolérance et l'ouverture d'esprit qu'elle apporte' (Accad et al. 2013: 170). In a way, and this would be the last and third point in this section, the omniscient narrator responds to Accad's quest of brotherhood as well. Accad discusses '(f)humaine' experience (Accad 1997: 17), where she places la femme or the woman in the heart of humanity. In that sense, she is close to Chedid, who rejects the binary divisions of male-female to adopt a more encompassing approach to humanity. In an interview with Deirdre Bucher Heistad, Sharon Meilahn-Swett and Bartley Meinke, Accad speaks of fémi-humanisme, which she defines as the movement of men and women working together for justice, reconciliation, harmony, peace, better understanding of all peoples, acceptance of one another, and, as such, acceptance and comprehension of the other sex: 'mouvement de femmes et d'hommes travaillant pour la justice, la réconciliation, l'harmonie, la paix, la compréhension entre les peuples, l'acceptation de l'autre et donc aussi l'acceptation et la compréhension de l'autre sexe' (Heistad et al. 2004: 23).

In the same interview, while discussing her texts *L'Excisée* and *Voyages en Cancer*, Accad confesses that it is difficult to use the first-person narrator as one feels exposed in front of the reader and that the third-person allows more distance: 'C'est difficile de dire Je, on s'implique advantage il me semble, on se met à nu devant le lectuer . . . alors que la troisième personne permet advantage de distance . . .' (Heistad et al. 2004: 29).

Ultimately, Chedid and Accad are writers who speak in the name of a universal humanity and shared values, who find it difficult to be in their characters' skin, and who resist confinement and alternate between different literary and artistic forms. As such, one can understand why they privileged the omniscient voice. It allows the writer to dodge (or perhaps attenuate) the perils of the feminist labelling; it speaks in women and men's names and as such does not aggravate the social divisions in an already war-torn country; it guarantees some distance between the writers and their characters especially since the topic is of a sensitive matter; and it offers a humanist approach to the war by offering multiple points of view.

La Maison sans racines, Le Message and Coquelicot du massacre

La Maison sans racines

La Maison sans racines was published in 1985, ten years after the beginning of the Lebanese civil war. According to Carmen Boustani, it was inspired by Chedid's novella called 'Un jour l'ennemie' in which a grandmother runs to rescue two girls who were wounded by a sniper, a little girl tricks her parents' vigilance, runs to the balcony and succumbs to violence, and a march for peace is organised (Boustani 2016: 255). Boustani also points out that a real march for peace was organised in Beirut in May 1984 by Imane Khalifeh, a member of the Institute for Women's Studies in the Arab World. The march was supposed to take place at Beirut's National Museum, which represented the demarcation line that separated Christian East and Muslim West Beirut. The idea behind the march was to unite the Christians and the Muslims. Intensive shelling put a quick end to the march and resulted in casualties. Boustani wonders whether Khalifeh was inspired by Chedid's novella or whether Chedid was inspired by Khalifeh's real march.

La Maison sans racines focuses on the outbreak of the Lebanese civil war in 1975 and tells the story of twelve-year-old Sybil and her grandmother Kalya. Sybil lives in the United States and Kalya lives in France. They chose to meet for the first time in what they consider to be the land of their ancestors. While Sybil discovers Lebanon for the first time, Kalya relives her childhood memories. Their peaceful vacation is interrupted by the brutal outbreak of the civil war, and the novel ends with the march's failure and Sybil's death. For Knapp, this novel 'dramatizes the deepest of trauma – the cutting down of a budding life, the destruction of future hope – in a stylistically innovative manner' (Knapp 1986: 358).

The narrative structure of the novel is complex. Divided into three time periods, July–August 1932, July–August 1975 and one morning in August 1975, the novel allows the development of three different stories located in different times and spaces. In the first story, Kalya stands by her window one morning in August 1975 to watch the march for peace organised by two young women, Ammal and Myriam. A shot rings out and one of the women is injured. Kalya runs to the rescue. While discussing this scene, Knapp argues that the novel begins very theatrically and Kalya's run becomes a long interminable march described in the smallest details (Knapp 1986: 358). The second story focuses on Kalya's childhood in 1932, when she and her grandmother Nouza left Egypt to spend their summer in Lebanon. The third story takes place between July and August of 1975 in Lebanon. It recounts Sybil and Kalya's arrival to Lebanon, their first meeting, their family reunion with Tante Odette and Slimane her faithful housekeeper and all the friendships they built within the community. This part of the novel shows all the elements that will lead to the outbreak of the civil war and that fatal day in August 1975.

Regarding the chronology in the novel, the three stories do not follow a coherent linear order; they are fragmented and frequently interrupted by analepses. For Elinor Ochs and Lisa Capps, '[s]ometimes chronology is artfully altered for rhetorical purposes, as when a narrator uses flashbacks or slow disclosures to enhance the dramatic effect' (Ochs and Capps 1996: 24).

Regarding the narrative voice, Kalya's childhood story from 1932 is told by a first-person narrator or the feminine 'I' and the other two stories from 1975 are told by an omniscient narrator. Why this shift in the narrative voice, one might ask? In fact, when the war begins, Kalya's feminine 'I' disappears just like her individuality. She becomes part of a larger group, the Lebanese society as whole. Kalya, who once witnessed history as a child, becomes a participant in the events. The abrupt change in the narrative voice underscores the disappearance of the feminine 'I' as well as peace in Lebanon. The omniscient narrator is therefore the consequence of Kalya's silence. It plays two important roles: it announces the war's arrival by signalling the disappearance of Kayla's personal voice; it stands at equal distance from all protagonists to identify the causes of the conflict (without accusing anyone), to deplore the acts of violence and the fratricide nature of the war and to express hope for the return of peace.

First: The Omniscient Narrator replaces the feminine 'I':

For classic narratology, the silence of the first-person narrator can be easily explained by the rise of technical needs such as the need for a larger point of view: Kalya has a very limited point of view and it is even more restricted during her march since she is almost frozen in time and space. These arguments are certainly true. However, to follow postclassical narratology's approach to the narrative voice, there is an undeniable symbolic meaning to this shift. In other words, the shift is not simply technical but is also representative of the limitations in times of war of the feminine 'I'. Kalya no longer tells her own story or remembers her childhood memories. As of July 1975, she becomes part of a larger group that is about to witness a violent repetition of its history. Consequently, she can no longer speak in her own name, and the omniscient narrator takes over the narrative to simultaneously reveal the connectivity of all characters and their shared collective history. They are all connected like the spokes of a wheel, and when Kalya's gaze and the omniscient narrator's voice overlap, they draw imaginary lines between her as the centre of the wheel/action and the other protagonist. For instance, during her march, she keeps looking at the building where her loved ones reside, then checks on the two wounded women: '[u]ne ligne médiane va de l'immeuble jusqu'au centre de la Place, un sillon mène de Sybil jusqu'à Myriam et Ammal, un axe conduit la vie. Un intervalle qui dure et dure. Une trêve, assaillie de questions, alourdie de souvenirs' (Chedid 1985: 172) / 'A line stretches from the apartment block to the centre of the square, a furrow from Sybil to Myriam and Ammal, a conductor of life. Time is suspended. A truce, under siege from questions, weighed down with memories' (Chedid 1989: 142). She also feels connected to all of humanity and the entire universe and feels everyone's sorrow: 'les angoisses de la terre, toutes ses lamentations' (Chedid 1985: 40) / 'all the anguish in the world, all its laments' (Chedid 1989: 30).

Despite this shift in the narrative voice, there is no disruption to the narrative itself. If the omniscient narrator indicates the limitations of the first-person narrator, it also reveals the fluid and repetitive aspects of history. It is a universal history that cannot be restricted to one individual, and it is a history that cannot be contained as it faithfully repeats itself.

Repetition in history is suggested to the reader through Kalya's early interest in religion. She asks whether God is for all human beings and whether he is only good and always without hatred: 'Dieu est pour tous les hommes? Dieu est sans haine, n'est-ce pas? Dieu est la bonté même? Sinon Dieu ne serait pas Dieu, n'est-ce-pas grand-maman?' (Chedid 1985: 69) / 'God is for all men? God is without hatred, isn't he? God is goodness itself? Otherwise God wouldn't be God, would he, Grandma?' (Chedid 1989: 54).

Her cousin Mitry explains the historical religious conflicts:

Mitry me raconta les disputes christologiques qui ensanglantèrent le passé, les querelles islamiques qui le déchirèrent. Histoire de ruptures et de réconciliations, de conquêtes, d'humiliations, de sang et de larmes . . . je remontais les allées des schismes et des unions, celles des batailles, des rétractations, des trêves; celles des massacres et des sanglots . . . de ces discussions houleuses embrouillées, autour de la succession du Prophète, autour du dogme de la Trinité, qui divisaient les uns et les autres jusqu'à l'exécration. Fallait-il être partisan d'Ali, cousin et gendre du prophète Mahomet; ou bien être fidèle au calife, son successeur choisir par consentement général? Fallait-il attribuer au Christ une ou deux natures, une ou deux volontés? Fallait-il être uniate, monothéiste, nestorien, chalcédonien, monophysite? Ces démêlés aboutissaient à des luttes assassines, à des carnages, à des meurtrières fureurs. (Chedid 1985: 70–1) / Mitry told me of the arguments over Christ which had bloodied the past, of the Islamic quarrels which had torn it apart. A history of schisms and reconciliations, of conquests, humiliations, blood and tears . . . I traced the paths of rifts and unions, of battles, of retractions, truces, of massacres and of tears . . . [of] stormy complicated arguments about the succession of the Prophet, around the dogma of the Trinity which divided peoples to the point of hatred. Should one be a partisan of Ali, cousin and son-in-law of the prophet Muhammad, or should one be faithful to the Caliph, his successor chosen by consensus? Should Christ be attributed one or two natures, one or two wills? Should one be Unicist, Monothelite, Nestorian, Chalcedonian or Monophysite? These disputes led to murderous struggles, to massacres and to deadly fury. (Chedid 1989: 55–6)

Mitry's explanations allow Kalya to understand the origins of the Lebanese conflict: the historical confrontations of the different religious communities, a history that will eventually repeat itself in 1975. Interestingly, Mitry warns his young cousin about repetition in history: '[j]usqu'aujourd'hui, dans ce pays, il y a quatorze possibilités d'être croyant, monothéistes et fils d'Abraham . . . C'est fragile. Chaque jour de paix est un miracle. N'oublie pas cette pensée. Où que tu sois, au plus profond de ta tristesse, elle t'aidera à sourire' (Chedid 1985: 71). / 'Even today, in this country, there are fourteen ways of being a believer, a monotheist and a son of Abraham . . . It's fragile. Every day of peace is a miracle. Never forget that thought. Wherever you are, in the depths of your sadness, it will help you smile' (Chedid 1989: 56).

This continuity in history is also suggested through the usage of the historical present tense to narrate summer 1932. According to Ochs and Capps, 'this rhetorical strategy renders the narrated events vivid and captivating. The use of the present tense to relate past events may indicate a continuing preoccupation; the events are not contained in the past but rather continue to invade a narrator's current consciousness' (Ochs and Capps 1996: 25).

For Anne-Marie Miraglia, the cyclic nature of history and the universality of the human condition in war are suggested though the mnemonic resonance of lexical terms, themes and characters: '[l]es résonnances mnémoniques au niveau lexical, thématique et au niveau des personnages facilitent l'enchaînement des séquences tout en insistant sur la nature cyclique de l'Histoire et de l'existence humaine' (Miraglia 1998: 33).

Second: The omniscient narrator at equal distance from all protagonists:

When writing about the civil war, how does one write about horrors committed by one's own community? How can one write without accusing anyone and without choosing sides? It would be a mistake to believe that all Lebanese women writers wrote from an apolitical point of view. For instance, and as we saw in Chapter 1, Etel Adnan adopts a leftist pro-Palestinian position in *Sitt Marie Rose*. According to Accad, Adnan 'glorifies the Palestinian cause' and 'romanticizes it to the extent of falsifying [it]' (Accad 1990: 73). Lina Murr-Nehmé in *Comme un torrent qui gronde* and Desirée Aziz in *Le Parfum du bonheur* speak from a conservative Christian point of view (Darwiche Jabbour 2007: 138).

For Chedid, the answer was precisely not to choose sides but instead to write in the name of peace for all. Chedid repeatedly spoke of hope and fraternity in her novels and poems and showed the devastation of war on all levels. According to Christine Germain, for Chedid, humanity begins within, from the inside of all things and all human beings and it expresses itself in the outside. This hopeful approach to humanity suggests a belief in an interior freedom, a self-affirmation that gives hope for the rebirth and reconstruction of the future:

> [l]'auteur propose une démarche humaine intérieure. Celle-ci consiste à retrouver le visage premier des choses et des hommes, à rejoindre dans leur nudité totale leur authentique réalité. Cette attitude suppose la liberté intérieure, l'affirmation totale de soi pour une renaissance et une construction de l'avenir. Elle s'enracine dans l'espoir. (Germain 1985: 69)

In her article "Andrée Chedid: quête poétique d'une fraternité", Renée Linkhorn shows the writer's strong belief in a cosmic brotherhood, one that connects all creations in time and space:

> [v]ision cosmique. Une vaste forme de fraternité unit la création tout entière. C'est une solidarité dans l'espace et dans le temps. Les images atteignent à cette vision cosmique en rapprochant entre elles, et en rapprochant de l'homme en particulier, toutes les composantes de l'univers. (Linkhorn 1985: 560)

She adds that for Chedid, brotherhood also means a shared destiny 'fraternité, c'est aussi partager un destin commun' (Linkhorn 1985: 561).

Chedid's belief in humanity and brotherhood may explain her narrative choice and her privileging of omniscience. In fact, in Lebanon, the first-person narrator (or in this case the feminine 'I') carries a religious identity that is either Christian or Muslim.[3] One can safely assume that Chedid was aware of this situation, and consequently chose the omniscient narrator to avoid choosing between the two religions. Situated outside the diegesis (to borrow Genette's terminology), the omniscient narrator offers a general view of all the protagonists that henceforth share a common destiny. Without accusing anyone and standing at a more or less equal distance from all protagonists, the omniscient narrator deplores the fratricidal nature of the conflict and advocates for love and hope.

At the beginning of the novel, the writer uses the voice of the omniscient narrator to foreshadow the beginning of the war. When Kalya and Sybil arrive in Lebanon, they take a taxi to go to Tante Odette's house. On their way there, they see some brownish tents, 'un amoncellement de tentes brunâtres' (Chedid 1985: 25) / 'a mass of brownish tents' (Chedid 1989: 17). When Sybil asks the driver about these tents, he says not to worry as they are temporary constructions: '[c]'est provisoire' (Chedid 1985: 25) / 'It's temporary' (Chedid 1989: 17). In fact, these tents refer to the Palestinian refugees who came to Lebanon in 1948 and 1967. In opposition to this scenery of poverty, the omniscient narrator describes the wealth and the luxury of coffee shops, casinos and restaurants by the beaches: '[c]afés, casinos, restaurants aux enseignes lumineuses paradent au bord des plages' (Chedid 1985: 25) / 'Cafés, casinos and restaurants with neon signs make a colorful splash along the sea front' (Chedid 1989: 18). It is interesting to note that it is not the protagonists that discuss the opposition between the two scenes but the omniscient narrator who seems to suggest that poverty and the refugee crisis will play an important role in the outbreak of war.

Religion plays an important role as well as it feeds sectarian violence.[4] For Tante Odette, religion is the most important element in Lebanon and in one's existence: '[i]ci, la religion prime tout, elle marque toute l'existence' (Chedid 1985: 66) / 'Here, religion dominates everything. It affects our whole lives' (Chedid 1989: 52). When Kalya says that faith is a personal and intimate question, Tante Odette laughs at her and says she is in the wrong country with the wrong people: '[s]i tu penses comme ça, alors tu te trompes de pays, de peuple, de contrée!' (Chedid 1985: 66) / 'It that's the way you think, you're in the wrong country, among the wrong people, in the wrong land!' (Chedid 1989: 52).

The omniscient narrator reports, through the protagonists and some-times with direct speech, the reasons behind the war without necessarily judg-ing. If it judges, it is to defend peace and to deplore the loss of lives. In fact, the omniscient narrator points out the growing discord between Myriam and her brother Georges. Myriam believes in Lebanese diversity while Georges has conservative Christian views. The omniscient narrator tells the reader about these. The fights are filtered through Mario's eyes (their father) and they reflect what is happening in the country in general:

> Mario – persuadé que seuls les liens familiaux résistaient aux épreuves – butait contre le mur qui s'élevait entre Myriam et Georges. Jusque-là son épouse était parvenue à le lui dissimuler. Les heurts traversés par le pays, par les régions avoisinantes, secouaient les deux adolescents, redoublant leur opposition. Leur père en fut ébranlé (Chedid 1985: 85) / Mario – convinced that only family ties could withstand hardship – had come up against the barrier that existed between Myriam and Georges. Until then, his wife had managed to hide it from him. The classes that occurred in the country, in neighbouring regions, shook the two young people, intensifying their oppo-sition to each other. It shattered their father. (Chedid 1989: 68)

> Le regard tendu, Mario parlait en haletant. Il ne pouvait plus dissimuler ses craintes pour le pays, pour ses enfants. Georges militait avec fièvre dans un parti. Myriam et Ammal cherchaient, en utopistes, à rallier toutes les com-munautés dans un même but ... Alerté par une expression de mépris sur le visage de son fils, par une colère intempestive chez sa fille, il se demandait comment parer au drame qui pourrait naître de leurs affrontements. (Chedid 1985: 133) / Mario strained his eyes, and spoke in a breathless voice. He could not conceal his fears for the country, for his children. Georges was an ardent militant in one party. Myriam and Ammal, ever the utopians, were trying to bring all communities together ... Alarmed by an expression of scorn on his son's face or by an outburst of anger from his daughter, he wondered how to ward off the impending tragedy. (Chedid 1989: 109)

The war has a more intimate side to it since it is a bloody fight between siblings. Despite the desperate situation, the omniscient narrator contin-ues to defend peace and brotherly love. The omniscient narrator's voice

accompanies Ammal and Myriam in their march for peace and reconciliation. When one of them is injured, the omniscient narrator does not distinguish between them. For the omniscient narrator, it does not matter who
was injured, since the consequences remain the same: '[l]aquelle, penchée au-
dessus de sa compagne, lui soulève le buste, s'efforce de la rappeler à la vie? La
question n'a presque pas d'importance. Ce matin, elles sont une, identiques'
(Chedid 1985: 8) / 'Which of them is leaning over her friend, raising her body,
trying to bring her back to life?' (Chedid 1989: 1–2). Despite their fall, the
omniscient narrator refuses to despair and continues to hope that the two
women will proceed with their march to save the country: '[i]l fallait sauver ce
que Myriam et Ammal avaient partagé; maintenir cet espoir qu'elles voulaient
porter, ensemble jusqu'au centre de la Place, où devaient bientôt converger les
diverses communautés de la ville. Sauver cette rencontre préparée depuis des
jours' (Chedid 1985: 10) / 'She had to rescue what Myriam and Ammal had
shared; maintain that hope which they had wanted to bring, together, to the
centre of the square, where the various communities of the town would soon
gather. Rescue this reunion which had been planned for days' (Chedid 1989:
4); '[i]l n'est peut-être pas trop tard. Malgré les violences de cette dernière
semaine, la paix peut encore être sauvée' (Chedid 1985: 19) / 'Perhaps it is not
too late. Despite the violence of the past week, peace might still be restored'
(Chedid 1989: 12).

It is important to note that in telling the stories of the march, the omniscient narrator repeatedly uses terms relevant to hope and peace. Its voice, which
at times overlaps with the writer's or Kalya's, takes the form of a supplication.
It sounds like it is praying or begging for peace to be restored, and its hope will
last for the duration of the novel, until the last pages when Sybil is killed by a
sniper. Sybil's death is hard to interpret or understand much like the reality
of a civil war. Does it imply the end of hope? One could argue that this is the
message intended by the writer, through the voice of the omniscient narrator, since the war will last for at least eight more years (from the date of the
publication).

The omniscient narrator faithfully reflects Chedid's cosmic vision of
humanity, the one according to which humanity shares a common destiny.
Under the weight of war and violence, Kalya's feminine 'I' is absorbed by the
group. Her individuality disappears and her narrative is told by an omniscient

narrator who attempts to continue in giving a message of hope and love. The war will put an end to its message.

Le Message

Chedid published *Le Message* in 2000, fifteen years after *La Maison sans racines*. It is based on a novella called 'Mort au ralenti' that Chedid published in 1993. Boustani quotes an interview with *Télérama* on 14 October 2000 in which Chedid says that the novella was inspired by a newspaper article called 'The lovers of Sarajevo', which tells the true story of a couple who died under the bombs. She was Muslim, he was Serbian. The story marked her deeply and her granddaughter encouraged her to transform her novella into a novel:

> En 1993, je découvre dans la presse un article titré « les amants de Sarajevo », la même histoire, mais véridique celle-là. Elle était musulmane, lui serbe. Ils s'aimaient au-delà des différences, des cultures, des conflits. Ils se jettent dans les bras l'un de l'autre, et tombent enlacés sous des balles. J'étais bouleversée. Ma petite-fille m'a incitée à retravailler la nouvelle pour en faire un roman. L'issue de l'histoire s'est transformée, et j'ai moi-même été surprise des réactions des personnes. (Boustani 2016: 277)

Le Message tells Marie and Steph's love story and conflicted relationship. When the city or the country in which they live slips into turmoil, they discover their love for each other, decide to meet on a bridge to leave together. Marie never makes it to their meeting point. Shot by a sniper, she struggles to stay alive. An older couple finds her and decides to help her deliver her love letter to Steph. They find him and when he comes to Marie, she is barely alive. She dies shortly after.

Le Message (*Message*) and *La Maison sans racines* (*Maison*) share commonalities on thematic and narrative levels. On a thematic level, both novels address the issue of war and violence against women. There is a certain resemblance between the two main protagonists. Just like Kalya, Marie is a photographer; they both take pictures to stop time and to document what they see: from a young age, Kalya realises how important it is to preserve happy moments. In watching her grandmother Nouza sleep, she realises that she wants a camera to record these times in her life: 'un appareil pour garder tous les instants qu'[elle] aime et les garder en vie' (*Maison* 138) and to protect her from old age 'cette décrépitude qui guette . . .' (*Maison* 138). Marie works as a photographer which allows her to deeply know her city: '[e]lle connaît à fond cette cité; elle y est née et y travaille depuis plus d'un an comme reporter – photographe, ses déplacements à travers d'étroites ruelles elle saurait en venir à bout' (*Message* 9). Despite Marie's attempt to freeze time, it eventually turns against her and repeats past events:

> [m]ais en ce jour l'Histoire avait eu raison de son histoire, Marie faisait soudain partie de ces vies sacrifiées, rompues, écrasée par la chevauchée des guerres. Les violences issues de croyance perverties, d'idéologies défigurées, de cet instinct de mort et de prédation qui marquent toutes formes de vie, avaient eu raison de sa petite existence. (*Message* 29)

Kalya and Marie show other similarities. Both enjoy dancing in their childhood: '[c]e soir là, la musique m'avait happée. Je m'étais envolée de ma chaise, où rien ni personne ne m'aurait retenue!' (*Maison* 78); '[l]es yeux mi-clos, Marie improvisait sa danse, inventait sa liberté. Marie tournait, tournait, jusqu'au vertige. C'était bien! C'était bon. Elle se sentait dans sa peau. Le rythme s'emparait de son corps, de son souffle. Elle était ailleurs. Ça ressemblait au bonheur.' (*Message* 14). Both women dance at first alone then meet their future partners on the dance floor. This detail could be an indication of these women's strong will and independence. For Carmen Boustani, Chedid identifies with both women. Just like Kalya, she questions her origins and the notion of roots, and just like Marie she has a strong love relationship with her husband, one that is full of ups and downs (Boustani 2016: 259, 283).

Also, Marie wears a yellow dress just like Ammal and Myriam: 'Ammal et Myriam, sveltes, souples, en larges vêtements jaunes' (*Maison* 7). The omniscient narrator explains that Marie chose to wear this colour to represent her love for Steph and her hope for a new life. However, Marie regrets her decision to wear such a bright colour for it drew attention to her: 'ce chemisier jaune, cette jupe fleurie ne pouvaient qu'attirer le regard. Elles les avaient choisis pour l'espoir, pour fêter cette réunion, pour célébrer cet amour' (*Message* 27). Hope is shot down just like Marie, Ammal and Myriam.

Some of the women protagonists have names that reflect hope: Ammal and Myriam in *La Maison sans racines* and Marie in *Le Message*. Ammal means hope in Arabic; Myriam and Marie refer to the holy figure of Virgin

Mary who is Jesus's mother in both Islam and Christianity (Accad 1990: 80). Both religions see Virgin Mary as an important figure; she represents the one who carries God's message and the one who accepts her destiny. Both Marie and Myriam carry important *messages* of love and peace.

Finally, to reach their loved ones, both Marie and Kalya have long journeys ahead of them. Marie holds on to hope, to the idea of reuniting with Steph on the bridge; she resists collapsing and forces her body to move: 'Elle s'agrippe à l'idée de ce pont qu'il lui faut, à tout prix, atteindre. Cet espoir la lancine, et fait surgir du fond de son être un dernier sursaut de volonté. Marie résiste à l'écroulement, à la chute, et se force à exécuter encore quelques pas' (*Message* 17); Kalya runs towards Myriam and Ammal to maintain hope, to reconcile the communities and to save what could be saved: 'Il fallait sauver ce que Myriam et Ammal avaient partagé; maintenir cet espoir qu'elles voulaient porter, ensemble, jusqu'au centre de la Place, où devaient bientôt converger les diverses communautés de la ville. Sauver cette rencontre préparée depuis des jours' (*Maison* 10); 'Kalya se mit en marche. Le chemin allait lui paraître interminable. La distance, infinie' (*Maison* 12).

On the narrative level, both novels have a similar structure. Just like *La Maison sans racines*, *Le Message* offers chronological transgressions in the diegesis. This disorder, often under the form of analepsis, allows the reader to better understand Marie and Steph's love story. According to Linkhorn, the narrative is constantly interrupted, and different scenes are quickly introduced just as in the movies which keep the reader in suspense: 'la narration se distingue par un art du discontinu. Les tableaux se succèdent comme autant de plans cinématographiques, passant d'un élément à l'autre du récit et tenant ainsi le lecteur en haleine' (Linkhorn 2002: 143). Also, this narrative style produces a sense of urgency and chaos like the ones produced by the war. The narrative does not follow a coherent order but instead reproduces a general ambiance of panic while breaking all the traditional narrative norms.

Unlike *La Maison sans racines* that allows only a small space for the first-person narrator, *Le Message* is entirely narrated by an omniscient narrator (aside from reported speech). Without necessarily reviewing all the technical merits of an omniscient narrator, one can say that the omniscient narrator plays four different roles in *Le Message*: it speaks for Marie who loses her voice; it tries to remain impartial, and shares all points of view including the one of a sniper; it expresses its outrage over the war; and finally it monopolises the voice to give the novel the aspect of universality and collectivity.

One: the omniscient narrator accesses everyone's thoughts, past and present and freely circulates between all protagonists without restrictions which is extremely important since one of the main characters is dying and unable to speak: 'Elle crie, elle crie. Sans écho. Dans le vide.' (Chedid 2000: 27) / 'She screams, she screams. Without echo. In the void. The omniscient narrator carries Marie's voice, and allows her to be heard. It carries her messages of love, regret and hope for the future.' In fact, some of the verbs in the paragraph below are conjugated either in the past or the present conditional tense, indicating regret or hope:

> Marie aurait voulu entonner tous les chants d'amour dont elle se souvenait. Elle aurait aimé effacer tous les sarcasmes, tous les doutes, toutes les craintes, toutes les inquiétudes. Elle s'alliait et se reliait à cet amour orageux mais robuste: déroutant mais tenace. Elle accepterait ses chemins escarpés, ses moments abrupts, ses colères ténébreuses, ses humeurs, ses errements, ses complexités, ses subtilités, ses chicanes, ses querelles, ses démêlés, ses vides. Elle ne se soucierait plus du jugement des autres. (Chedid 2000: 66) / Marie would have wanted to start singing all the songs of love that she remembered. She would have loved to erase all the sarcasms, the doubts, the fears and the worries. She attached and reattached herself to this stormy but robust love: disconcerting but tenacious. She would accept its steep paths, its abrupt moments, its dark angers, its humours, its erring ways, its complexities, its subtilities, its squabbles, its quarrels, its troubles, its emptiness. She wouldn't worry anymore about the others' judgements.

The omniscient narrator allows the reader to access her most intimate thought right before she dies: '[e]lle aurait voulu lui dire le bonheur de sa lettre, combien il avait raison, que la seule force vive était celle de l'amour. L'amour, elle le vivait en cet instant, intensément, même si la mort devait suivre. La mort suivant toujours . . .' (Chedid 2000: 121) / 'She would have wanted to tell him about the joy of his letter, how he was right, that the only force alive is the one of love. Love, she was living it in that moment, intensely even if death must follow.'

Two: the omniscient narrator attempts to remain impartial as it does not endorse a specific political or religious view. It gives all the protagonists the opportunity to tell their stories, including Gorgio the sniper. The omniscient narrator reveals three aspects of Gorgio's life: first, it tells us about his sad past and his father's rejection and humiliation: '[s]es études avaient été médiocres. Son père, avocat de renom, issu d'une famille modeste, avait fait son chemin, sans aide, en luttant. Il se désolait des incapacités de son fils, qu'il ne pouvait s'empêcher de harceler et d'humilier: Tu ne seras jamais personne!' (Chedid 2000: 70). Additionally, the omniscient narrator tells us about Gorgio's cruel participation in the war: '[d]e temps à autre, pour se donner l'impression d'exister, de prendre part au combat, il visait un passant ou les pneus d'une voiture égarée. Il tirait de plus en plus juste et ratait rarement sa cible ... Gorgio n'éprouvait aucun scrupule à les descendre, il ne ressentait plutôt de la fierté' (109). Finally, the omniscient narrator reveals Gorgio's remaining humanity when he tries to get rid of his weapon: 'cette mitraillette. Il chercha à s'en débarasser. Elle lui pesait soudain, déformant, trahissant sa propre personne. Il cherche à s'en défaire sans parvenir. Qui était-il au fond? Il ne l'avait jamais su, il se sentait perdu' (110); and when he tries to save Marie by finding an ambulance: '[i]l sauta sur le sol, chercha des yeux la jeune femme blessée. Il était impatient de la retrouver, de lui annoncer qu'il venait lui porter secours et qu'il était bien décidé à la sauver' (125). In revealing Gorgio's story, the omniscient narrator invites the reader into a violent world, hoping perhaps for a better understanding of the origins of violence and for a more human verdict. Without necessarily excusing Gorgio's violent behaviour, the omniscient narrator seems to imply that it was the result of humiliation, bad parenting, constant rejection and lack of love.

Three: the omniscient narrator expresses its outrage regarding the war. It expresses its frustration and deplores all the lives lost in vain:

> Comment définir cette contrée, comment déterminer ses frontières? Pourquoi cerner, ou désigner cette femme? Tant de pays, tant de créatures, subissent le même sort.
>
> Dans la boue des rizières, sur l'asphalte des cités, dans la torpeur des sables, entre plaines et collines, sous neige et soleil, perdus dans les foules que l'on pourchasse et décime, expirant parmi les autres ou dans la solitude:

les massacrés, réfugiés, fusillés, suppliciés de tous les continents, convergent soudain vers cette rue unique, vers cette personne, vers ce corps, vers ce cœur aux abois, vers cette femme à la fois anonyme et singulière. À la fois vivante, mais blessée à mort.

Depuis l'aube des temps, les violences ne cessent de se chevaucher, la terreur de régner, l'horreur de recouvrir l'horreur. Visages en sang, visages exsangues. Hémorragies d'hommes, de femmes, d'enfants . . . Qu'importe le lieu! Partout l'humanité est en cause, et ce sombre cortège n'a pas de fin.

Dans chaque corps torturé tous les corps gémissent. Poussés par des forces aveugles dans le même abîme, les vivants sombrent avant leur terme. Partout.

Comment croire, comment prier, comment espérer en ce monde pervers, en ce monde exterminateur, qui consume ses propres entrailles, qui se déchire et se décime sans répit? (Chedid 2000: 18) / How to understand this land and its borders? Why choose this woman? So many countries and creatures suffer similar fate. In the mud of the rice fields, in the cities' asphalt, in the laziness of sands, between plains and hills, under snow and sun, the massacred, the refugees, the executed, the tortured of all the continents get lost in the crowds, breathe their last breaths among others or in solitude, and converge suddenly toward this unique street, toward this person, toward this body, toward this cornered heart, toward this woman simultaneously anonymous and unique. Simultaneously alive and yet injured to death.

Since the dawn of time, violence continues, the reign of terror, the horror to cover up the horror. Bloody faces, livid faces. Hemorrhaging of men, women, and children . . . the location does not matter! Humanity is in doubt everywhere, and this dark procession does not end.

In every tortured body there are bodies that groan. Pushed by blind forces into the abyss, the living succumb before their time. Everywhere.

How to believe, how to pray, how to hope in this perverse world, in this exterminator world that consumes itself, that tears and decimates itself without a break?

The omniscient narrator repeatedly interrupts the narrative and the protagonists' direct discourses to ask questions about the war. This is by no mean an expression of its limited knowledge. If anything, it reflects the omniscient narrator's feelings about the war (and clearly Chedid's by extension).

Four: the omniscient narrator deliberately monopolises the narrative voice in a world of violent cacophony where all voices claim to know God and to hold the one true religion. It is the 'God-like' voice that rises to hush the other belligerent voices and to speak in the name of collective humanity and shared values rather than individuality. The omniscient narrator becomes thus this universal voice of sanity in a mad world.

The universality of the narrative voice and its humanist message are also reflected in the anonymity of the city or the country where the action takes place. For Linkhorn, Chedid never names the city as similar events take place in so many different places that they become generic: '[l]a romancière ne nomme jamais la ville; ces événements d'aujourd'hui se déroulent en tant de lieux qu'ils en deviennent génériques, et c'est l'essence même des faits qui importe' (Linkhorn 2002: 143). For Boustani, Chedid wanted to show the universality of violence and war. The location does not matter, and the goal is to show the number of people who suffer the same fate in different countries at war: 'L'auteur a tenu à donner une image de l'universalité de la violence et de l'horreur de la guerre. Qu'importe le lieu, son objectif est de montrer que de très nombreuses créatures subissent le même sort dans les pays en guerre' (Boustani 2016: 275).

Coquelicot du massacre

Evelyne Accad published *Coquelicot du massacre* with L'Harmattan in 1988, and the story focuses on the lives of three women during the Lebanese civil war: Nour, Hayat and Najmé. Nour wants to cross Beirut with her son Raja to reach a safer place; Hayat is a university professor who is in love with a Muslim man named Adnan; Najmé is a young college student who is addicted to drugs.

The novel's title reflects these women's struggles in Lebanon during the civil war. When asked about the choice of the title, Accad says that the poppy is a very delicate red flower that grows in the wild fields in Lebanon and among the ruins of war. It can be used as a narcotic, and its red colour can represent blood. Above all, it is a beautiful flower that survives despite all the hard conditions:

le coquelicot, c'est cette fleur délicate, rouge, qui pousse dans les champs sauvages du Liban et qui poussait dans les ruines de la guerre. C'est aussi le pavot de la drogue et c'est aussi le symbole du sang. Par-dessus tout, c'est une fleur belle et délicate qui peut survivre dans des conditions difficiles. (Heistad et al. 2004: 35)

Structurally, the narrative and story time are fragmented, and rotate between the three stories of Nour, Najmé and Hayat. In the prologue (although it is not named as such), the omniscient narrator introduces two unnamed protagonists, the Man and Her (Accad 1988: 5). In the epilogue, the same two unnamed protagonists resurface as Her with the American (Accad 1988: 149). Retroactively, the reader will understand that Her is referring to Hayat who eventually leaves Lebanon to live in Chicago. For Mary-Angela Willis, the fragmentation of the narrative reflects the individuality of the war experience but at the same time its collectivity. It also gives room for more women to speak-up and share their stories (Willis 2004: 176–7).

All the stories are told by an omniscient narrator who, from a technical point of view and as mentioned before, circulates freely between the protagonists, time and space. In addition to being gender neutral and at equal distance from all protagonists, the omniscient narrator contributes into the widening of women's space of expression since not one woman monopolises the narrative voice. (One must acknowledge the irony here where the counterargument could be that the omniscient narrator is monopolising the narrative voice and depriving women from expressing themselves as first-person narrator. This counterargument could be valid if the writer's intent is, in fact, to hijack women's voices. Clearly, this is not the case.)

Just like the omniscient narrator in Chedid's *La Maison sans racines*, the omniscient narrator in *Coquelicot du massacre* indicates the limitations of the feminine 'I' in times of war. Unlike *La Maison sans racines* where the feminine 'I' has its own dedicated chapters and time in the narrative, *Coquelicot du massacre* is almost entirely narrated by the omniscient narrator with a few minor abrupt exceptions of the feminine 'I', which particularly appears in the *mise en abîme* in Hayat's and Najmé's writings.

These shifts in the narrator's person are available right from the beginning of the novel when the unnamed woman 'Elle' speaks; they are marked not only by the change in the person but also by the added spaces between the paragraphs:

> Ils marchent dans l'herbe, pas séparés, mur qui vient de se dresser, silence qu'elle ne peut plus briser . . .
>
> J'aurais pu, j'aurais pu vivre cet amour avec toi, mais tu n'as pas voulu. Tu me demandais des calculs, un échange d'intérêts. Tu voulais de moi une fin. Tu demandais que je prenne ce que tu prenais. Tu ne pouvais accepter un élan sans loi, regard sans frontiers. J'ai entrepris un voyage intérieur pour tenter de t'expliquer. (Accad 1988: 7) /

> They walked on the grass, taking separate strides; a wall had just been erected, a silence she could no longer break . . .
>
> I could have, I could have lived that love with you, but you didn't want it. You asked me for a calculated exchange of interest. You wanted me as a means to an end. You asked me to take what you were taking. You couldn't accept a leap of faith, an unlimited gaze. I searched deep inside to find a way to explain it to you. (Accad 2006)

They are also available in Hayat's story. At the beginning of the novel, Hayat is the object of the omniscient narrator's gaze, who describes her and her life often employing terms related to silence and mutism. Gradually and as the narrative progresses, Hayat gains visibility and access to the narration. She speaks against fatalism and passivity which she considers to be the reasons behind the Lebanese civil war: Her feminine 'I' appears at this point, but in the form of a direct speech reported by the omniscient narrator: '[m]on indifférence ne me fait pas accepter n'importe quoi. Je rejette la violence, mais aussi la passivité. Et je désavoue surtout les jeux de pouvoir' (Accad 1988: 56) / 'My indifference doesn't make me accept just anything. I reject violence, but also passivity. And I especially renounce power politics' (Accad 2006: 102). It is only in her poems and songs, and through the *mise en abîme*, that the feminine 'I' breaks free from the omniscient narrator and speaks for itself: 'Peut-être, par ce processus, réussira-t-elle à trouver les causes secrètes de la tragédie de son pays. Peut-être qu'en recomposant les évènements qui l'ont marquée, elle arrivera à démêler la complexité d'une situation qui semble sans issue' (Accad 1988: 88); 'J'écris tout cela alors que je suis au Liban, pays déchiré d'enfants conçus dans la haine et la vengeance, mais aussi dans la joie, les vœux d'amour et l'espoir d'un monde meilleur' (Accad 1988: 89) / 'She thought perhaps, through this process, she would find the hidden causes of her country's tragedy, that in reconstructing events that marked her, she would come to untangle the complexity of a situation that appeared to have no solution' (Accad 2006: 162); 'I write all this while in Lebanon, a country torn apart with children conceived in hatred and vengeance, but also in joy, oaths of love, and in the hope for a better world' (Accad 2006: 164).

The omniscient narrator wonders whether Hayat writes in the hope of finding the secret causes to the tragedy in her country or maybe to understand the complexity of a hopeless situation. Hayat answers that when she is in Lebanon, a country torn apart by children conceived in hatred and vengeance but also in joy, she writes wishes for love and hope for a better world. This sudden shift in the narrative voice is indicated not only in the change in the narrating persons, speech and tenses but also visually through the added space between the paragraphs.

One can argue that these *mise en abîme* of Hayat's writings in Accad's narrative allow an overlapping of different narrative voices: it is Hayat re-appropriating the space of expression and speaking in her own voice; it is Accad speaking through Hayat, and arguably it is the omniscient narrator reporting directly Hayat's writings (although one must acknowledge that the brackets are missing). This overlapping offers a wider space of expression and, to a certain extent, enlarges the first-person narrator's points of view since it allows it to borrow from the omniscient narrator.

It is interesting to note that Accad identifies with Hayat. In the interview with Deirdre Bucher Heistad, Sharon Meilahn-Swett and Bartley Meinke, Accad says that the name Hayat means life in Arabic, and that the root of her own name is Eve which also means life. She explains that she wishes to represent herself at times through this name without necessarily using the feminine 'I': 'Hayat en arabe signifie Vie. La racine de mon nom Eve veut aussi dire Vie. J'ai donc choisi ce nom pour me représenter quelques fois au lieu de dire Je' (Heistad et al. 2004: 38). Just like Accad, Hayat writes and reads poetry, sings and asserts herself as a woman through different artistic forms and despite the surrounding chaos; and just like Accad, Hayat leaves Lebanon to live in Chicago. Najmé, like Hayat, is unable to assert herself as a woman and narrator in a war-torn society. Born into a wealthy Lebanese family, Najmé, whose name means star in Arabic, uses drugs as a temporary relief from the daily aggressions of the armed conflict and of her family. They allow her to assert herself and to escape what surrounds her in the most destructive way.

Najmé's drug addiction is reported first by the omniscient narrator who describes her as a sick, irresponsible person who is willing to drive under the bombs to get her heroin fix: '[e]lle se précipite dans sa voiture . . . Elle appuie sur l'accélérateur. Le compteur de vitesse monte à cent. Elle fonce, aveuglée par la démence de son pays, elle-même prise par la folie et la frénésie de dompter la mort en la frôlant, en la narguant' (Accad 1988: 36) / 'She jumped into the car . . . She stomped on the accelerator. The speedometer climbed to 100. She pushed harder, blinded by the insanity of her country, herself taken in by the frenetic madness of cheating death while thumbing her nose at it' (Accad 2006: 66). The omniscient narrator declares that she is as crazy and irresponsible as the country in which she lives. She is also generous with her drugs and is always willing to share: 'Najmé est connue pour sa générosité. Elle partage toujours ce qu'elle a, même la poudre que les autres cachent et gardent jalousement pour elle, surtout dans les moments de bombardements, quand elle est rare, qu'il est difficile de s'en procurer' (Accad 1988: 36) / 'Najmé was known for her generosity. She always shared what she had, even the powder that others hid and guarded jealously for themselves, especially during the bombings, when it was rare and difficult to come by' (Accad 2006: 66).

The omniscient narrator wonders whether Najmé will tell Hayat, her university professor, about her addiction. Najmé hesitates and is ashamed. Deep down, she felt like she was enslaved by the drugs and she wanted to break free: 'Najmé hésite. Doit-elle parler à cette femme, son professeur, de son problème? . . . Najmé a honte de son état. Au fond d'elle-même, elle se sent esclave de la drogue et aimerait en être libérée' (Accad 1988: 75) / 'Najmé hesitated. Should she talk to this woman, her professor, about her problem? Najmé was ashamed of her condition. Deep inside, she felt she was a slave to the drug and wanted to be free of it' (Accad 2006: 136).

Najmé's feminine 'I' surfaces in the assignment she submits to Hayat and where she speaks up using the first-person narrator. Her admission of her addiction comes straight from her to the reader and not via the omniscient narrator. She says that it all began three years ago when she started using heroin. It helped her silence her soul's noises. When she took it, she felt high and above all suffering: 'Tout a commencé lorsque je me suis mise à prendre de l'héroïne. Il y a trois ans . . . La drogue m'a aidée à taire les bruits de mon âme. Quand j'en prenais, je planais au-dessus de la souffrance de notre drame' (Accad 1988: 98) / 'It all began when I started taking heroin. That was three years ago . . . The drug helped me to silence the rumblings of my soul. When I was using it, I flew high above the suffering of our common tragedy' (Accad 2006: 178).

This interruption in the narrative voice is important; through the *mise en abîme*, it suspends the omniscient narration and allows the first-person narrator to speak up. Najmé, just like her professor Hayat, attempts to assert herself in a violent environment through her writing. However, her attempt to break free is short-lived. She will be forced into marriage and the passages describing her wedding are reported by the omniscient narrator: 'Dès lors, son visage sera toujours coloré, dessiné, souligné, et la flamme de ses yeux s'éteindra lentement, mais pour toujours cette fois. Ses gestes lui seront imposés et elle adoptera petit à petit des habitudes de soumission dans la dépendance' (Accad 1988: 125) / 'From then on, her face would always be colored, drawn, underlined, and the flame in her eyes would burn out slowly, definitively. Her gestures would be imposed and she would adopt little by little the routines of submission through dependence' (Accad 2006: 230). The omniscient narrator's voice is interrupted by the abrupt emergence of the first-person singular and plural pronouns: 'Si tu nous revenais, Najmé . . . Si j'avais pu . . . Si j'avais eu les moyens . . .' (Accad 1988: 126–7) / 'If you came back to us, Najmé . . . If I could have . . . If I had had the means . . .' (Accad 2006: 232–4).

Najmé's story is marked by these last interruptions in the narrative voice and ends with a short poem suggesting that it is Hayat speaking, or perhaps the writer through Hayat's voice. It is as if Hayat witnessed Najmé's wedding and decided, at the last minute of her story, to interject and to tell the rest of the story in lieu of the omniscient narrator. It is the last attempt of the feminine 'I' to speak out before complete silence.

Unlike Hayat and Najmé, Nour's story carries a hint of hope. The omniscient narrator recounts Nour's journey with her son Raja fleeing the growing violence in one side of the city; it tells us about Nour's tenacity, courage and fears. It reports some of her most intimate thoughts as it penetrates her unconscious to describe her nightmares (Accad 1988: 30, 95 / Accad 2006: 56, 174).

The novel carries multiple references to hope, and the omniscient narrator does not stay immune to these contagious messages. Nour and Raja are Arabic names that respectively translate into light and hope. Their journey is symbolic as it shows one's ability to break the wall of hatred and to cross to the other side. Protagonists in the novel admire their courage and ask them to carry messages to their 'brothers' on the other side, to tell them that they are with them, that they do not want this division, and to ask them to work with them for the reconstruction and reunification of the city: '[s]i vous arrivez à l'autre côté, dites à nos frères que nous sommes avec eux. Dites-leur que nous ne voulons pas de cette division. Demandez-leur de travailler avec nous à la reconstruction de la ville et de sa réunification' (Accad 1988: 47) / 'If you get to the other side, tell our brothers that we are with them. Tell them we don't want this separation. Ask them to work with us on reconstruction of the city and its reunification' (Accad 2006: 86).

The hope they incarnate is powerful; the omniscient narrator tells us about it mostly through reported speeches between the protagonists but also in its own description. In fact, the omniscient narrator frequently refers to them as 'the mother' and the 'son' as if they were a holy family invested with a message of salvation. It even acknowledges that both Nour and Raja are attempting to create a 'miracle' (Accad 1988: 65 / Accad 2006: 118).

Music is another element that suggests hope in the novel. It accompanies Nour and Raja in their journey and silences the sounds of fear and war. Alison Rice notes the availability of music in both Accad and Chedid's texts (as well as Assia Djebar's) (Rice 2004: 87).[5] In *La Maison sans racines*, music becomes the thread that connects different generations and nationalities. In her youth, Kalya loved dancing: '[e]mportée par la mélodie, je me suis faufilée parmi les danseurs. Toutes les joies de la terre et du ciel me possédaient. Je virevoltais, tourbillonnais. J'étais au-delà de toute parole' (Chedid 1985: 51)/ 'Carried away by the music, I threaded my way among the dancers. I was possessed by all earthly and heavenly joys. I pirouetted and twirled. I was beyond words' (Chedid 1989: 40). Sybil shares her grandmother's passion for music and dancing: 'Moi, je serai danseuse! . . . [u]ne pirouette, un entrechat, un jeté. La nappe de ses cheveux planait autour d'elle. Elle termina par une cabriole, suivie d'un grand écart" (Chedid 1985: 110–11) / 'I'm going to be a dancer! . . . A pirouette, an entrechat, a jeté. The pale sheet of hair fanned out around her. She finished with a cabriole, followed by splits' (Chedid 1989: 86–7).

Music is also a form of international language that unites different people regardless of their differences. Sybil could not talk to Slimane, the Sudanese butler, because of their language differences. However, they manage to communicate through their love for music. Slimane teaches her a lullaby from his own childhood (Chedid 1985: 135 / Chedid 1989: 111). Music can heal the broken souls and unite people from different backgrounds, languages, religions and nationalities. This is precisely why the protagonists Hayat, Najmé and especially Nour are accompanied by music, as it provides them with an alternative space of self-expression. Hayat and Najmé are unable to tell their stories using the first-person narrator, but they can write poetry and sing.

The hope that music carries is so powerful that it suspends the omniscient narrator's voice and gives room for the feminine 'I' to express itself:

'Je veux vivre pour effacer la peur

Je veux vivre pour effacer la haine' (Accad 1988: 71) /

'I want to live to erase fear

I want to live to erase hatred' (Accad 2006: 130);

J'ai compris dans la souffrance

J'ai trouvé dans les larmes

J'ai crié dans le désert

Le chemin s'est ouvert

Et j'ai vu l'étoile de vie

Et j'ai bu l'eau des sources

De mon pays fleuri. (Accad 1988: 122) /

I have understood in suffering

I have found in tears shed

I have cried out in the desert

That the way is open

And I have seen the star of life

And I have drunk water from the source

Of my country in blossom again. (Accad 2006: 226)

In fact, the feminine 'I' appears frequently through reported speech but most importantly in the songs. One can argue that there is no real interruption of the omniscience. This may be true. However, the songs are reported in their own paragraphs, and are visually separated from other paragraphs. Unlike reported speech, paragraphs of songs do not begin with a dash or a bracket, suggesting thus a clear interruption in the narrative voice.

When Nour learns that the music school has been destroyed, her voice overlaps with the omniscient narrator's voice, and they both wonder why it was necessary to destroy the country's music so viciously. Why aim at the heart of its music? 'Pourquoi s'être acharné avec tant de haine sur la mélodie de ce pays, déjà tellement atteint? Pourquoi avoir visé, au cœur même de sa chanson?' (Accad 1988: 122) / 'Why had they wreaked so much havoc on the music of this country already so badly damaged? Why did they aim at the heart of its song? (Accad 2006: 226–8). The music is dead and Nour's hope, voice and first-person narrator are shattered. Despite it all, Nour decides to continue her journey with Raja. When crossing the demarcation line, they decide to sing and to raise their voices in the battle: 'ils élèvent leurs voix dans la bataille' (Accad 1988: 143) / 'They raised their voices during the battle' (Accad 2006: 264). At the end of the novel, the omniscient narrator finds an ally in music and concludes the story on a more hopeful note. Accad herself admits that she did not want to write a sad, hopeless ending: 'j'ai terminé sur une note positive. La femme qui traverse la ville arrive à être sauvée avec son fils, il y a donc plus d'espoir . . .' (Heistad et al. 2004: 40).

To conclude, it is important to remind the reader that it is almost impossible to know the absolute reasons for which Chedid and Accad opted for the omniscience rather than the first-person narrator. However, postclassical narratology along with literary analysis allow us insight into this narrative choice alongside the effects it produces. We can say, like Dawson (2013), that we are dealing with a 'moralist omniscient narrator' or a 'social commentator' or, as I call it, a humanist omniscient narrator, which indicates, not only the technical limitations of the feminine 'I', but also its metaphoric restrictions in terms of free expression in war-torn patriarchal society. It attempts to remain at equal distance from all protagonists and shows different points of view, even those of morally corrupt protagonists. It does not name any of the belligerent parties and strictly defends peace and love; however, most importantly, it adopts a moralist superior point of view and monopolises the narrative to silence the sounds of the war.

Notes

1 Dawson traces the history of the analogy between God and the omniscient narrator. He says: 'The analogy stems from the Renaissance comparison of the poet with God in which, unlike classical antiquity where he is inspired by God, the poet possesses a faculty of imagination like that of God.' He continues to show that this analogy was considered blasphemous before the sixteen century and the omniscient narrator became somewhat secularised in the twentieth century (Dawson 2013: 35).

2 Dawson defines the free indirect discourse as:

> generally understood as a phenomenon of speech and thought representation which appears to merge the perspective of both narrator and character . . . FID is traditionally defined as a syntactic unit in which a character's 'original' utterance or thought has undergone a pronominal and tense shift of the grammar of the narrative discourse, typically from first to third person, and present to past tense, and is marked by an absence of tag clauses or reporting verbs. (Dawson 2013: 168)

3 This is what Philippe Lejeune refers to when he argues that the first-person pronoun is ultimately the carrier of a serious identity problem (Lejeune 1980: 35).

4 For Carine Bourget, the novel *La Maison sans racines* 'promotes a clash of religion interpretation of Lebanese civil war, since the internal socio-economic as well as external factors (the Palestinian refugees) are only indirectly surfacing in the course of the narrative' (Bourget 2010: 70).

5 It is interesting to note that Accad writes and plays music and that Chedid wrote for her grandson, the French artist Mathieu Chedid, the song called 'je dis aime'. The song came out in France in 1999.

PART II

THE NARRATIVE BODY

3

The Evil, Sick and Disabled Female Body

In this chapter, I examine the representations of the female body in war in Vénus Khoury-Ghata's *La Maîtresse du Notable* and Hyam Yared's *La Malédiction*. Following the guidelines of postclassical narratology, particularly feminist and postcolonial narratologies, I argue that the body, just like the voice, plays a role in the narrative structure. In fact, in these novels, the war stories are told through or by the body. The narrative voice remains available. However, the female body tells the war story around which the narrative is built. In Khoury-Ghata's novel, the female body is the source of evil and the reason behind the war. The foreign body spreads fear among the natives. It is the generative body that produces monsters and it is the Western body that settles in the East. In Yared's novel, the female body is the oppressed sick body that, like Lebanon, lives an internal conflict and becomes self-destructive.

It is interesting to note that both novels focus on the mother figure as an agent of oppression to both male and female bodies, which goes against the old feminist discourse that portrays men as the enemy, the 'sexual brutes' and the 'cultural dominators' (Bordo 1993: 23). As Susan Bordo stipulates, the old feminist discourse seems at times inadequate in its simplistic dichotomies of man/woman, oppressor/oppressed. Additionally, this argument shows women as passive and lacking agency (Bordo 1993: 23). In this regard, Vénus Khoury-Ghata and Hyam Yared differ from the mainstream feminist discourse in pointing out the role women play in women's oppression, particularly during war time.

La Maîtresse du Notable or The Evil Female Body

La Maîtresse du Notable tells the story of Flora, a white woman living in an unnamed war-torn city. Married to a Christian man, she has three children: Fredéric, Bébé and an unnamed daughter who also acts as the narrator. Flora lives in a building located at the demarcation line between the Christian and the Muslim sectors. She has different neighbours with different stories: Mlle Liliane, who was previously engaged to Flora's husband; Mme Evguénia, called Mme Vava; M. Nahum, the disabled Jewish building owner; his black Muslim servant, Mourad; two Spanish lesbian nuns, Lucia and Anunciad; and a sniper who lives on the rooftop. The novel opens with Flora leaving her household to join her wealthy and powerful Muslim lover, referred to as the Notable.

The novel is structured around Flora's character. She is the main link between all the protagonists. She does not speak and her story is told by other protagonists. Her past is gradually revealed through the narrator's memories, conversations between neighbours and through the finding of old photographs. We are never told where Flora lives, but it is clear that she lives in Lebanon during the civil war because of the many cultural and historical references pointing in that direction. Flora had met the Notable when she was single and worked at a dance club. The Notable instantly fell in love with Flora and took her home to introduce her to his mother, but their first encounter did not go well. Afraid of the mother's Islamic traditions, poverty and overwhelming fascination with her whiteness, Flora ran away. The Notable never forgave Flora this humiliation, and the novel suggests that he developed a fixation on her and vowed to have her one day. Flora went on with her life, married her Christian husband, whose name is never told, and had three children with him. The Notable resurfaces in her life when she is pregnant with her third child. She sees him from her window and recognises him immediately. She abandons her family and leaves with him shortly after giving birth.

Flora is an absent protagonist. Even so, her departure is the central event that triggers all her neighbours' stories and gossip. In the neighbours' eyes, Flora has shamed her family and broken her husband's heart; she has pushed her oldest son into drugs and homosexuality[1] and her daughter into promiscuity. They hold her responsible for having broken the fragile peace between the

Christian and the Muslim sectors. She is also blamed for Mourad's death and for the Notable's misery. Everything that happens to the neighbours is her fault. Flora never leaves the Notable's house. At the end of the novel, she ages suddenly and loses her mobility. She dies shortly after Fredéric, when he was trying to get to her. He was killed by the Muslim sector.

As Susan Bordo says, women's bodies, even when silent, are 'speaking' and Flora's body seems to be speaking a language of evilness (Bordo 1993: 6). She is the fallen mother who does not perform her excepted duties, and the foreign body that threatens the natives. She is also the female generative body that gives birth to hybrid subjects, and she embodies the destructive power of the West in the East. These images of Flora's body build the war narrative. They tell the war story.

Flora, the Fallen Mother

Flora is depicted as a bad mother; she neglected Fredéric for so long that she did not notice that he was addicted to drugs or that he had transitioned from boy to girl: 'Ma mère ne remarqua pas la transformation de son fils en fille . . . Il marchait à l'ombre de Georges, se cachait derrière son dos d'athlète. Sa récompense: un sachet de coke . . . Flora fermait les yeux sur ses absences' (Khoury-Ghata 1992: 25). She is also deaf to her children's call: 'nous avons appelé « maman », d'une même voix. Notre appel s'est perdu entre les deux secteurs. Nous avons appelé « maman » tout au long de la journée mais la femme visible à travers les sycomores n'a pas répondu à nos appels' (110). By abandoning her family, Flora earned a bad reputation that she passed on to her children. The neighbours consider the children genetically predisposed to copy their mother's poor behaviour. When Flora's underage daughter (the unnamed narrator) has sex with the sniper, the neighbours call her a sinner, as she has inherited her mother's urge to fornicate: 'La fornication c'est génétique' (151); 'T'as de fortes chances d'y retrouver ta mère, une autre pécheresse, elle va t'y précéder. Elle a offensé Dieu bien avant toi' (204). When Fredéric returns home from France, Mme Vava suspects that he paid his ticket back through prostitution. He is, after all, Flora's son: 'La même mauvaise graine que sa mère' (228).

The topic of bad motherhood goes against the traditional construction of femininity which suggests that women are warm and kind. As Paula Ruth

Gilbert puts it, women are typically seen as maternal, gentle and protective, and they are not expected to be heinous, evil or murderous (Gilbert 2013: 7). In *The Second Sex*, Simone de Beauvoir explains that the topic of cruel maternity has been known but 'hypocritically attributed to the figure of the cruel stepmother, punishing the offspring of a "good" mother who is dead' (de Beauvoir 1989: 514). Estela V. Welldon discusses at length how society in general and psychology in particular focus on male perversion and ignore the perverse behaviour of women (and mothers) simply because they assume that women are incapable of such acts:

> There is still no acknowledgement of female perversion, though the evidence is that male perversion is often the result of early faulty mothering. Why is it so difficult to conceptualize the notion of perverse motherhood and other female perverse behavior according to a separate, completely different psychopathology which originates from the female body and its inherent attributes? Male assumptions have made it difficult to understand some female behavior, including female perversions, sometimes to the extent of denying all evidence that female perversion exists. (Welldon 1988: 5–6)

Looking back at the history of psychology, Welldon blames Freud for this faulty assumption. Perversion, whether carrying moral implications or a sexual component, has been traditionally assigned to the male body. In her interpretation of Freud, Welldon argues that male perversion is the result of:

> [U]nresolved Oedipus complex which has castration anxiety as its central and main component. When the oedipal male reaches manhood, he is unable to reach genital primacy with a person of the opposite sex, since his mother is still in his unconscious mind, and he feels in extreme anxiety of being castrated by his father. He then denies the differentiation of the sexes and creates a phallic mother. (Welldon 1988: 5)

For Welldon, following Freud's logic, since women do not have a penis, they can suffer neither from the Oedipus complex nor from the fear of castration. They are already castrated and, as such, they are incapable of perversion. This gendered view of perversion made its way into the traditional construction of femininity; consequently, women are falsely assumed to be unable to perform immoral or sexually perverse acts. Flora, however, does so when she abandons

her husband and children to join her lover, and this representation compli-
cates the meaning of the novel as the reader is taken by surprise. Flora is not,
by any means, what one would expect of a mother.

In addition to being depicted as a bad mother, Flora is not given the
appropriate space to explain herself or to justify her actions, which is not
necessarily surprising. In general, feminist discourse has been unkind in its
representation of motherhood. Brenda O. Daly and Maureen T. Reddy argue
that it mostly focuses on the daughter's voices. This 'daughter-centricity', as
they call it, either ignores the mother's experiences or simplistically portrays
her as a victim of her own society (Daly and Reddy 1991: 2). Khoury-Ghata
adopts the daughter-centricity approach, which adds two dimensions to the
text: on the one hand, Flora's silence represents the silence of Western countries during the civil war; on the other hand, when coupled with Flora's body,
her silence allows the story to be told from her child's perspective.

Also, feminism has resisted the idea of motherhood as it represents the
loss of subjectivity and personal control over the body. For Adrienne Rich,
we also live in a culture of somatophobia, or fear of the body; we privilege the
brain over the body, which explains why some feminists completely reject the
idea of motherhood and see it as a contradiction to their own values (Rich
1995: 18).

Traditionally, mothers in literature are not given the right space to
express themselves, and Flora, in that respect, perpetuates this custom.
Always described from afar, she is a shadow figure who exists in the confined space of a window, a mirror,[2] a photograph, or a water puddle. There
is always an obstacle between her and the protagonists' gazes, and her few
words are frequently indirectly reported to the reader. Flora exists as a photograph, enclosed in a specific frame, and her understanding completely relies
on whoever is looking at her. Susan Sontag points out that photographs are
a form of narrative that potentially carry multiple meanings: 'Photographs
had the advantage of uniting two contradictory features. Their credentials
of objectivity were inbuilt. Yet they always had, necessarily, a point of view'
(Sontag 2004: 26). Flora, just like a silent photograph, presents the reader
with multiple points of view. She is the white foreign beauty that is seen as
a threat by the natives, and the feared generative female body that defiles the
city with its impurity. Finally, she is a representation of the West's destructive

presence in the Middle East in general and in the Lebanese civil war in particular.

Flora, the White Strange Body

In descriptions of Flora's body, her whiteness is always emphasised. When the Notable's mother meets her for the first time, she thinks she is a houri from paradise as her whiteness is unreal: 'La mère prononça trois fois le nom d'Allah, suivi de celui de son prophète. La créature devant elle n'était pas une vraie femme, mais une houri du paradis. Sa main calleuse effleura l'avant-bras de Flora. Elle voulait s'assurer que tant de blancheur n'était pas truquée' (Khoury-Ghata 1992: 29). When the Notable's governess comes to the Christian sector to meet with Flora's husband and to ask for her divorce, she tells him how the servants fight among themselves to serve Flora because they are amazed by her whiteness and blondness: 'C'est rare les vraies blondes. Ses servants disent sa touffe dorée et roses les aréoles de ses seins. Tout ce velours, toute cette soie et nacre éveille leur curiosité. Elles se battent pour l'épiler, mais Flora refuse qu'on touche à sa toison' (73). During his wedding ceremony to another woman, the Notable sees a seagull whose white belly reminds him of Flora's white beauty; he abruptly interrupts the ceremony to go find Flora: 'Une mouette en pleine nuit, chose jamais vue auparavant. Son ventre blanc s'étale impudique sur une couche d'air. Il pense au corps de Flora et donne l'ordre d'arrêter la fête. Le notable n'est que soumission devant les ventres blancs' (235).

Susan Brownmiller discusses the different meanings traditionally attributed to female whiteness and blondeness. Blonde hair has been associated with innocence and purity in literature and arts. In opposition to the dark-haired or dark-skinned women, a blonde woman is portrayed as the fragile urban beauty who is gentle and yet dynamic (Brownmiller 1984: 70). Similarly, white skin and fair, pale beauty has been associated with virginity and aristocracy. It implies that the woman has been sheltered all her life and has not been exposed to the outside world (Brownmiller 1984: 130).

However, in *La Maîtresse du Notable*, whiteness and blondness are not an indicator of Flora's innocence or virginity but are instead emblematic of her dangerous otherness. She is the foreign female with distinctive physical traits, and her foreignness constitutes a threat to the natives. For Mlle Liliane, who was previously engaged to Flora's husband, Flora is a white woman who easily stole her fiancé (Khoury-Ghata 1992: 15). For the Notable's mother, Flora is the royal blood that should not be mixed with the Muslim black blood: 'Cette femme est faite d'une autre argile que nous. Son sang est bleu, le nôtre est noir, de la couleur de la Kaaba. Même le Prophète est incapable de mélanger nos deux races' (132). She is the white female that fornicates with a dark Muslim (53).

Flora is the stranger that does not belong, and her unbelonging is signalled to the reader with a vocabulary specifically related to vegetation. Symbolically, Flora is the *flora* or the plant that is foreign to the region and that destabilises the soil's fragile balance (Khoury-Ghata 1992: 61). She has flourished in an unhealthy environment, in a cabaret called *Les Palmiers* (which translates into palm trees) and is dying in the Notable's house like an etiolated fetid flower (131). She is the barren Mother Nature that controls rain and flooding (64), carries thorny bushes in her womb (50), and buries her foetus under a destructive eucalyptus tree that grows into the Notable's house (129–30). She is the foreign vegetation that gets rooted in the Notable's home (147) and becomes painful like a thorn under the nail: 'Elle s'est enracinée dans nos murs comme l'épine sous l'ongle' (251). She is a tomb and as such requires decorative flowers (147).

In examining the concepts of nation and identity in Arab women's writing, Mona Fayad shows the relationship between the concept of nation, the female body and earth:

> Woman as historical metaphor is most commonly represented through the allegory of mother/earth/country. Such a representation involves a reinscription of ancient Middle Eastern mythology. The original sacrifice of the god of fertility Adonis/Baal for his people, his dismemberment as he is scattered onto the earth, and his resurrection by the goddess-mother-consort Ishtar have been displayed from the god to Woman's body, specifically Woman as mother. Consequently, the mother is cast in a dual role: she must carry within her body both the dismemberment and the re-membering. Through this double role, Woman is written into history as the necessary blood-sacrifice that precedes the birth of the nation – *al-umma*, abstract feminization of *al-umma*, the mother, whose original name carried no sexual marker. (Fayad 1995: 148)

Although it is very common to equate the mother's body with earth and nation,[3] Vénus Khoury-Ghata uses this equation differently. In the case of *La Maîtresse du Notable*, earth and female body are not warm and kind but dangerous and destructive, particularly when they are foreign to the native land in which they live and grow.

Flora, the Impure Generative Body

Flora's body is compared to a bitch in heat (Khoury-Ghata 1992: 165), to a blue-eyed, smart devil (50), and feared for what it can reproduce. Through her pregnancy, she can entrap the Notable: 'Elle a piégé son amant avant qu'il ne se lasse d'elle. Elle l'a enchaîné avec un héritier . . . Elle lui a jeté son ventre tel un os à un chien affamé' (99). She can also alter the fate of the Muslim generations to come: 'Elle est chrétienne. Elle peut dévier le cours de sa progéniture. Ses doigts qui prient dessinent des croix. L'Islam n'aime pas les croix' (50).

Historically, the female body has been feared for its generative power. It is an unstable body that can change in shape. As Margaret Shildrick points out, 'the pregnant body is not one vulnerable to external threat, but actively and visibly deformed from within. Women are out of control, uncontained, unpredictable, leaky: they are, in short, monstrous' (Shildrick 2002: 31). The physical deformation of the pregnant body defies the concept of 'fixed *bodily* form, of visible recognizable, clear and distinct shapes' and provokes male anxiety since it goes against the stereotype of feminine passivity (Braidotti 1997: 64).

It is also a body with generative power, a threatening power that Julia Kristeva examines at length (Kristeva 1982: 77). In fact, the pregnant body destabilises the boundaries between bodies, between the subject and the Other. For Tory Vandeventer Pearman, the pregnant body 'represents the subject-in-process; the birthing body, when it expels the child – or more aptly, when the child separates itself from its mother – demonstrates abjection. The fear of the generative power is ultimately a fear of collapsing boundaries between the self and Other' (Pearman 2010: 25). Iris Young considers the pregnant body as 'decentered, split, or doubled in several ways'; its borders are temporarily suspended in time and space, split between the past and the future (Young 1998: 274).

It is also a body that may produce a deformed being, a monster. Rosi Braidotti defines monsters as:

> human beings who are born with congenital malformations of their bodily organism. They also represent the in between, the mixed, the ambivalent as implied in the ancient Greek root of the word 'monsters', *teras*, which means both horrible and wonderful, object of aberration and adoration ... The monster is the bodily incarnation of difference from the basic human norm; an a-nomaly; it is abnormal. (Braidotti 1997: 62)

The pregnant body blurs the lines between the self and the Other, between the praised subject and the feared monster.[4] It collapses traditional social boundaries between the self and the Other: the Other gestates within the self and is expelled, at some point, out of the self. Pearman points out that there has always been a superimposition between femininity and monstrosity:

> The monster, itself a 'deformed' and excessively physical creature composed of human and unnatural characteristics, is directly analogous to the female body in its Otherness and its sensuous fleshiness ... [which] is intricately linked to the defectiveness of women in male – authored discourses. (Pearman 2010: 24)

It is interesting to note that Flora's pregnancy is described using the language of deformity: 'le ventre de ma mère, déformé par sept mois de grossesse' (Khoury-Ghata 1992: 11) / my mother's belly was deformed by seven months of pregnancy; her screams during childbirth are like the screams of a slayed beast: 'ce cri de bête égorgée qui fit trembler les vitres du troisième étage. Cri qui écartela le ventre maternel et plia en deux l'homme de la guérite' (13) / the cry of a slayed beast that shook the third-floor windows. A cry that tore the maternal womb apart and broke in two the man in the sentry box. Flora is the monster that produces other monsters: children with mixed blood and mixed religions.

Finally, Flora defiles the city with her monstrous bleeding body, and brings misfortune to its inhabitants. In fact, the pregnant body is perceived as an impure body because it bleeds during and after childbirth. Kristeva, following the British anthropologist Mary Douglas's examination of purity and pollution, shows a strong link between abjection, the female body and the pregnant body. She notes that cultures have imposed specific rituals to pre-serve the borders between polluted and pure bodies in order to avoid defile-ment, and through these rituals, the female body was considered impure and therefore inferior to the male body. In the chapter on 'Semiotics of Biblical Abomination', Kristeva provides examples from Leviticus to show a woman's body has been labelled impure after childbirth:

> Because of her parturition and the blood that goes with it, *she* will be 'impure': 'according to the days of separation for her infirmity shall she be unclean' (Leviticus 12: 2). If she gives birth to a daughter, the girl 'shall be unclean two weeks, as in her separation' (Leviticus 12: 5). To purify herself, the mother must provide a burnt offering and a sin offering. Thus, on *her* part, there is impurity, defilement, blood, and purifying sacrifice. (Kristeva 1982: 99)

Flora transgresses the rituals that apply to the pregnant female body. She leaves her newborn when her breasts are still heavy with milk and her belly still contains black blood (Khoury-Ghata 1992: 9) and joins her Muslim lover when she is still bleeding impure Christian blood (50). She brings malediction to the city: 'C'est malsain, une accouchée qui se balade dans la nature. On les enfermait dans son pays. Quarante jours, pas un de moins. Le lait tournait à leur seule vue et la pâte refusait de lever' (65). Her body becomes the reason behind all ills: the war, her son's addiction, her daughter's promiscuity, her husband's weakness, her lover's obsession with her, Mlle Liliane's loneliness and the deaths of Mourad and Mr Nahum.

Flora, the Destructive Western Power

Flora's white body is also a representation of the West's historical role in the East in general and in the Lebanese civil war in particular. Flora is Polish. The choice of her country of origin may be innocent. Lebanon and Poland do not necessarily share strong historical ties; however, one could argue that Flora's nationality functions as a reference to the Second World War, which started with the German invasion of Poland.[5] The novel briefly and indirectly makes a reference to the Second World War: 'Flora . . . avait de l'expérience. A seize ans, elle était riche d'une autre guerre, et d'autres bombardements. Varsovie l'avait endurcie' (Khoury-Ghata 1992: 55) / Flora . . . had some experience.

At sixteen, she lived another war and other bombings. Warsaw hardened her. In referencing Poland, Flora becomes the point of origin of all the destruction that follows, especially in the East. She embodies the Western power that sets artificial borders between the previously colonised Middle Eastern countries and disturbs the natural relations between the Jews, Christians and Muslims which ultimately leads to the civil war in Lebanon. This complex relationship between the West and the region's different religious communities is represented in the novel through two different love triangles, the first of which involves Mr Nahum, Mourad and Flora, and the second one features the Notable, Flora and her husband.

The first triad of Flora, Mr Nahum and Mourad represents the role of the West in the rise of the Arab–Israeli conflict. Mr Nahum is the disabled Jewish man who heavily relies on his black Muslim servant Mourad. Mourad pushes Mr Nahum's wheelchair around, often from one floor to another. Occasionally, he carries him to places that are inaccessible by wheelchair. They depend on each other: Mr Nahum needs Mourad for transportation, and Mourad relies on Mr Nahum for financial support. The novel suggests that each is a slave to the other: 'devenu l'esclave d'un esclave . . . M. Nahum tient à son valet. Mourad est l'ombre debout de son corps avachi' (Khoury-Ghata 1992: 66–7). When Mourad is killed by the Muslim sector for having sent Flora Koranic verses on adultery, Mr Nahum seeks revenge. Mourad's death deprives Mr Nahum of his faithful servant and therefore his mobility within the city. He subsequently finances the Christian militia in its fight against Flora and the Muslim sector: 'La mort vivant affalé sur sa chaise roulante réclame vengeance pour son domestique. Il est prêt à doubler la mise: deux Kalachnikovs à Georges au lieu d'un, comme s'il pouvait tirer à la fois des deux mains' (106). Also, Mr Nahum was led to believe by Mme Vava that Bébé, Flora's third child, is his (56). Mr Nahum has now two reasons to support the Christian militia in its fight against the Muslim sector: Mourad's death and his own Christian-Jewish child. One could argue that the odd couple of Mourad and Mr Nahum represents the Palestinian–Israeli conflict that spilled over into Lebanon and fuelled the Lebanese civil war.

The second love triangle of Flora, her husband and her lover represents the conflicted relationship between the predominantly Christian West and the divided East with its Muslim majority and Christian minority.

The Notable is described as a dark limping figure who is always in Flora's shadow. He and Flora share a long history; he even appears in her old photographs: 'Au pied d'un escalier en bois. L'homme sombre sortait de là' (Khoury-Ghata 1992: 201). He is simultaneously Flora's stalker and lover. He is a respected community leader whose men and women faithfully serve and obey him. He is the mirror image of the weak, Christian husband who is fragile, unstable and delusional at times. Flora's husband is unable to control his wife or family members, and he is mocked by his community including Mlle Liliane, his son, his son's lover Georges and the Christian militia (40). Flora is a Helen of Troy whose beautiful white body is a source of conflict for two men and their respective sectors (89). She is the sun that blinds all men (11), and the Notable is the man who is drawn to this sun and its rays that reflect off his teeth (18). The Christian militia is deeply troubled by the sun, their prime enemy (172).

This representation of a conflicted Middle East as a dichotomy between Christian/Muslim, weak/strong and feminine/masculine is faithful to Edward Said's definition of orientalism. Orientalism is the ethnocentric imperialist repertoire that depicts the Orient as inferior or completely unfamiliar to the European traditions. It is the discourse that has a 'paternalistic or candidly condescending' approach to the Orient that is either praised for its classical cultures and ancient civilisations or deplored for its modern state of affairs (Said 1979: 204). Within the orientalist discourse, the Orient is frozen in time, unable to change, unstable, dangerous and despotic (207–8). The Orient is also feminine, subject to male domination, sensual and exotic. It is the 'Eastern bride' seen only through veils. It is the 'Inscrutable Orient' (222). In the Western Christian imagination, the East is also evil. The Orient in general and the Near East in particular represent terror, devastation and barbarism. For Said, this image is rigorously tied to the rise of Islam in the seventh century: its military conquests and religious and cultural hegemony stretching from that time period through the Ottoman Empire and until today (59–61).

The Notable and the husband embody this mixed representation of the Orient. If the Muslim Notable represents the dark, strong, dependable and masculine aspects of the East, the Christian husband stands for the unreliable, powerless and feminine sides. For Vénus Khoury-Ghata, this ambivalence in the Orient's representation may explain its inability to exist in peace. It is interesting to note that while Khoury-Ghata adopts an orientalist lens to describe the Orient (more precisely Lebanon), her depiction of the West is equally unflattering. Through the image of Flora, the West is depicted as self-ish and only caring for its own interests: 'Flora, personne ne l'ignore dans la grande maison, n'a jamais aimé le notable. Elle aime l'amour qu'elle lui inspire' (Khoury-Ghata 1992: 182) / 'No one ignores Flora in the big house, she never loved the Notable. She loves the love she inspires in him'; 'Flora a pleuré Flora qui ne sait pas aimé . . .' (236) / 'Flora cried for Flora, the one who does not know how to love'; 'Elle se nourrit de sa rage, s'alimente de son désespoir et remâche sans arrêt sa désillusion' (252) / 'She feeds off his rage, despair and his disillusion.' Finally, it is the West that is simultaneously the queen and the slave of the East: 'Elle est à la fois sa victime et son bourreau, son esclave et sa souveraine' (192).

Flora is also the Christian West that presumably shares similarities with the Christian minority in the East that has a problematic relationship with the Muslim majority. This compatibility between the Christian West and the Christian Eastern minority is hinted at through the topic of reproduction. Flora is able to produce three children with the Christian husband but is unable to carry her pregnancy to term with her Muslim lover. One wonders if Khoury-Ghata is, in fact, suggesting the viability of hybridity or métissage between the Christian West and the Christian East but its impossibility with the Muslim East.[6] While the possibility of hybridity among Christian subjects may be suggested, it is not however suggested in a celebratory way. In fact, all the hybrid subjects in the novel – whether hybrid through a Christianity that is equated with the West or through their lineage – are represented as broken. They are shown to be torn between their Middle Eastern identity and their Christian Western values. Their hybridity rendered them, as Kristeva says, monsters on the crossroad (Kristeva 2019: 46). They are all hybrid monsters produced by Flora, by the Christian West with whom they identify and yet by which they are rejected.

As for the Muslim East, Flora has a conflicted relationship with it. She is depicted as different and resistant to Islamic traditions: 'Elle résiste à leurs coutumes, ne mange pas de mouton, n'observe pas le jeûne', (Khoury-Ghata 1992: 181) / 'she resists their costumes; she does not eat sheep nor does she fast'. When she meets the Notable's mother for the first time, she feels overwhelmed by the mother's fascination with her whiteness. She throws away the tiara she is offered and runs away. The mother feels humiliated (51) and the Notable vows to find Flora and to punish her: 'Il préparait le terrain pour la conquérir, pour la chattier. Il lui fallait cette femme dans sa vie et dans son lit, pour cracher sa semence dans son ventre et rendre sa fierté à son sexe humilié' (52).

They engage in a love–hate relationship; the Notable is fascinated by Flora, in love with her, but he also wants to humiliate her. Although twenty years have passed, he still wants her to apologise to his mother (50). He is also frustrated by her constant refusal to enjoy their sexual encounters (51). He wants her on his own terms. He wants her to want him and to submit to him. She, of course, remains defiantly silent and sexually unsatisfied.

Flora's rejection of the Notable's mother, her silence and her sexual frustration represent more than a woman's simple rejection of a man. Flora effectively rejects the Notable's entire religion and culture, beginning with her rejection of the mother figure who is traditionally perceived as the guardian of these values. As Frantz Fanon says in his discussion of the relationship between a man of colour and a white female:

> By loving me, she proves to me that I am worthy of a white love. I am loved
> like a white man.
> I am a white man.
> Her love opens the illustrious path that leads to total fulfilment . . .
> I espouse white culture, white beauty, white whiteness.
> Between these white breasts that my wandering hands fondle, white
> civilization and worthiness become mine. (Fanon 1967: 45)

Although Fanon's example is of a black man with a white woman, his sentiment could be extended to describe the power struggle between a dark-skinned Muslim man and a white Christian woman, between the Muslim East and the Christian West. Flora, in rejecting the Notable and his family, rejects the entire Muslim community and makes them all feel unworthy of her white Western body and culture. Her body stands for the Christian West that is loved and hated by the East. It is the Christian West that never apologises or kneels to any Eastern man, whether Christian or Muslim. It is the mother that produces hybrid children in the East and abandons them at birth. Finally, it is the manipulative female body that silently destroys the lives she touches.

La Malédiction

Born in the seventies and growing up in a violent Lebanon, Hala,[7] the narrator and the main protagonist, finds herself constantly torn between her mother's teachings about the female body and the social expectations of her own body and personal views on the matter. Oppressed by both her mother and her Catholic schooling, she compensates by overeating and engaging in a lesbian relationship with her schoolmate Fadia. Constantly feeling inadequate and out of place, she accepts a marriage proposal at the age of eighteen naïvely believing that doing so would enable her to escape her mother's grip. She soon comes to realise that she only traded one oppressor for another. She simply replaced her mother with a mother-in-law. Hala's husband is also under his mother's thumb. Deprived of his voice and diagnosed with the fictional medical condition of erosion, he gradually fades away. When he is pronounced dead, the mother-in-law sues Hala for the custody of her two daughters. She blames Hala for the death of her son and labels her an unfit mother. At the court hearing, Hala is unable to properly communicate her views to the five male judges who clearly have preconceived ideas on femininity. After reciting an irrational speech at court, Hala loses the case. She retreats in silence, kills her daughters and dies by suicide thereby refusing to abide by traditional social rules.

Hala's suffering, the oppression of her body by her mother and her subsequent illness and disability are in fact the story of the civil war in Lebanon. In order to understand this link between Hala's body and the war narrative, it is important to start by examining the conflicted mother–daughter relationship.

Foucault's theory on the docile body is useful in understanding the problematic nature of the mother–daughter relationship. In fact, Hala's mother functions as the pacifying institution that seeks to transform her daughter into a docile body in order to maximise its effectiveness and its value in an old-fashioned society. Hala on the other hand is a resisting subject who rejects her mother's and subsequently her society's views of the female body. She manifests her resistance and claims her body through her sexuality and her eating disorder. Her awareness of her body comes with the rise of her political consciousness. Hala notices that her body, just like her country, is sick and broken and her mother, who to a certain extent represents the older generation, is blind to both. Hala's realisation makes her even more vulnerable to the traditional expectations of her gender. Unable to live within this paradigm and unable to defend herself, she chooses to leave this world with her daughters by her side.

The Mother or the Pacifying Agency of the Daughter's Body

In his examination of modern society, Foucault studies the link between discipline and the body. Considered to be the centre of power, the body is 'manipulated, shaped, trained' in order to maximise its utility and forces (Foucault 1995: 136). The body becomes thus an investment for its institution just like the soldier for the military, the student for the school, or the prisoner for the prison. As a valuable investment, the body requires control. Foucault identifies three important aspects of control: the scale of control, the object of control and the modality of control. For the scale of control, the coercion must be discreet and subtle enough to create the illusion that one is acting upon one's own free will when in fact, one is acting within a group performing en masse. For the object of control, what truly matters is the efficiency of the movements that should occur in a way to maximise the utility of the body. Finally, for the modality of control, it must be constant and codified in space and time in order to form a discipline. These elements are available, for example, in monasteries, schools, military and other institutions that are highly codified. The codes of conduct or disciplines create what Foucault calls 'practiced bodies, "docile" bodies', where the body becomes a machine that is possible to control, explore and repair (Foucault 1995: 138). It is a docile machine at the service of a rigid discipline.

Control over the docile bodies must be constant and 'highly ritualized' (Foucault 1995:184). It occurs through what Foucault calls the 'normalizing gaze', which is 'a surveillance that makes it possible to qualify, to classify and to punish' (184). A similar principle has been observed in Jeremy Bentham's panopticon, a prison that consists of an annular building with a tower in the centre.[8] The building itself contains the prison cells with wide windows that allow the supervisor in the tower to observe the inmates. The prison cells are backlit, which guarantees clear visibility from the tower and 'induce[s] in the inmate a state of conscious and permanent visibility that assures the automatic functioning of power' (201). Power that leads to discipline and punishment when infringed is both visible and invisible. It is visible through the pure exist-ence of the tower, a constant reminder of authority in the eyes and minds or the inmates. However, it is invisible as the inmate never really knows when he or she is being observed. Consequently, '[p]ower has its principle not so much in a person as in a certain concerted distribution of bodies, surfaces, lights, gazes . . .' (202).

Foucault's examination of the role of the body in modern society is certainly of extreme importance. However, he neglected to consider differ-ences in gender and their relationship to power. He studied the body as a homogeneous entity without distinguishing between male and female bodies and their respective relations to discipline, power and punishment. This could lead to the false assumption that their relations are similar. Perhaps this is the most important point of contention with feminism according to which bodily practices are much more demanding of women in comparison to men, and therefore the control over the female body is much higher.[9]

Sandra Lee Bartky re-examines Foucault's theory of 'docile bodies' within a gendered frame because '[t]o overlook the forms of subjection that engen-der the feminine body is to perpetuate the silence and powerlessness of those upon whom these disciplines have been imposed' (Bartky 1997: 132). She demonstrates that modern societies impose far more discipline on women's bodies in comparison to male bodies. She divides these disciplinary practices into three different categories: practices related to body size and configura-tion, practices related to gestures, postures and movements, and finally prac-tices relevant to the body as an ornament to display. Regarding body size and configuration, Bartky shows how the image of the female body has changed through time and cultures. Today, we live in a world in which obesity is 'met with distaste' (Bartky 1997: 132). Fashion imposes a certain image of what it considers to be a beautiful female body by obsessively encouraging women to diet. Dieting by itself is a form of imposed discipline on the body that aims to maximise its utility. It certainly has beneficial health values; however, it is often done in order to fit into the image of the perfect female body rather than out of concern for fitness. It is interesting to point out that frequently fashion magazines tailor their diets toward women and not necessarily to men.

Regarding bodily comportment, women's gestures are more restricted than men in the way they walk, talk, sit, or move their hands, and so on: 'the female gaze is trained to abandon its claim to the sovereign status of seer. The "nice" girl learns to avoid the bold and unfettered staring of the "loose" woman who looks at whatever and whomever she pleases' (Bartky 1997: 135). Women are taught from a young age to control their bodies, to move with grace and modesty and to avoid eye contact or any suggestive behaviour that may be perceived as erotic.

Finally, a woman's body is considered an ornament that requires certain disciplinary practices such as hair removal, skin and hair care, cosmetic surgery and make-up: 'Woman lives her body as seen by another, by an anonymous patriarchal Other' (Bartky 1997: 140). It is evident to us that unlike male bodies, female bodies are subjected to greater and stricter disciplinary practices. However, if the disciplinary practices vary according to gender, the control itself remains genderless as it is exercised by everyone: by men and women and by society as a whole.

There are sanctions to female bodies that do not conform to expected societal practices: a woman 'faces a very severe sanction indeed in a world dominated by men: the refusal of male patronage. For the heterosexual woman, this may mean the loss of a badly needed intimacy; for both heterosexual women and lesbians, it may well mean the refusal of a decent livelihood' (Bartky 1997: 144). Women have reacted differently to the imposed male image of the female body. Some women have completely internalised the patriarchal discourse on the female body while others have adopted the opposite position and rejected it entirely thus running the risk of being shamed and alienated. Some women have taken a less extreme position by arguing that some traits, although first imposed by men, today constitute an undeniable part of their female identity and should remain as such.

By applying Bartky's reading of Foucault's docile bodies to *La Malédiction*, we can clearly see how the mother functions as the institution that works to pacify her daughter's body through the implementation of a strict code of conduct related to body size, its movements and its display within society (which are the three categories identified by Bartky). The mother considers her daughter to be inferior simply because she is female, but also because she fails to properly perform what is expected of her gender. She also views her as dirty and impure. Because of what she sees as inferiority and impurity, the mother takes control over her daughter's body. She mocks her weight, neglects her sexual education (as it is best to leave her unaware of her body) and treats her differently than her brothers.

The conflicted nature of the mother–daughter relationship appears right at the beginning of the text when Hala explains that she loves her mother and fears her at the same time: '[l']amour maternel est une forme de terreur. Certaines mères sont à l'image de Dieu" (Yared 2012: 11) / 'A mother's love is a form of terror. Some mothers are godlike.' Her brother urges her to distance herself from her mother by avoiding the possessive pronoun and by only referring to her as 'the mother': 'Ne dis pas Ma mère, dis La mère. Ne t'approprie rien' (15). For Hala, the mother assumes the role of a judgemental God who tests his sinful creatures. In the Christian faith, 'the beginning was the word, and the word was with God' (John 1: 1), but for Hala the beginning starts with a candy box provokingly displayed by the mother in the living room: 'Elle avait trouvé, en la qualité de la bonbonnière, un arbre de la connaissance *pavlovien*. Sa progéniture lui tenait lui d'Adam et Ève et elle rejouait tous les jours la Chute originelle' (9). It is interesting to note the reversal of gender roles in Hala's version of Genesis. God is female and the first sin is committed by a male. Her brother, desperate to see a naked female body, asks Hala to undress. He bribes her with some candy and claims to be examining her in the name of science (10). Drawn to the candy like Eve was drawn to the apple, Hala displays her body for her brother and joins him in committing the mortal sin of disobeying 'the mother'.

The mother – in all her godly powers – sees Hala's femininity as inferiority. She is inferior by birth but also for her inability to abide by the rules that define her gender. The mother thinks that her daughter is overweight, which, in the mother's mind, is a reflection on the daughter's inability to conform to the traditional standards of female beauty. She criticises her, makes fun of her and compares her to a balloon and different animals: 'Tu es aussi grasse qu'une oie. Tu devrais cesser de manger . . . Tu t'es regardée? On dirait une vache enceinte' (13) / 'You are as fat as a goose. You should stop eating . . . Have you looked at yourself? You look like a pregnant cow'; 'Tes cuisses vont ressembler à des jambonneaux si tu t'acharnes à vouloir manger gras et non allégé' / 'Your thighs will look like hams if you continue eating heavy food and not fat free' (21); 'Mon petit ballon de baudruche' (83) / 'My little balloon.'

When Hala was born, the mother was disappointed and the nurse asked her not to worry because God is good and the next one will be a boy: 'Ne vous en faites pas, Dieu est bon. Le prochain sera un garcon' (13). When her brother Hicham was born, the mother was so proud, especially because he was a blond male in comparison to his dark-haired siblings. It is a moment of redemption for the mother who realises that her body can, in fact, produce what she sees as perfection in opposition to the common (brown-haired boy) and to the inferior (girl).

Susan Brownmiller examines the meanings and the cultural representations of the naked female body: hair, clothes, voice, skin, movement, emotion and ambition. She shows the historical evolution of each of these body elements and argues that beauty standards in general and female beauty standards in particular have been set by white culture, or what she calls the 'tyranny of Venus' (Brownmiller 1984: 23). Venus, the goddess of love, represents the perfect body of a white, golden-haired female. Anything that does not fit within these standards of beauty is to be considered less beautiful.

> Blonde hair has been associated with the goodness of sunshine, the preciousness of spun gold, the purity of the Madonna, the excitement of paid-for love, and the innocent, pastoral vision in literature, myth and art ... Golden hair was definitely an attribute of feminine beauty in Imperial Rome, where it became fashion for prostitutes and wealthy matrons to wear blonde wigs made of hair brought back from conquered Gaul. In fifteenth-century Florentine art, reddish gold and flaxen were the colors of choice to grace the heads of Botticelli's pagans as well as his Madonnas, and for the Annunciations, Adorations and Virgins with Child of Fra Angelico and Filippo Lippi. (Brownmiller 1984: 70)

It is interesting to note that in *La Malédiction*, the mother associates Hicham's blondness with purity, and opposes it to his sister's dark hair and impurity. When Hala tells her brothers about her menstrual blood, the mother is particularly angry with her for having tainted Hicham's innocence. For Hala, Hicham is the favourite one with chaste ears '[u]n favori aux oreilles chastes' (Yared 2012: 54).

Brownmiller discusses the historical preference for fair skin and shows how it was praised as the signature of perfect beauty: 'Beautiful skin – sweet-smelling, lily-white, rosy-cheeked, soft and dewy and free of blemish – is a sentimental attribute of virginal innocence and aristocratic fragility' (Brownmiller 1984: 130). She examines the historical evolution and cultural meanings of standards of beauty through a gendered lens to explain how these tropes are still in play in our modern society and inform our current construction of femininity. However, if we take her analysis temporarily out of the gendered context to place it within the frameworks of colonialism and postcolonialism, we can see how it can be used to justify the superiority of white European culture. As Fanon argues, unconsciously the colonised subject believes the coloniser to be culturally superior. Before independence, the Western, colonising bourgeoisie living in the colonies identifies with the culture of the mother country and has some legitimacy in doing so. The native bourgeoisie, identifying with the coloniser, tries to imitate the Western bourgeoisie. During the period of unrest and after the independence, the native bourgeoisie adopts 'unreservedly and with enthusiasm, the ways of thinking characteristic of the mother country' (Fanon 1963: 178).

The mother, a middle-class Christian from Lebanon, believes in the superiority of Western culture, particularly French culture, which explains her exceptional pride in giving birth to a blond male. Hicham's blond hair makes him superior to his common-looking brother and inferior sister. For the mother, her own body has finally produced perfection. She has paid her dues to society.

The mother also sees impurity in her daughter's femininity. When Hala menstruates for the first time, the mother does not explain the female reproductive system; she simply describes menstrual blood as dirty, intimate and shameful: 'Je t'explique. À ton âge, les filles ont du sang une fois par mois. Ça s'appelle les règles. C'est sale. Je te passerai des serviettes pour ne pas tacher les fauteuils. Et il ne faut jamais en parler à personne. Jamais. C'est intime' (Yared 2012: 50). When Hala violates the golden rule of silence and tells her brother about her menstruation, her mother takes the bloody pad and wipes it across her mouth; she wants Hala to taste her own blood so that she will always remember how repulsive it is: 'Ouvre la bouche, lèche. Tu aimes ça? C'est dégoûtant, n'est-ce pas?' (55).

In her examination of purity and cleanliness, Mary Douglas shows the link between dirt, impurity and social structure, and examines the impact of pollution beliefs on social life. Communities, based on local consensus and wide complicity, have labelled some practices as taboo. A taboo, according to Douglas, is:

> [A] spontaneous coding practice which sets up a vocabulary of spatial limits and physical and verbal signals to hedge around vulnerable relations. It threatens specific dangers if the code is not respected. Some of the dangers which follow on taboo-breaking spread harm indiscriminately on contact. Feared contagion extends the danger of a broken taboo to the whole community. (Douglas 2002: xiii)

What is denounced as taboo is also considered to be dirty, dangerous and impure. As a result of this codifying of some behaviours, a certain social order was installed to distinguish between pure and impure, dirty and taboo.

Dirt is understood to be related to hygiene but also to the respect of social conventions. 'Shoes [adds Douglas] are not dirty in themselves, but it is dirty to place them on the dining-table; food is not dirty in itself, but it is dirty to leave cooking utensils in the bedroom' (Douglas 2002: 45). So, dirt by itself is 'not necessarily dangerous' (xi). However, it becomes dangerous when it reflects disorder:

> There is no such thing as absolute dirt: it exists in the eye of the beholder. If we shun dirt, it is not because of craven fear, still less dread of holy terror. Nor do our ideas about disease account for the range of our behavior in cleaning or avoiding dirt. Dirt offends against order. Eliminating it is not a negative movement, but a positive effort to organize the environment. (Douglas 2002: 2)

> Dirt then, is never a unique, isolated event. Where there is dirt, there is a system. Dirt is the by-product of a systematic ordering and classification of matter, in so far as ordering involves rejecting inappropriate elements. This idea of dirt takes us straight into the field of symbolism and promises a link-up with more obviously symbolic systems of purity. (Douglas 2002: 44)

Dirt came to exist linguistically, but also as a result of the labelling of some social practices as dirty following certain disciplinary rules relevant to hygiene, health and medicine, religion and other institutions.[10]

Building on Sartre's essay on stickiness, Douglas argues that dirt brings out our own anxieties as it is an anomaly that escapes classification. It is neither a solid nor a liquid; it defies the boundaries between the self (and the society) and what is considered to be dirt. For example, when 'a monstrous birth occurs, the defining line between humans and animals may be threatened' (Douglas 2002: 49). Once identified as dirty or as an anomaly, the question would be how to deal with it. According to Douglas, one can treat it negatively by ignoring it, pretending it does not exist or condemning it – or positively by acknowledging its different existence which could eventually alter our own reality.[11]

In *La Malédiction*, the mother views her daughter's femininity as dirty and an anomaly to the male ruling form. This explains why she mocks her weight and compares her to a cow and a pig. The mother's anxiety regarding her daughter's femininity expresses itself when her daughter hits the age of puberty and has her period for the first time. The mother is suddenly confronted with her daughter's reality and the blood functions as a tangible reminder of what she sees as inferiority. For Simone de Beauvoir in *The Second Sex*, 'the blood, indeed, does not make woman impure; it's rather a sign of her impurity' (de Beauvoir 1989: 150). If the shoes, for Douglas, are not dirty by themselves but when on a dining table they are, then the same logic applies or can be applied to blood. The impurity comes from the context in which blood exists, which in this case is the female body. Consequently, the female body is declared impure and dirty. For that, it should be hidden away which explains why the mother asks Hala not to speak of it to her brothers.

In her examination of Mary Douglas's work, Kristeva argues that Douglas neglected to elaborate on the meaning of dirt as a border element, particularly for other systems such as psychology and economics (Kristeva 1982: 66). Kristeva approaches dirt from a different perspective, one which pays particular attention to gender. In her chapter, 'From Filth to Defilement', Kristeva shows how religious prohibitions, the protection of the sacred and the ritualisation of defilement accompany sex separation that empowers men over women. If men are seen as powerful, rational and clean, women are perceived to be irrational, uncontrollable and dirty. Consequently, '[t]hat other sex, the feminine, becomes synonymous with a radical evil that is to be suppressed' (Kristeva 1982: 70). Kristeva gives different examples of body fluids:

> Neither tears nor sperm, for instance, although they belong to borders of the body, have any polluting value . . . Menstrual blood, on the contrary, stands for the danger issuing from within the identity (social or sexual); it threatens the relationship between the sexes within a social aggregate and, through internalization, the identity of each sex in the face of sexual difference. (Kristeva 1982: 71)

In comparison to menstrual blood, sperm has no polluting value as it does not threaten the boundaries between the two sexes. Blood comes from within and blurs the bodily borders of the inside and the outside. It is also a visible reminder of sex differences, which is why it is considered to be dirty and defiling in a society that simultaneously wants to control and beautify femininity, but also to pacify it to the point of invisibility. Interestingly enough, for Kristeva, the '[m]aternal authority is the trustee of that mapping of the self's clean and proper body' (Kristeva 1982: 72) The mother is in charge of the primal mapping of the body that predates language. The body thus becomes a territory with lines, areas and orifices that are either controlled and cleaned or dirty and neglected. In other words, the mother sets the rules of what is dirty and what is not for her non-verbal infant.

Acting as the pacifying agency, the mother, in addition to labelling her daughter fat and inferior, keeps her in the dark when it comes to the proper functioning of her body. For instance, the mother never really explains to her daughter the menstrual cycle. Another example would be when the son lured his sister to undress, he alone was reprimanded by the parents. Hala, who was eight years old at the time of the incident, was excluded from the discussion that took place behind closed doors:

> [M]on corps avait basculé d'un coup dans l'indifférence . . . Un sentiment d'injustice s'empara de moi. Je voulais avoir les mêmes droits de comparution que mon frère. J'étais exclue de tout. Honte. Péché. Punition. Langage. J'en convins: le trou détenait un secret dont je n'avais pas la clé. / My body suddenly fell into the indifference . . . I was shaken by a sentiment of injustice. I

wanted to have the same rights as my brother. I was excluded of everything. Shame. Sin. Punishment. Language. I was convinced: the hole had a secret to which I did not hold the key. (Yared 2012: 17)

Hala's ignorance is so pervasive, and she is so oblivious to her bodily functions that she believes herself to be pregnant from the butler's kiss: 'J'avais la conviction que la salive d'Edward m'avait engrossée' (Yared 2012: 72).

In the mother's mind, the daughter's body requires her strict control due to its inferiority and impurity. This control is practised by keeping the daughter ignorant of her body but also by treating her differently than her brothers. For instance, she punishes her differently:

Deux doigts comme deux pinces. Cette manière de molester, la mère me la réservait. J'étais la seule à être du même sexe qu'elle. De ses doigts, elle m'attrapait le lobe de l'oreille qu'elle pinçait en me tirant jusqu'à elle, afin que mon visage, proche du sien, sente son souffle et son regard. Elle se servait de la colère comme d'une virilité compensatoire à ce qu'elle considérait être une faiblesse: la féminité. / Two fingers like pliers. This way of molesting me, the mother reserved it to me. I was the only one to share her sex. With her fingers, she grabbed my ear lobe and pinched pulling me towards her so my face would be close to hers and so I could feel her breath and see her expression. She used anger as a compensatory virility for what she considered to be weakness: femininity. (Yared 2012: 12)

Unable to understand her mother's hostile attitude towards her, Hala concludes that her mother must hate her own femininity. Hala thinks that she is nothing more than her mother's extension in the world: 'La mère souffrait d'automutilation retournée sur autrui. À travers moi, elle punissait son propre sexe' (Yared 2012: 27). Despite the lack of communication between the mother and the daughter, Hala gradually comes to realise that her mother's behaviour is simply unfair. The mother wants to control every aspect of her daughter's body by forcing her to go on a diet and take swimming lessons; and yet, she fails to see that her daughter was sexually molested by the swimming trainer (34). By forcing her to conform to a body image imposed upon women by society, the mother actually erases the real existence of her daughter: 'Efface-moi tant que tu y es. Gomme-moi, comme on corrige une faute dans une rédaction. Fais-moi passer du visible au néant' (54). Hala is very much aware of these sentiments. She is invisible to her mother and as such decides to take control over her body hoping to get her mother's attention.[12] She develops an eating disorder and becomes severely ill. Her resistance against her mother takes the form of a self-inflicted illness that disables her and destroys her just like the war disabled and destroyed Lebanon.

Eating Disorder as a Form of Resistance

Hala's mutiny starts when she notices contradictions between her mother's discourse and her religious teachings. She is told that her female body is sinful and unworthy, yet she must protect it for the greater good of society. She is asked not to speak about sex and yet the topic of sex is everywhere. Finally, she hears that God creates perfection, but she is told that her female body is imperfect and inferior.

At school, Sister Paule de la Croix[13] tells her students that masturbation will render them blind and that they must renounce the body in order to see the light: 'La masturbation vous rendra toutes aveugles. Le renoncement à la chair, seul, rend la vue' (Yared 2012: 36). After telling them that their bodies are sinful, she stresses the importance of their role in reproducing little Christians since they are at war with the Muslims: 'C'est grâce à vous, mes filles, que nous résisterons par le nombre aux invasions des *autres*. Il faut faire plein de petits chrétiens' (161).

Although the word 'sex' is taboo in Hala's family, Hala (who does not really understand what it means) notes that the word exists everywhere in her society: among the frustrated youth, in the hateful language of daily life and in her father's curse words:

> En famille, le mot « sexe » était tabou. Pourtant les manifestations du sexe à travers le déni, le refoulement, la surveillance et les allégories de substitution pour le désigner, étaient nombreuses. Dans la rue, mon Orient n'était que sexué. L'insulte, la haine, les murs criblés de tirs de roquettes et de graffitis. (Yared 2012: 46)

Finally, Hala is told that her body does not matter, and yet her mother panics when she thinks that Hala lost her virginity after inserting a hose to urinate standing; she immediately takes her to a gynaecologist who finds the hymen intact. From the incompatible nature of these messages, Hala concludes that God is sexist and narcissistic for creating women inferior to men and for equipping them with a sex that does not really belong to them. God and his religion are nothing more than a colonial power to the female sex. They are also the reasons behind the war in Lebanon:

> Dieu avait-il un prépuce quand il créa Adam sexué? Le créa-t-il par amour de lui-même, de son ego, de son image? Sexiste et narcissique, Dieu devait déjà l'être depuis son ciel, là-haut. Il créa l'homme, masculin à son image, et réduisit la femme à naître d'une côte d'homme, avec, en sus, une castration reproductive . . . Mon sexe ne m'appartenait pas. A la naissance déjà je ne l'avais pas choisi . . . Dès la naissance, nos entourages manifestent le désir de découvrir ou de rejeter nos corps, en tout cas, occupés. Nos sexes colonisés, annexés aux pères, aux fils, aux mères, aux frères . . . Nos sexes sont des galets, érodés, effacés, fantomatiques. (Yared 2012: 49)

With this awareness comes Hala's first rebellious act: she offers her bracelets to a classmate in exchange for candy (Yared 2012: 25). Believing her to be obese, Hala's mother puts her on a strict diet but Hala finds ways to get food. She begs her classmates, steals from their backpacks or digs through the garbage. One time, Hala pays for candy with golden bracelets her mother gave her as part of the family heritage. Hala's trading of the bracelets for candy shows her rejection of the way her body is treated as an ornament to be displayed in society and, by extension, a rejection of her mother's traditional view of her body.[14]

It is interesting to note that Hala feels invisible in her mother's eyes that only see her as overweight. As a reaction to her invisibility, she turns to self-mutilation, self-cutting and nail biting:

> Plus la mère nous rationnait, plus la privation me conférait un air d'affamée. Une faim comme un plat. Je portais mes ongles à mes dents et arrachais tout ce qui dépassait. Les cuticules. La peau. J'aurais pu détacher mes doigts . . . je m'emparais d'un ciseau pour faire des saillies dans la peau. Les gouttes de sang qui giclaient s'accompagnaient d'une sensation de bien-être. (Yared 2012: 23–4)

She also makes the decision to become obese and dirty:

Et si je décidais d'être putride, immonde, grasse, débordante et que, par excès, mon corps cessait d'exister? Être écrasante au point qu'on ne me verrait plus? Je me mis à espacer mes douches. Un soir oui, un soir non . . . Puis une fois par mois. Je voulais être invisible par excès de négligence. (Yared 2012: 63)

Fadia plays an important role in educating Hala about her body and in raising her sexual and political awareness. Abused by a father who is proud of his illegal militia's activities, Fadia is severely anorexic; she finds consolation in reading literature and is very well read. She passes on her knowledge to Hala and teaches her about the menstrual cycle, reproduction, sexuality, eroticism and eating disorders.

Fadia might be Hala's alter ego. She represents everything Hala is not. She teaches her how to become bulimic; she encourages her to eat pizzas, to drink sparkling water and to vomit afterward. She tells her she will feel light and free: 'Tu te sentiras légère. Délivrée' (Yared 2012: 88). Scared of the unpleasant feeling of nausea and the emptiness generated by vomiting, Hala soon learns to enjoy the experience as an expression of control over her body. From that moment on, Hala alternates between anorexia nervosa and bulimia.

Susan Bordo examines the relationship between the female body and eating disorders.[15] Our society, Bordo argues, is constantly pursuing the image of the ideal female body. Women are always asked to change and to improve their bodies through fashion, make-up, diet, cosmetic surgeries and other practices.

> [Our] [c]ulture not only has taught women to be insecure bodies, constantly monitoring themselves for signs of imperfection, constantly engaged in physical 'improvement'; it also is constantly teaching women (and let us not forget, men as well) how to *see* bodies. As slenderness has consistently been visualized glamorized, and the idea has grown thinner and thinner, bodies that a decade ago were considered slender have now come to seem fleshy. (Bordo 1993: 57)

Women thus live under the pressure to be thin, or, as Kim Chernin calls it, the 'tyranny of slenderness' (Chernin 1985).

Slenderness carries multiple meanings. In medieval times, fasting to the point of starvation was strongly linked to willpower, discipline and purity.

Women who starved themselves and survived on prayers and little food qualified for sainthood for their abilities to rise above the needs of their female bodies (Bell 1985; Brumberg 1988). Today, slenderness conveys a similar meaning, and a woman on a diet is praised for her strong will and her ability to control her body. Slenderness also implies that women can control their appetite and eat as little as possible while nurturing and feeding others, which preserves the stereotypical image of the caring woman.

Eating disorders come as a reaction to the cultural expectation of thinness and to the traditional discourse on femininity.[16] They often erupt:

> in the course of what begins as a fairly moderate diet regime, undertaken because, someone, often the father, has made a casual critical remark. Anorexia *begins* in, emerges out, what is, in our time, conventional feminine practice. In the course of that practice, for any number of individual reasons, the practice is pushed a little beyond the parameters of moderate dieting. The young woman discovers what it feels like to crave and want and need and yet, through the exercise of her own will, to triumph over that need. In the process, a new realm of meanings is discovered, a range of values and possibilities that Western culture has traditionally coded as 'male' and rarely made available to women: an ethic and aesthetic of self-mastery and self-transcendence, expertise, and power over others through the example of superior will and control. The experience is intoxicating, habit-forming. (Bordo 1997: 100)

The anorexic female feels liberated. Through the intensive practice of conventional feminine behaviour, she is able to enter the privileged male world.

For Bordo, eating disorders are sometimes linked to sexual abuse. Women who have suffered from deep humiliation and/or sexual abuse in their childhood are very much aware of the sexual vulnerability of the female body. They hold themselves responsible for the 'unwanted advances and sexual assaults. This guilt festers into unease with [their] femaleness, shame [their] bodies, and self-loathing' (Bordo 1993: 8). As a result, they starve themselves or binge-eat and then vomit in order to erase their traditional feminine curves (such as breasts and hips) and to cultivate the image of an androgynous body which, in their minds, represents the perfect intersection of the masculine values and the female body (Bordo 1997: 97).

Eating disorders are thus multidimensional. They are heavily related to the social expectations of the female body, but they are also intertwined with one's personal past. Women with eating disorders do not realise that they actually suffer from an illness and find the experience of starvation or binge-eating and vomiting to be liberating. They literally cannot see their bodies as extremely thin or dangerously unhealthy. Also, they are unaware that their eating disorders are a form of protest which renders the protest counterproductive as it is only self-destructive.

Sexually abused by her brother early in life and constantly humiliated by her mother, who sees her as a deformed, unattractive, lazy female, Hala engages in self-destructive behaviour during which she alternates between starvation, binge-eating and vomiting. Her eating disorder starts right after she is discovered naked in the bathtub with Fadia. Her non-normative sexuality (although experienced only briefly), her being overweight and her griminess are diametrically opposed to the conventional definition of femininity, which traditionally implies heterosexuality, slenderness and cleanliness. As a reaction to her mother's hurtful comments, Hala decides to embrace the conventional definition of femininity and make it her own by pushing it to the extreme. By doing so, she challenges her mother and sets her own terms of femininity. She accepts to be thin and to eat less but she will determine how thin she will be and how little she will eat:

> Je maigrissais comme on régresse vers la perte de l'amour. Mes formes perdaient de leurs rondeurs. L'absence de Fadia m'occupait toute entière. En maigrissant, j'avais l'impression d'extraire de mon surplus de chair son squelette absent. Grossir devint ma hantise. Manger mon réflexe. Je jumelais les deux en vomissant après chaque séance de gavage. (Yared 2012: 99)

By losing weight when she turns eighteen, Hala gains social visibility and is declared marriable. Her aunt Violette arranges a meeting between Hala's family and her future mother-in-law. Although Hala is very critical of the practice to the point of comparing it to human trafficking, she does not resist. In her mind, she protests through her eating disorder which allows her to retain control over her body. However, and as Bordo (1993) argues, this form of protest is counterproductive; society is oblivious to its true meaning and will either praise the body for being slender or criticise it for looking sickly.

Therefore, Hala's eating disorder will go unseen just like her resistance. She notes her manoeuvre's invisibility when she meets her future mother-in-law for the first time. The future mother-in-law inspects her, sees she has white teeth but fails to see Hala's diseased gums and eroded teeth from the constant vomiting and acidity:

> Ma future belle-mère n'écoutait rien et calculait tout. Le nombre de caries. La qualité de la salive. L'épaisseur du sang. Elle s'assurait du milieu buccal où la langue de son fils ira traîner. Elle ne soupçonna rien dans mon hygiène dentaire . . . Mes dents exposées tout à tour à l'acidité de la bile perdaient de leur émail. En apparence, elles étaient blanches. En réalité, leur surface se réduisait au fur et à mesure de mon rétrécissement. Je n'arrêtais de vomir qu'au moment où je reconnaissais le goût amer de la bile. (Yared 2012: 102–3)

Once Hala is married, she deliberately gains weight: 'A peine mariée, je me mis à manger comme on court après la consolation, en s'abrutissant' (Yared 2012: 135); 'J'ingérais toutes formes de nourriture en pensant à la fable de la grenouille qui, voulant devenir aussi grosse que le bœuf, explosa' (136). Thinking that she has escaped her mother's grip and feeling that she has satisfied the social requirements of her gender, she allows her body to take a break from excessive dieting and frequent vomiting. However, this feeling of fulfilment is short-lived as Hala becomes increasingly aware of her new social duty, which is to have children, particularly boys, so that they can ensure the family's continuity. She only partially fulfils this social obligation as she produces, to her mother-in-law's complete dissatisfaction, two girls.[17]

The Sick and Disabled Body as the War Storyteller

As mentioned in the Introduction, Hala's story is in many ways the story of Lebanon, and her body represents the story of the civil war. Just like Lebanon, Hala experiences violence from the people entrusted to protect her. Through her eating disorder and pregnancies, Hala becomes aware of this parallelism between her body and her country. The more she feels her body suffers, the more she is able to recognise the extent of Lebanon's devastation.

Early in the novel, Hala wishes to become blind and yet gradually she comes to see her body and her country in a different light. She recognises the pain in both and designates her mother, Syria and religion as oppressors. From the beginning of the text and as previously discussed, Hala's mother privileges the whiteness and slenderness of Western standards of female beauty. Due to her Christian faith, the mother identifies with the West and rejects her Arab identity that she associates with Islam. She hates Arab countries and blames Syria and Palestine for the civil war in Lebanon. She considers the word 'Palestine' to be a curse word and forbids her children from saying it: 'un gros mot. Je ne veux pas l'entendre ici' (Yared 2012: 29). She also compares her daughter's obesity to the Syrian invasion of Lebanon: 'Les acides gras et la Syrie étaient ses pires ennemis. Les deux présageaient, selon elle, des invasions suivies d'occupation irréversible et le pire des pièges consistait à céder du terrain à ces deux tumeurs' (22). She rejoices when Lebanon is compared to Switzerland or France: '*Suisse de l'Orient, Paris du Moyen-Orient* . . . Elle applaudissait à la perspective d'un pays surnommé la Suisse ou le Paris de n'importe quel nom d'après pourvu que l'Orient fût relégué aux oubliettes' (85).

If the mother sees Hala's body as a representation of the enemy within her household, Hala sees her mother as an oppressive power. For every time she oppresses her, Hala is reminded of her suffering country: when her mother forces her to go on a diet, Hala cannot help but think of the hungry refugees (Yared 2012: 33); when her mother punishes her, she compares her living body with the dead bodies piled up in the streets (32); when her mother reminds her she is overweight, she thinks of the shrinking size of her country (83).

Ironically, Hala compares her mother to Syria, a country that the mother obviously hates. If Syria wants to invade Lebanon and control it, so does the mother with her daughter's body (97). These binary relations of Syria/Lebanon and Mother/Daughter make Hala compare her country and her body to a dysfunctional digestive tube that cannot work properly or exist in peace:

> La Syrie ne supportait pas non plus que le Liban fût séparé d'elle. Elle caressait le rêve de digérer ce pays qu'elle n'avait de cesse d'ingérer en compétition avec Israël. A force d'être envahi, mâché, revisité, abandonné, ce pays dut finir par penser que son unique destin était celui de sa transformation en merde déféquée. J'avais pour hantise de digérer. Vomir m'évitait d'être un

agent transformateur. Je voulais décanter la vie et les aliments le moins possible. N'être qu'un tube digestif dysfonctionnel. (Yared 2012: 125)

Comparing the female body to a country is not necessarily a novel idea. In fact, many literary texts have made that link, and many critics have demonstrated how the female body functions as a representation of national identity within patriarchal nationalist discourse.[18] The originality of *La Malédiction* resides not so much in the conflation of female body and country, but instead in its identification of the abusive authority which generates this conflation. Traditionally, the female body is equated with nation within the patriarchal discourse which justifies men's control over women's bodies. Typically, men's control of women is viewed as part of the political agenda and the reservoir of national identity. However, for Yared this control is exerted by women on women. Indeed, men are rarely seen or heard in this text; however, women are heavily present and extremely vocal. Regarding the father figure, Hala seems to have a good relationship with her father and later with her father-in-law. She shares positive memories of her father, including memories of them eating together (Yared 2012: 32) or teaming up against her mother (56). As for the father-in-law, she describes him as being in his wife's shadow. Aloof, he enjoys collecting butterflies and prefers working in silence rather than engaging in social activities (143). As for Hala's husband, completely dominated by his mother, he seeks her approval in everything even in intimate matters related to his wife and household. The husband has no name and ends up dying from a rare fictional medical condition called erosion:

Que Rayon X l'aimât ou le sermonnât, mon mari s'érodait . . . Les premiers symptômes de sa maladie remontaient à l'enfance. Au début, aucun médecin ne put détecter l'origine de son mal. Les diagnostics avaient fusé: eczéma, nervosité, stress . . . Le spécialiste plus avisé que ses confrères, avait décrété mon mari atteint d'une maladie rare jamais contractée à ce jour: l'érosion. (Yared 2012: 152)

As for the judges, they cause harm to Hala not because of their masculinity but rather because of their false interpretation of and attachment to religion (and as mentioned above, for Hala, religion is also another form of colonisation, one that she equates with Western colonial powers, Syria and her mother).

In opposition to the three somewhat harmless male figures, Hala describes most of the women in her life in unflattering terms. The only exceptions to this negative portrayal are her paternal grandmother, her friend Fadia and her own daughters. The paternal grandmother is described as a warm and loving grandmother. After a serious horse injury and a diagnosis of Alzheimer's, she loses her ability to speak; however, despite her illness and silence, Hala finds her love radiant, which is not the case of her maternal grandmother who is described as an insincere snob (Yared 2012: 58–61). Hala finds her maternal grandmother's touch as cold as tentacles; she also compares her to a praying mantis who devours the male while copulating (101). As for her mother-in-law, her last name is 'Fagotaka' (107) which vaguely rhymes with the word phagocyte, a term used in cellular biology to refer to the destruction or the ingestion of a cell by another (which is very appropriate in this case implying that the mother-in-law wants to ingest her son along with Hala). Hala also gives her the nickname of 'Rayon X' for her ability to perceive, intervene and control everything.

Clearly, Hala's world is dominated by women. Men, although present in her life, are not necessarily involved in the decision making. When organising the wedding, for example, the mother and the mother-in-law negotiated everything. The bride and the groom were not involved and were only asked to attend the wedding and say their vows. This is not to say that the mother and the mother-in-law function as a united front against men and children. They are very possessive of their respective families, and they seek to maintain their powers over their children despite the fact that their children are adults and married. The mother-in-law wants to control her son's life just like Hala's mother wants to control her daughter's body. It is interesting to note that for Hala, control of the body seems to be more of a mother-child issue rather than a gender issue. Her husband, although male, is controlled by his mother as much as she is controlled by hers and just like she drew the link between her body and Lebanon, she compares her husband's fading body and lack of will to the disappearance of a free and independent Lebanon:

Dans le flou de leur souffrance rarement énoncée, mon mari et mon pays se rejoignaient. Leur honte d'avoir grandi sans visage – de plus s'en souvenir – n'avait d'égale que leur gentillesse. Plus ils perdaient leurs traites, plus ils se montraient gentils avec leurs camarades, obéissant avec leurs maîtres, serviles avec leurs voisins. (Yared 2012: 123)

As a result of all the injustices in her life committed against her body and against her country, Hala is finally able to see clearly (which ironically reminds us of her wish to go blind). When her husband dies, her mother-in-law sues for custody of the two girls. The ecclesiastical court, composed of five male priests and judges, meets five times to examine the case. The sessions, scattered throughout the novel as if to imply that Hala's entire life is on trial, are printed in a different font. During these sessions, the mother-in-law manages to destroy Hala's reputation. She accuses her of killing her son. She also accuses her of immorality for raising her children in a manner that does not conform with Catholic teachings, but also for once engaging in a lesbian relationship. She even calls upon Fadia's father to testify. It is worth mentioning that the father-in-law speaks up in Hala's defence and against his wife, in a way to prove that the oppression of women in Lebanon and the greater Middle East does not necessarily generate from patriarchal discourse but rather from the mothers' reproduction of traditional views of femininity.

Hala refuses to appoint an attorney and decides to represent herself, naïvely believing that she will be heard. She genuinely thinks that the judges will see the injustices committed against her, that they will see her. Quickly, she realises her mistake, and the body and country she fought for rapidly lose their visibility. Just like her husband, they are threatened with permanent erosion. In a way, her fight for visibility, for the control of her body and for the justice in her country rendered her vulnerable in a society that does not see the need for change and only cares for the status quo of traditional values.

Facing serious charges, Hala does not answer the judges' questions but instead accuses the church of being the coloniser and then gives them a speech on femininity and love (Yared 2012: 116–17). Her answers seem irrational to everyone in the courtroom and unfortunately give credibility to her mother-in-law. She loses the custody case. Desperate to keep her daughters with her, she bakes a cake with pesticide and shares it with them. One could argue that her act, although horrifying, is an indicator of deep love. She truly believes that she is sparing her daughters from the curse or la malédiction of being born female and living with the consequences of what society considers to be a defective birth. She believes that she is protecting them from a long life of shame and submissiveness and chooses for them all, herself included, a different and maybe less violent route.

This pessimistic ending is heavy with meaning. It tells us that a woman's body, just like Lebanon, will never be free. Violence with social and religious oppression will always win. Women's bodies and Lebanon will continuously be at war. This conclusion raises a series of serious questions: how can one break away from this vicious cycle? Is suicide or *tabula rasa* the only available option to end this curse?

To conclude this chapter, the two novels of *La Maîtresse du Notable* and *La Malédiction* focus on the female body and indicate the different ways by which the female body tells war stories. For Khoury-Ghata, the female body is a metaphoric body that naturally inserts itself within a foreign society and silently brings calamity. It is a body that is feared for its strangeness, reproductive powers and Western values. For Yared, the female body is the oppressed, broken, and disabled body that, just like Lebanon, attempts to resist its oppressor and fight against the mother-institution that constantly reproduces oppressed bodies. It is a body at war against itself. Alone against the flow, it fails in its mission and dies.

Notes

1 The figure of the troubled brother is a recurrent topic in Vénus Khoury-Ghata's writings. It is in fact based on her real-life brother, Victor. In an interview with Bernard Mazo, Khoury-Ghata talks about him:

> Poète en herbe, rédigeant toutes ses rédactions en alexandrins, mon frère Victor a fui le toit familial dès l'âge de 18 ans pour Paris où on lui avait promis de publier ses poèmes. Il revint au Liban deux ans plus tard, Paris n'a pas publié ses poèmes, mais l'a initié à la drogue. Au lieu de l'envoyer dans un hôpital de désintoxication, notre père l'emmena dans un hôpital psychiatrique. Deux fuites où il arrivait les pieds en sang, souvent la nuit; son père l'y ramenait. Des séances d'électrochoc massives, peut-être une lobotomie (à la demande du père) en firent un être résigné mais diminué. Il n'a plus fui, n'a plus cherché à revenir à la maison, se croyait en colonies de vacances. De mon frère poète qui mordait la vie à pleines dents ne restait qu'un légume qu'on déplaçait d'un endroit à

l'autre. Il est mort il y a deux ans. Mon roman *Une Maison au bord des larmes* (éditions Balland) décrit son calvaire. (Mazo 2002: 26)

Just like Victor, Frédéric lives in a broken home. He is a poet who writes in French and wants to travel to France to publish his poems. His project fails. He gets addicted to drugs and his father sends him into a psychiatric hospital. Under the treatment, Frédéric loses his personality, his interest in life and his will. He runs away from home and attempts to find Flora but dies trying.

2 For Barthes, the mirror, made by the Occident, is the 'very symbol of narcissism' (Barthes 1976: 138). Flora is often depicted as sitting in front of or looking at herself in the mirror. Taking Barthes's statement into consideration, one could argue that Flora stands for the narcissist West.

3 In *The Second Sex*, Simone de Beauvoir discusses the ambivalent assimilation of the female body to nature. She is the nature that is needed by all men but is also exploited and crushed by them. She is the enemy and the ally; she is the nourishing mother-nature and that gives birth to life but also destroys it. She is the nature that transforms the gods into falling men and dooms them to live and die (de Beauvoir 1989: 145–7).

   Also, ecofeminism draws the link between gender and nature and shows the relationships between the oppression of women and nonhuman entities. For more information, see: Gaard 2010: 643–65; Warren 1997: xi–xvi.

4 For more on monsters, see Cohen 1999.

5 Fisk 2001. See Chapter 1 'Sepia Pictures On A Wall' on the relationship between Poland, the Holocaust and the Lebanese civil war.

6 On hybrid identity, see Bhabha 1994.

7 'Hala' means beauty in Arabic.

8 As Foucault describes, 'Bentham's *Panopticon* is the architectural figure of this composition. We know the principle on which it was based: at the periphery, an annular building; at the centre, a tower; this tower is pierced with wide windows that open onto the inner side of the ring; the peripheric building is divided into cells, each of which extends the whole width of the building; they have two windows, one on the inside, corresponding to the windows of the tower; the other, on the outside, allows the light to cross the cell from one end to the other. All that is needed, then, is to place a supervisor in a central tower and to shut up in each cell a madman, a patient, a condemned man, a worker or a schoolboy. By the effect of backlighting, one can observe the tower, standing out precisely against the light, the small captive shadows in the cells of the periphery. They are

like so many cages, so many small theatres, in which each actor is alone, perfectly individualised and constantly visible. The panoptic mechanism arranges spatial unities that make it possible to see constantly to recognise immediately. In short, it reverses the principle of the dungeon; or rather its three functions – to enclose, to deprive of light and to hide – it preserves only the first and eliminates the other two. Full lighting and the eye of a supervisor capture better than darkness, which ultimately protected. Visibility is a trap. (Foucault 1995: 200; Foucault 1980: 146).

9 For a detailed analysis of the contention between feminism and Foucault, see Ramazanoğlu 1993.

10 According to Mary Douglas, 'no one knows how old are the ideas of purity and impurity in any non-literate culture' (Douglas 2002: 5).

11 In fact, Douglas identifies five ways of dealing with dirt as an anomaly: one can consider the anomalous element as what defines the individual as a whole; one can seek to eliminate the anomalous element; one can avoid it altogether; one can label it as dangerous, and finally one can incorporate in order to redefine the existence of the group as a whole. In her examination of disability, Rosemarie Garland Thomson takes Douglas's five ways of dealing with dirt and applies it to disability (Garland Thomson 1997a: 33).

12 Hala feels invisible to her mother and this makes her want to go blind. In his investigation of blindness as a cultural construction in medieval England and France, Edward Wheatley (2010) points out that blindness, whether figurative or physical, in medieval Christian discourse, was rarely described as advantageous as it was a reminder of the sinful, fallen body. A rare exception for medieval Christians occurs when Jesus asks the married man who lusts after another woman to pluck out his eyes rather than commit adultery: 'If thy right eye scandalize thee, pluck it out and cast it from thee. For it is expedient for thee that one of thy members should perish than that thy whole body be cast into hell' (Matthew 5: 29). Self-mutilation is therefore a better option than gazing with temptation (Yared 2012: 19). Hala's wish to go blind can be interpreted in two ways: on the one hand, she prefers to go blind rather than violate her mother's instructions and religious teachings. However, the temptation is there and Hala, with the help of her friend Fadia, steadily sees her body, her mother's mistreatment and her society's oppression. On the other hand, and just like Oedipus, this new reality is too much to bear and makes her wish to go blind. Seeing and knowing do not empower Hala. On the contrary, they render her even more vulnerable in a society where daughters are expected to blindly follow the rules no questions asked.

13   It is interesting to note that the person in charge of educating children on their bodies carries the name of a Saint (Saint Paul) known for his hard views on the body as the site of sin.

14   The treatment of the body as an ornament reminds us of Bartky's analysis, in which she distinguishes between three different categories of bodily practices: there are ones are related to the body size, others to its movement and others to the treatment of the body as an ornament (Bartky 1997).

15   Bordo argues that eating disorders were not examined within a gendered frame up until 1983, when Carol Gilligan and Susan Orbach presented their ground-breaking findings during a conference on 'Eating Disorders and the Psychology of Women'. Summarising Orbach, Bordo says:

> the anorectic embodies, in an extreme and painfully debilitating way, a psycho-logical struggle characteristic of the contemporary situation of women. That situation is one in which a constellation of social, economic, and psychologi-cal factors have combined to produce a generation of women who feel deeply flawed, ashamed of their needs, and not entitled to exist unless they transform themselves into worthy new selves ... The mother-daughter relation is an important medium of this process. But it's not mothers who are to blame ... for they too are children of their culture, deeply anxious over their own appe-tites and appearances and aware of the fact – communicated in multiple of ways throughout our culture – that their daughters' ability to 'catch a man' will depend largely on physical appearance, and that satisfaction in the role of wife and mother will hinge on learning to feed others rather than the self – metaphorically and literally. (Bordo 1993: 47).

Bordo shows how Orbach's work was criticised and misunderstood as entirely placing the blame on mothers. Regardless of the reaction it generated, it was the first to make the link between the construction of femininity and eating disor-ders. Some researchers have rejected these findings arguing that some men suffer from eating disorders. Others have argued that men and women are exposed to the same culture and therefore eating disorders are purely biological (Bordo 1993: 49).

16   Bordo argues that hysteria, agoraphobia and anorexia nervosa are all forms to protest conventional discourse on femininity and male dominance. Hysteria can be traced back to the Victorian era. Agoraphobia, anorexia nervosa and bulimia made their appearance in the second half of the twentieth century (Bordo 1997: 93). Ironically, our modern society has failed in understanding the reasons

behind these disordered bodies and assigned them with the exact meanings that these bodies are trying to fight against. The hysterical female body has been associated with the feminine mystique, the agoraphobic body has been interpreted as the normal women's attachment to domesticity and the anorexic body has been, to certain extent, glorified as the achievement of the perfect slender female body. However, these bodies carry the opposite meaning assigned by society. By the loss of the voice, hysteria becomes a form of linguistic protest, the refusal to talk to a male-dominated world. By the loss of mobility, women take the boundaries of domesticity to the extreme by refusing to leave the domestic space originally assigned to them. By the loss of healthy appetite, the anorexic and the bulimic female body fight the traditional perception of the nurturing female that is expected to ignore her personal needs and learn how to cook and feed the others. In a way, these female bodies question the value of their participation in a patriarchal society: why speak when one is not heard? Why leave the house when one is only allowed to do so within specific conditions? And why eat when one is expected to deny the self in the name of others? For more information on agoraphobia see Seidenberg 1962.

17 It is interesting to note that when Hala first becomes pregnant, she expresses mixed feelings: she is amazed by her body's ability to produce life when she thought it only contained emptiness. She is also scared of her body, a body that she thought she finally knew and is able to control: 'je fus horrifiée à l'idée de ne plus porter le vide' (Yared 2012: 141); 'Ne plus avoir le monopole de ma propre déformation me sembla être le comble de l'emprisonnement. J'aurais bien voulu d'un déni de grossesse mais l'expansion de mon corps confirmait mon état' (142). Lacking a good example of motherly love, Hala is afraid of turning into her mother and potentially fostering a conflicted relationship with her own children: 'L'enfantement m'angoissait. Devenir la mère, à mon tour' (142). It is her father-in-law who addresses her fear and comforts her; he assures her that love is not necessarily a mimicry (143). She eventually comes to realise that she does not have to be like her mother if she did not want to. She willingly embraces motherhood by loving her daughters with all the love she never received.

18 Accad 2001; Accad 1990; cooke 1997; cooke 1994–5: 5–29; cooke 1982: 124–41; Fayad 1995: 147–60; Ghandour 2002: 231–49; Hamdar 2014; Zeidan 1995.

4

The Magical Body and the Grotesque Body

In Chapter 3, I discussed two representations of the female body and the way by which they contribute to the construction of war narratives. I examined the evil female body: a metaphoric body that by its silence spreads calamity and feeds the already existing violence among the protagonists. I also examined the ill female body in a war-torn environment, an illness resulting from an abusive mother–daughter relationship and from conservative patriarchal values.

In Chapter 4, I focus on the grotesque female body as represented in Hyam Yared's and Vénus Khoury-Ghata's writings and study the way by which the carnivalesque body and the magical body build war stories.

Mary Russo says that to live with the grotesque is to live a 'claustrophobic experience' (Russo 1994: 1) as the grotesque references the cave, the grotto. Historically, the grotesque has been associated with the female body as both are perceived as sharing similar traits. They are dark, obscure, hidden and earthly. For Russo, the association of the grotesque to the female body reveals a long misogynistic approach to the female body; it is an abject body that produces bodily fluids such as blood, vomit and excrement and is governed by its lower stratum. However, the grotesque has also been used in other contexts. As Bakhtin shows in *Rabelais and His World*, the term 'grotesque' was used to describe strange Roman ornaments that were discovered in the fifteenth century during the excavation of Titus' baths. These ornaments playfully combined 'plant, animal, and human forms. These forms seemed to be interwoven as if giving birth to each other. The borderlines that divide the kingdoms of nature in the usual picture of the world were boldly infringed' (Bakhtin 1984: 32). For Bakhtin, although the term grotesque first appeared in the discovery context in Rome, it actually existed throughout different periods of time from antiquity to the Middle Ages and the Renaissance.

As Russo (1994) demonstrates, the grotesque is visible in Christian art – Raphael's designs in the Vatican for instance – where the grotesque sits side by side with the sacred. This juxtaposition of the sacred and the grotesque allows us, as Russo argues, to highlight the perfection of the first and the monstrosity of the latter.

Also, according to Russo, feminist discourse of the 1990s has largely contributed to the invisibility of 'grotesque bodies' by indirectly adhering to the binary division of male/normal–female/abnormal discourse. In fact, feminist discourse of the 1990s had a very narrow view of the female body and thought of it as one homogenous body – specifically a white, abled, heterosexual body. This excluded unfamiliar bodies like ethnic minorities, disabled bodies or homosexual bodies, all of whom have historically been associated with the grotesque. Consequently, any female body that is different than the norm has been marginalised and excluded from the general homogenous definition of the female body.

Russo continues to show that the grotesque manifests itself under two forms of the uncanny: the magical and the carnivalesque. Borrowing Russo's definition of the grotesque body and its two subcategories, this chapter examines magical realism and grotesque realism as they appear in *L'Armoire des ombres* by Hyam Yared, *Vacarme pour une lune morte* and *Les Morts n'ont pas d'ombre* by Vénus Khoury-Ghata.

In these novels, magical realism and grotesque realism provide the authors with alternative spaces of magic and carnival to expose the war, to address the serious issue of violence and to criticise Lebanese society for its conservative patriarchal values. Magical realist bodies and carnivalesque bodies (with focus on female bodies) reveal a chaotic violent world, one that cannot be understood by traditional rules of logic, time and space.

L'Armoire des ombres

Published in 2006, *L'Armoire des ombres*, which translates into 'The Wardrobe of Shadows', tells the story of a divorced woman who, desperate to pay her rent, auditions for the leading role in a play. Encouraged by her friend Yolla, the unnamed woman, who is also the narrator goes to the theatre scared and not knowing what to expect. Before she gets on stage, she is asked to leave her shadow in the dressing room. She argues against this absurd request but eventually does as told. On stage, she finds a wardrobe full of shadows and as she unfolds them, she tells the stories of their owners: Greta the prostitute, Léna the lesbian bartender and Mona the abused wife. The lives of these three women, along with the lives of the narrator and her friend Yolla, gradually become connected, and toward the end of the novel the reader realises that there is in fact one woman: the Lebanese woman in the war and the post-war periods.

While the play itself takes place in post-war Lebanon, the stories of the different women occur during the war. The fragmentations of time, space and stories along with the uncanny elements of removing one's shadow and finding a wardrobe full of shadows create the mysterious environment that is typical in magical realist texts. Magical realism allows the narrative voice to break away from the traditional patriarchal discourse, a dominant discourse that remained intact during the war and post-war period in Lebanon and to mock it from a marginal and magical space; it is important to first revisit the definition of the genre of magical realism and then examine its effects in constructing a woman's war narrative.

Definition of Magical Realism

Traditionally, magical realism has been associated with Latin American writers, who were among the first to develop the concept and popularise it as a genre. Eva Aldea (2011) offers a succinct history of magical realism. The grandiose visibility of magical realism has been attributed to Gabriel García Márquez after the publication of *One Hundred Years of Solitude* in 1967. However, as Aldea demonstrates in examining the works of the Cuban-born literary critic Roberto Gonzáles Echevarría, the term magical realism has been around longer than that.

According to Gonzáles Echevarría, the term 'magical realism' first appeared in 1925 in an art article on post-expressionist painting. The term itself was attributed then to the German art critic Franz Roh who drew a distinction between the fantastic and reality. However, it remained attached to the world of painting. In 1949, it surfaced in the literary field when the Cuban writer Alejo Carpentier 'call[ed] for a "marvelous real" literature in

America' in the forward to his novel *Kingdom of This World* (Carpentier 1975: 2). Magical realism makes its big appearance in 1955. In examining Latin American romantic literature, the Mexican writer Angel Flores notes the existence of mixed elements of fantasy and realism. He calls the mix 'magical realism' (qtd in Aldea 2011: 2).

A Postmodern or a Postcolonial Genre?

For Gonzáles Echevarría, as Aldea states, there are two types of magical realism: phenomenological magical realism and ontological magical realism. In phenomenological magical realism, magic appears from the interaction between one's own subjectivity and perception of reality. In ontological magical realism, magical realism derives from the marvellous. The distinction between these two types of magical realism raises the issue about whether magical realism implies the existence of magic or whether it is simply a question of perception. For Aldea, answering this question is vital as it allows the reader to fully understand the circumstances in which a magical realist text is born. If magical realism is merely a question of perception, then one should only look at the textual features of magical realist texts and analyse them from within without necessarily looking at the framework of the text. If magical realism is an opposition between the real and the supernatural, then the reader must examine the socio-geographic factors that led to the text. As a result of this binary approach to magical realism, critics have labelled it either a postcolonial or a postmodern literature. Postcolonialism concerns the conflicted relationship between coloniser and colonised and the hegemony of colonial culture in the postcolonial world; postmodernism focuses first on textual features such as time, space, narrative voice, historical elasticity and other elements before it inserts itself into the relationship between the real and fiction.

Stephen Slemon argues that magical realism is a postcolonial literature as it reveals a power struggle between two languages, two different forces and two different narratives embedded in the same text. While one reflects the colonial imperialistic discourse, the other one reflects the fragmentation of the postcolonial subject.

> colonization, whatever its precise form, initiates a kind of double vision or 'metaphysical clash' into colonial culture, a binary opposition within lan-

guage that has its roots in the process of either transporting a language to a new land or imposing a foreign language on an indigenous population . . . for some, the dream of historical process is that over time a process of trans-mutation will occur which will enable this language, the cognitive system it carries, to articulate the local within a 'realist' representational contract. In a postcolonial context, then, magic realist narrative recapitulates a dialectical struggle within language, a dialectic between 'codes of recognition' inher-ent within the inherited language and those imagined, utopian, and future-oriented codes that aspire toward a language of expressive, local realism and a set of 'original relations' with the world. (Slemon 1995: 411)

Rawdon Wilson argues that magical realism can be considered a postcolonial discourse:

as the mode of a conflicted consciousness, the cognitive map that discloses the antagonism between two views of culture, two views of history (European history being the routinization of the ordinary; aboriginal or primitive his-tory, the celebration of the extraordinary), and two ideologies. (Wilson 1995: 223)

For Wendy Faris, magical realism is a postcolonial genre as it offers a counter narrative to the dominant Western discourse where the 'postcolonial subject is suspended between two or more cultural systems' (Faris 2004: 135). It clashes against realism which is a Western literary creation that promotes a Eurocentric culture, history and language. By blurring the lines between realism, the fantastic and the marvellous, and by including different cultural traditions, it destabilises dominant Western discourse and exposes the hybrid nature of the postcolonial society (Faris 2004: 1). She also suggests that magical realism is an important component of postmodernism. In fact, Faris argues that although it has a postcolonial nature, magical realism constitutes 'a strong current in the stream of postmodernism' (Faris 1995: 165). It allows us to redefine the relationship between the Western culture that is considered as the centre and its peripheral regions such as Latin America, the Caribbean, India or Eastern Europe. This peripheral literature pushes the boundaries, displaces the centre and takes its place, and yet it still speaks from a peripheral position.

Brenda Cooper argues that magical realism is a hybrid genre. The political environment in which magical realism is born is postcolonial as it manifests a clash between different cultures, specifically between pre-capitalist and capitalist cultures in developing countries. Magical realism is also postmodern for its use of postmodern textual features such as the fragmentation of time and space, a carnivalesque spirit and an ironic narrative voice. The hybridity of magical realism is comparable to Homi Bhabha's third space where the cultures of the coloniser and the colonised meet.[1] Cooper calls this space the 'third eye' as the writer of magical realist texts sees the world as a combination of clashing cultures and values. 'Why "seeing with a third eye"?' Cooper asks. She adds that:

> Magical realism strives, with greater or lesser success, to capture the paradox of the unity of opposites; it contests polarities such as history versus magic, the pre-colonial past versus the post-industrial present and life versus death. Capturing such boundaries between spaces is to exist in the third space, in the fertile interstices between these extremes of time or space. (Cooper 1998: 1)

Theo L. D'haen examines the works of Douwe Fokkema, Allen Thiher, Linda Hutchean, Brian McHale, Ihab Hassan, David Lodge, Alan Wilde, among others, to conclude that magical realism and postmodernism share common traits: 'self-reflexiveness, metafiction, eclecticism, redundancy, multiplicity, discontinuity, intertextuality, parody the dissolution of character and narrative instance, the erasure of boundaries, and the destabilization of the reader' (D'haen 1995: 192–3). He argues that it is becoming increasingly hard to distinguish between the two categories. To a certain extent, they overlap, and some novels use postmodern techniques to create a magical realist world. They are both 'ex-centric'; they speak from the margins.

> Magic realist writing achieves this end by first appropriating the techniques of the 'centr'-al line and then using these, not as in the case of these central movements, 'realistically', that is to duplicate existing reality as perceived by the theoretical or philosophical tenets underlying said movements, but rather to create an alternative world *correcting* so-called existing reality, and thus to right the wrong this 'reality' depends upon. Magic realism thus

reveals itself as a *ruse* to invade and take over dominant discourse(s). (D'haen 1995: 195)

In response to this analysis, Eva Aldea argues that the elements given to define postmodern magical realism are the same used to define it as postcolonial:

Again we are given a description of magical realist texts via a list of literary devices such as intertextuality, metatextuality, deformation of time and space, bifurcation of plot, and so on, that are identified as postmodern, and that allow these novels to subvert existing views of reality. However, this subversion is also what critics reading magical realism from a postcolonial perspective identify in the genre. (Aldea 2011: 8)

As a matter of fact, it is possible to argue that magical realism is the place where postmodernism and postcolonialism meet since they both strive to disrupt the dominant discourse and grant a marginalised voice control of the narrative. I would also argue that the text in hand, *L'Armoire des ombres*, is simultaneously a postcolonial and postmodern writing as it presents the reader with textual features that are specific to postmodernism while conveying a postcolonial message that permits the deconstruction of the dominant narrative in the name of the subaltern.

The Five Elements of Magical Realism

Today, there is no dispute that magical realism is a well-established genre that may, at times, bleed into other genres such as fantasy or speculative fiction. Faris provides perhaps the most useful and concise definition of magical realism: 'Very briefly, magical realism combines realism and the fantastic in such a way that magical elements grow organically out of the reality portrayed' (Faris 1995: 163).

Magical realism is an oxymoron by its nature: it is realism mixed with magical elements that remain unquestioned by the characters in the text. Lois Parkinson Zamora and Wendy B. Faris argue that in magical realist texts, 'the supernatural is not simple or obvious matter, but it *is* an ordinary matter, an everyday occurrence – admitted, accepted, and integrated into the rationality and materiality of literary realism' (Zamora and Faris 1995: 3).

For Zamora and Faris, magical realism differs from realism by its intention. Realism portrays the world as one objective reality, while magical realism disrupts this narrative and offers an alternative world that transcends conventional borders of logic, time and space:

> Realism intends its version of the world as singular version, as an objective (hence universal) representation of natural and social realities – in short, that realism functions ideologically and hegemonically. Magical realism also functions ideologically but . . . less hegemonically, for its program is not centralizing but eccentric: it creates space for interactions of diversity. In magical realist texts, ontological disruption serves the purpose of political and cultural disruption: magic is often given as a cultural corrective, requiring readers to scrutinize accepted realistic conventions of causality, materiality, motivation. (Zamora and Faris 1995: 3)

Magical realism resists classification and cannot be contained in a structure or category. It is a literary genre that defies reason and goes beyond the laws of nature. It superposes different worlds and allows the coexistence of spaces and times to which the reader does not belong. The reader is often positioned outside the magical realist world and when invited in, is placed in an uncomfortable position as he or she will have to suspend the Cartesian way of thinking in order to fully grasp the magical realist experience, that is to say in order to understand madness, one has to be mad.

This is a very general introduction to magical realism. Faris provides a detailed analysis of the genre and identifies five primary traits that go into the construction of magical realism:

> First, the text contains an 'irreducible element' of magic; second, the descriptions in magical realism detail a strong presence of the phenomenal world; third, the reader may experience some unsettling doubts in the effort to reconcile two contradictory understandings of events; fourth, the narrative merges different realms; and, finally, magical realism disturbs received ideas about time, space, and identity. (Faris 2004: 7)

Faris argues that magic exists in the text as a reality that cannot logically be explained. It disarrays the realistic Western narrative and unsettles the reader who finds it hard to believe the unnatural elements revealed, and cannot logically find evidence of their existence. The narrative voice, on the other hand, provides a detailed description of these elements as if they were an everyday occurrence and as if there was nothing extraordinary about them. In doing so, the narrative voice relies on traditional or folkloric narratives which contribute even more to the postcolonial hybridity of the narrative and in the disruption of Western realism. It creates a space where the ordinary and the extraordinary, realism and magic coexist. This is not to say that magic naturally blends into the narrative as it still produces an effect, or multiple effects, on the reader. If the narrative voice makes it sound very natural, the reader remains surprised by the magical component and constantly attempts to suspend logical belief to fully grasp the text and penetrate its world. As Faris argues:

> In short, the magic in these texts refuses to be entirely assimilated into their realism; it does not brutally shock but neither does it melt away, so that it is like a grain of sand in the oyster of that realism. And because it disrupts reading habits, that irreducible grain increases the participation of readers, contributing to the postmodern proliferation of writerly texts, texts co-created by their readers. (Faris 2004: 9)

Also, Faris demonstrates that the insertion of magical elements into the real not only disrupts the dominant realist narrative as we know it, but also ridicules it and makes it, at times, sound trivial. In fact, magic realism displaces realism into a new and unfamiliar context. Realism thus becomes devoid of its traditional meaning and may very well turn into a parody of the real, a mockery, or a caricature. In short, the real becomes derisory.

The phenomenal world is the second trait that goes into the definition of magical realism. Realism, as Faris argues, describes the world as we know it with all its conventional rules about time, space, life and death. To borrow Barthes's phrase, realism produces 'un effet du réel'; it portrays a world that is parallel to the reader's world and implies that the fictional story could plausibly take place in the real world (Faris 2004: 14). However, in magical realist fiction, the magical elements are described in great details and in such a way that they clearly represent a divorce from reality and constantly remind the reader of their imaginary status.

The real and the magical become intertwined in such a way as to constantly interrupt the narrative but also to rewrite history. In fact, real life events are referenced in magical realist texts. However, they are attached to magical elements which allows their revision. To put it differently, magic not only interrupts the dominant discourse, but also subverts it in order to present the reader with an alternative reality and history. History is thus written from a marginalised perspective. Cooper adds:

> In the ideal magical realist plot, there is no gothic subtext, no dark space of the unconscious, no suppressed libidinous attic space, in which a mad-woman is concealed. The mysterious, sensuous, unknown and unknowable are not in the subtext, as in realist writing, but rather share the fictional space with history. The alternative histories, the mysteries, dreams, pain, bewilder-ments and nightmare labyrinths, struggle to be visibly inscribed within the text's surfaces. (Cooper 1998: 36)

Clearly, this reinscription of history questions the credibility of the nar-rative voice. To what extent can the reader believe this voice, especially when it departs from the real to argue in favour of 'real magic'? And what if the narrative voice is simply mad? To these legitimate questions, Cooper says that one must read the magical realist text keeping in mind that the characters do not necessarily reflect the author's position and that the omniscient narrator may not always be trustworthy (Cooper 1998: 36). This fair warning does not necessarily undermine the message behind magical realism. In fact, magical realism does not seek to deceive the reader for the sake of deception but rather to encourage criticism of the reality expected and to raise awareness of the existence of an alternative one. In other words, when the reader questions what is learned from the narrative voice, the dominant discourse that has so far been accepted as fact is also questioned. When this occurs, one can say that magical realism has served its purpose.

The relationship between the reader and the magical realist text consti-tutes, in fact, the third aspect identified by Faris. She calls it the 'unsettling doubt' where 'the reader may hesitate between two contradictory understand-ings of events, and hence experience some unsettling doubts' (Faris 2004: 17). The hesitation derives from the clash encountered within the narrative between the belief in what is real and what is magic; and for Faris, the level of hesitation varies according to one's own beliefs and culture.

The question of hesitation in reading a narrative is central to Tzvetan

Todorov's study *The Fantastic: A Structural Approach to a Literary Genre.*
In fact, magical realism is not always easy to pick out and dissociate from its
neighbouring genres such as the fantastic, the uncanny and the marvellous.
For Todorov, the fantastic implies uncertainty whether the narrative is experienced is reality or a dream, a truth or an illusion.

> In a world which is indeed our world, the one we know, a world without
> devils, sylphides, or vampires, there occurs an event which cannot be
> explained by the laws of this same familiar world. The person who experi-
> ences the event must opt for one of two possible solutions: either he is the
> victim of an illusion of the senses, of a product of the imagination – and laws
> of the world then remain what they are; or else the event has indeed taken
> place, it is an integral part of reality – but then reality is controlled by laws
> unknown to us. Either the devil is an illusion, an imaginary being; or else he
> really exists, precisely like other living beings – with this reservation, that we
> encounter him infrequently.
>
> The fantastic occupies the duration of this uncertainty. Once we choose
> one answer or the other, we leave the fantastic for a neighboring genre, the
> uncanny or the marvelous. The fantastic is the hesitation experience by a
> person who knows only the laws of nature, confronting an apparently super-
> natural event. (Todorov 1975: 25)

At this point one wonders who is the subject of the hesitation? Is it the reader
or is it the hero in the narrative? For Todorov, both the hero and the reader
could hesitate. However, the first and absolute condition of the fantastic is for
the reader to hesitate. If the reader is aware of an alternative reality, he or she
would read the text differently. For that, the reader must be integrated into the
hero's uncertain world regardless of the hero's anxiety about the true nature
of events (Todorov 1975: 31).

For Todorov, the existence of the fantastic may be threatened when the
hesitating reader interprets the narrative events as allegorical. Consequently,
for the fantastic to exist, three conditions should be met: (1) The reader
must accept the world of the characters and hesitate between a natural or
supernatural explanation for the events occurring in the narrative; (2) The
hesitation may be felt by the hero with whom the reader may identify; (3) The
reader must reject allegorical or poetic interpretations of the text (Todorov

1975: 33). For Todorov, the first and the third conditions are a must for the fantastic genre. The reader's hesitation may also result from questioning his or her own understanding of the text. In this case, the reader is doubtful not so much of the nature of events (natural or supernatural) but rather of his or her own comprehension of the events. This uncertainty, as Todorov says, may create a conflict between the characters and the reader to which the reader reacts and considers the characters mad (Todorov 1975: 37).

For Todorov, the fantastic lives for the duration of the uncertainty. It is like the present time: slippery and only available for a brief period. The fantastic exists precariously and could easily slip into another genre: once a logical explanation is given, it becomes the uncanny; if the laws of nature remain suspended at the end of the narrative, it turns into the marvellous. As for its relationship with magical realism, Faris seems to suggest that two genres of magical realism and the fantastic overlap. They share the doubting reader as a common trait. However, if doubt is always present in the fantastic, there are times where it is less obvious in a magical realist narrative especially when the narrator offers an explanation to put the reader at ease. This does not necessarily mean that the reader will accept the explanation and often the reader remains sceptical. Nevertheless, the difference between the magical realism and the fantastic can be seen in the layers of unsettling doubt.

The fourth component of magical realism, for Faris, is what she calls 'merging realms', where the real is confronted with the supernatural consequently creating a space of uncertainty: 'In terms of cultural history, magical realism often merges ancient or traditional – sometimes indigenous – and modern worlds. Ontologically, within the texts, it integrates the magical and the material. Generically, it combines realism and the fantastic' (Faris 2004: 21). The borders of the magical realist space are fluid and porous; they are hard to draw with precision, and they do not obey the rules of logic. For instance, the worlds of the living and of the dead could intersect.

> The magical realist vision thus exists at the intersection of two worlds, at the imaginary point inside a double-sided mirror that reflects in both directions. Ghosts and texts, or people and words that seem ghostly, inhabit these two-sided mirrors, many times situated between the two worlds of life and

death; they enlarge that space of intersection where a number of magically real fictions exist. (Faris 2004: 21–2)

The separation of fact from fiction and natural from supernatural is not easy within a magical realist world where time, space and identity are constantly disrupted and frequently altered. This is, in fact, the fifth and last component of magical realism where time, space and identity obey natural and supernatural rules; they bend differently to deconstruct the world as we know it and to create multiple worlds with multiple times, spaces and identities.

Regarding space as a geographical location, it is difficult to firmly identify its contours; it is a mobile, hybrid space that calls on different cultural elements particularly ones from the coloniser and the colonised. Consequently, magical realism provides a multicultural space that defies cultural homogeneity and hegemony. With regard to time, it does not necessarily move in a linear way. Often fragmented, it breaks away from routine and rewrites history by offering alternative stories. As for identity, the characters in magical realist fiction are far from being stagnant and they do not necessarily present the same traits from beginning to end. In fact, magic interferes with their world to present them under a new light. This new presentation may come as a surprise to both the characters and the reader who, as we have seen before, may question the legitimacy of the event and the credibility of the narrative voice. Consequently, characters in magical realist fictions have multiple identities as they evolve in contested time and space.

Finally, and in addition to the five primary characteristics of magical realism, Faris adds a list of secondary traits (Faris 1995: 175): (1) Contemporary magical realist texts are often metafictional as they refer to themselves through, for instance, the use of *mise en abîme*. This narrative strategy makes the reader and possibly the characters highly conscious of the narrative itself and of the distinction between reality and fiction. (2) 'The reader may experience a particular kind of verbal magic – a closing of the gap between words and the world, or a demonstration of what we might call the linguistic nature of experience' (Faris 1995: 176). In this case, magic appears when a metaphoric image or a proverb is turned into a real event. Faris gives an example from *One Hundred Years of Solitude* by Márquez where, when José Arcadio Buendía shoots himself, a drop of his blood goes down the street until it reaches

Buendía's house and his mother's kitchen. This image is a literal reminder of the adage that says that blood is thicker than water. (3) In some cases, the narrative appears childlike or primitive to today's reader. Just like a child accepts a story, magic is told and accepted without any explanation. (4) Repetition is also another secondary trait; it becomes available to the reader either through symbolic or metaphoric references or just simple redundancy. Repetition allows a return to the point of origin where a new story will take place; it is like the hero who every time he falls asleep experiences something new only to wake up again and again in the same time and place.[2] The availability of mirrors in a text may also open the door for the repetition of certain images; however, the image projected by magical realism is not always faithful to the original and may be distorted to better reflect the parallelism between two different worlds such as the ghostly and the living worlds. (5) Metamorphose is a recurrent theme in magical realist texts; this allows the intersection and coexistence of different worlds with constantly changing characters. (6) Magical realist texts often carry an antibureaucratic message that questions the established order. In many cases, and as Faris demonstrates, magical realist texts have been written against totalitarian regimes. She cites multiple examples, such as *The Tin Drum* by Günter Grass or Toni Morrison's *Beloved*, written to expose slavery. Faris argues that these texts:

> open the door to other worlds, respond to a desire for narrative freedom from realism, and from a univocal narrative stance; they implicitly correspond textually in a new way to a critique of totalitarian discourses of all kind. Scheherazade's story is relevant again here, for even though she narrated for her own life, she had the eventual welfare of her state on her shoulders as well, and her efforts liberated her country from the tyranny of King Shariyar's rule. (Faris 1995: 180)

The last three secondary characteristics of magical realism are: (7) references to ancient beliefs and local or indigenous tales that not only remind the reader of the space in which the event is taking place but also of the cultural confrontation between the coloniser and the colonised or the powerful and the powerless. (8) Magic is often felt and lived by a collectivity rather than as an individual memory, dream or illusion. (9) Magical realist texts often exhibit a carnivalesque spirit and use precise language to reference gruesome, extravagant realities. This point of the carnivalesque spirit will be examined in more detail in the second section of this chapter.

Magical Realism in *L'Armoire des ombres*

Considering all the characteristics presented by Faris, including the five primary traits and the secondary traits, *L'Armoire des ombres* is without any doubt a magical realist novel.

The text opens on an irreducible element of magical realism. When the unnamed narrator goes to the audition, she tries to take her shadow with her. When she gets to the theatre, the staff tells her that she does not need her shadow for the stage, and that she ought to leave it in the changing room (Yared 2006: 7). An element of magical realism is promptly introduced to the unprepared reader; it is inserted into the real world as if it were always part of it. The narrator confides in the implicit reader and shares her real-life problems: she has troubles with her landlord and is behind in her rent; she is separated from her husband and struggles to support her child. In contrast to these real-life events, the narrator lives in a world where shadows can be removed, folded over a hanger and placed in a wardrobe.

Consequently, the ordinary and the extraordinary coexist right from the beginning, and while the reader may find it difficult to fully penetrate the narrator's world, the narrator herself accepts her magical reality and agrees to the theatre's request to remove her shadow. In fact, at no point does she wonder about the impossibility of such a request; instead, she questions the implications of such a removal. For instance, she becomes anxious when the backstage team (to whom she only refers as they) abruptly folds her shadow. She worries they might make a mistake and that she will leave with the wrong shadow. What if they give her a chair's shadow instead? (Yared 2006: 10–11).

Once on stage, the narrator pulls different shadows from the wardrobe. Wearing them, she tells their stories. The first shadow she removes is her mother's. She tells us that her mother finds her bizarre and a disappointment: for being born female and not male, for being different from other Lebanese girls and for being divorced.

The second shadow the narrator takes out of the wardrobe belongs to Marguerite, nicknamed Greta after Greta Garbo (Yared 2006: 41). Raped at sixteen by her neighbour, Marguerite runs away from her abusive brother, Tony, who chose to believe the neighbour over her. She finds refuge in a convent but only for the duration of the pregnancy, and after she gives birth, the nuns ask her to leave. Illiterate, with nothing but her beauty, Marguerite becomes Greta, a girl who wears high heels and sells her body for money.

The narrator puts on a third shadow, one belonging to Lena, a lesbian bartender who works at the bar with Greta. For a time during the war, Lena was married to a British doctor who volunteered with Doctors Without Borders. Their marriage was never consummated as Lena was afraid of intercourse. After ten years of marriage, her husband left her, and Lena became a bartender. She loves her job for she serves illusions to her clients. She is also deeply in love with Greta.

Mona is the fourth shadow the narrator reveals. Her parents died in a car accident when she was very young. Her paternal grandparents, a very wealthy family from the south, despised her mother for coming from a humble family from the north. Raised by her unloving grandparents, who clearly preferred her brother, Mona marries her father's cousin who turns out to be abusive. He beats her and rapes her regularly. After having two children with him, she decides to take contraceptive pills. When he finds out that she has been taking the pills for a while, he becomes extremely violent and beats her up. She runs away and goes to a police station to report abuse. The officers do not believe her and hint that she probably deserved the beating. Aided by a friend, Mona escapes to Cyprus where she leads a successful life and gets pregnant from her Greek boyfriend.

In all these performances, the irreducible element of magic exists primarily through the unfolding of the shadows; each shadow allows the depiction of a phenomenal world that coexists with and intersects the real world. The coexistence and intersection of the two ordinary and extraordinary worlds, or the two realms, as Faris calls them, are conveyed through the blending of magic and material, fiction and fact.

The phenomenal world appears first when the narrator is asked to remove her shadow before stepping on stage. However, without her shadow she has no story to tell as her shadow represents her identity. Furthermore, the director does not provide her with a script. To supplement this absence, she goes to the wardrobe and finds the shadow of the closest person to her, the one person who knows her identity well: her mother.

The conflicted mother–daughter relationship allows the narrative to continue but also for the phenomenal world to persist. In fact, the mother finds the narrator to be different and 'marginale' (Yared 2006: 32) as the narrator has always wanted to understand her own shadow. The mother is not at all surprised by the absurdity of the narrator's quest but rather by its different nature. No one or at least no woman has ever wanted to examine her shadow. Alarmed, the mother calls the doctor; she asks the narrator to sleep in the dark, so she will not see her shadow anymore (31). However, the narrator perseveres in wanting to understand it. She tells the reader that her fascination with shadows goes back in time; it started during the civil war when she was just a child. She heard someone cry and she could tell from the crying that the person was injured but not dead. She wished for the person to become a shadow as shadows do not die and do not cry. Shadows live on walls even when the walls are full of bullets (32). Another incident occurred fuelling the narrator's fascination with shadows. It started at puberty when she wore stiletto shoes for the first time. She felt empowered and fell in love with the shape of her shadow in high heels. Her mother hated her shadow and said it looked slutty (30). She buys her daughter new shoes, but the narrator finds them horrendous. From then on, the narrator decides to begin what she calls the high heels revolution. She lies to her mother, wears the ugly shoes at home, then she changes them for the stilettos in the school bus.

The mother–daughter relationship declines even more when the narrator gets a divorce. Her husband leaves simply because he did not like her toes: 'Bahij, lui, n'a pas aimé mes orteils. Il n'était pas sûr de pouvoir vivre avec eux pour le restant de ses jours' (65). Her mother blames her for her failed marriage; had she followed the road that had been traced for her and had she walked properly like any Lebanese girl, had she 'walked in the shoes' of every Lebanese girl, she would not be divorced today.

The magical image of the shadow along with the multiple realist references to shoes, feet and toes contribute to the creation of an extraordinary world where magic and reality collide. Clearly, the shoes and toes references are a reminder of the traditional gender role for females in Lebanese society.

However, the narrator rejects that expected role. Unlike Cinderella, she does not wait for the glass slipper to magically appear nor does she wait for it to fit.[3] She takes matters into her own hands and if her husband does not like her toes, it is his problem not hers.

From this magical space, the narrator criticises the role of mothers who act as guardians of patriarchal values. As we have seen in Chapter 3, mothers are the mechanism through which the daughters are trained to accept their social roles and to obey social requirements and expectations without questioning them. By clinging to her shadow, the narrator objects to her mother's oppression. She refuses to 'fit in the shoes' that were made for her and rebuffs what she calls the sheep mentality and the culture of 'yes': 'Tu m'as toujours refusé une vie, quelle qu'elle soit, qui ne serait pas conforme à une morale prêt-à-porter, une morale pour moutons qui paissent dans le respect de l'ordre. Je ne suis pas mouton' (59). She resents the culture of 'yes', a culture where women accept everything. She and her shadow had tried to live with this culture of 'yes' and they became three living in one body. They could not survive as the 'yes' crushed them all to the point where she could not speak anymore:

> Le oui, répondais-tu. Dire oui. Un seul mot. Nous avons essayé mon ombre et moi. De le dire. Depuis lors, nous faisons ménage à trois, mon ombre, oui et moi. Par la suite le oui a très vite doublé de volume, a gonflé, a pris toute la place. Écrasées par le oui, je et mon ombre avons essayé d'écarter les lettres les unes des autres . . . Révolte stérile. Culture du oui. Je ne sus plus où le ranger. Le oui. C'est moi qui me suis rangée. Le problème, c'est que oui n'a pas d'ombre. Je m'en suis rendu compte plus tard. J'ai plongé dans un grand mutisme après ça. (Yared 2006: 62)

The shadows of Greta, Lena and Mona also participate in the creation of an extraordinary world that coexists with the real world. On the surface, Greta, Lena and Mona are, in order, a prostitute, a lesbian bartender and an unmarried pregnant woman. However, down in the darkness of their shadows they are much more than this, and they represent all the untold stories of sexual assault, and verbal and physical abuse against women. By shedding the light on their shadows (which interestingly sounds like an oxymoronic image), by putting them on stage, the narrator reveals the 'reality' of these women with their pasts, presents and futures. She traces their identities and, in a way, gives them a sense of dignity. The reader, at this point, can no longer be judgemental of these women and dismissive of their stories, but can only sympathise with them as they have been deeply wronged and misunderstood in the real world.

The ambiance of magical realism reaches its climax toward the end of the text when the narrator realises, while performing on stage, that all the shadows she has encountered are in fact hers. She is all these women; she is also Yolla (initially introduced in the novel as her best friend). It is true that the narrator never found Yolla's shadow in the wardrobe. However, Yolla is frequently, if not always, represented as shadowing the narrator and accompanying her in all her social events. She magically appears in the narrator's apartment, she shows up uninvited to her wedding, she travels to Berlin with her, she goes clubbing with her, she even shares her lover, Erik. Many times in the novel, the narrator hints that she and Yolla may be one. She says:

> J'ai souvent cherché l'ombre de Yolla dans l'armoire. Parfois le temps d'un acte. Jamais pu la dénicher. Au début, ça me révoltait. Je ne comprenais pas pourquoi Yolla avait été exclue des planches. J'estimais légitime de lui faire une place sur le mur, avec les autres. Après tout, il y avait une Yolla en chacune de nous. Potentiellement dormante (Yared 2006: 71) / I often tried to find Yolla's shadow in the wardrobe. Occasionally during an act. Never found hers. At the beginning, this infuriated me. I could not understand why Yolla was excluded from the stage. I think she has her place on the wall with the others. After all, there is a Yolla in each one of us. Potentially dormant.

Therefore, the narrator is simultaneously the oppressed daughter, the raped sister, the abused wife, the lesbian lover and the illiterate prostitute. Despite their differences and irrespective of their religions and sexual orientations, these women have one thing in common: they are all oppressed. Their oppression occurs in different times and spaces, and comes from their mothers, fathers, brothers, grandparents, spouses, neighbours and society as a whole both during and after the war. The multiplicity of the narrator's identity allows for these experiences to become shared ones. The narrator is no longer alone. In fact, no woman is alone anymore as all women become one group with similar stories joined in the realm of magic.

It is important to note that the stage is the space where the narrator's metamorphosis takes place. For Wilson, there are three different fictional spaces. The first is a space that uses geometrical and geographical discourse easily understood by the reader, that is comparable to the reader's own world. The next space is a fantasy world that has its own rules, where, for example, the interior could be bigger than the exterior or where time is reversible. The final space is a hybrid space where the natural and the abnormal take place and where 'the narrative voice bridges the gap between the ordinary and bizarre, smoothing the discrepancies, making everything seem normal' (Wilson 1995: 220). In this hybrid place, Wilson continues, eruption of the magical in the real suddenly occurs and vice versa. In *L'Armoire des ombres* the theatre is the narrator's hybrid space in which she breaks away from the real world to enter the magical world. Through the aspect of a precise ritual that takes the form of repeated moves of going to the theatre, leaving her shadow in the changing room and stepping on stage, the narrator accesses the extraordinary world of shadows and performs the role of another woman.

The stage is also the hybrid space from which the narrator can speak up against the traditional order of Lebanese society. Mary Russo shows the danger that society has assigned to women in a public space. A woman might 'make a spectacle out of herself', which means that she might inadvertently expose herself and act beyond the boundaries of her gender (Russo 1994: 53). The narrator of *L'Armoire des ombres* seems to be fully aware of this danger and is willing to run the risk of 'making a spectacle out of herself' in the name of women's rights. The stage thus becomes not only the space for the narrator's metamorphosis and not only her gateway into the magical realm, but also her subversive space from which she positions herself higher than the rest of society (or the audience) and into the light to expose issues that Lebanese society regards as taboo. From her stage, she openly talks about sex, rape, physical and verbal abuse, reproductive rights, and many other topics that are traditionally confined to the private space. By exposing herself, by making a spectacle out of herself, she brings into the light issues that have long been hidden in the shadows of Lebanese society. With carnivalesque spirit, she breaks the borders between the public and the private and creates a world of magic where women are placed on stage and as a priority.

There are two other spaces that are diametrically opposed to the narrator's stage: the first is with the audience inside the theatre, and the second is outside the theatre with the protesters whom the women regularly encounter. With regards to the protesters, they first appear when the narrator goes on stage for the first time. She notices that she has no audience. There is no one in the theatre besides her, the make-up artist who helps her take off her shadow and the light engineer (Yared 2006: 26). Everyone else has left to join the group of people gathered outside the theatre to protest in the name of truth. It is unclear what exactly they are protesting and what specific truth they are seeking. The narrator does not provide an explanation as she does not understand the situation: 'J'affirmai timidement que la vérité n'existe pas. Cela importait peu du moment qu'il avait une cause pour laquelle manifester' (Yared 2006: 26).

The size of the protest seems to grow as the narrative progresses; it also becomes increasingly dangerous and menacing. The protesters get weapons and shoot in the air to celebrate the Independence Day, an independence that does not seem to exist for the narrator (Yared 2006: 29). They continuously harass the narrator on her way to work at the theatre: 'Je n'en pouvais plus de me faire agresser tous les soirs en reentrant chez moi. Je les croisais toujours. Immanquablement ils m'invitaient à me joindre à leur cause. C'est rigide une cause. Leur sit-in était sur mon chemin' (39). They even shout at Greta when she is working the street (42) and protest against Mona who gives birth on stage to a baby shadow of undetermined sex (148). At first, they think that Mona is the name of a virus spelled M.O.N.A. and immediately start an awareness campaign against her. When they realise that she is an unmarried woman with a baby, they alter their agenda and protest the independence of the uterus. They accuse women of going against their cause and call for the implementation of serious sanctions against women like Mona (149–50). They finally go after the narrator. One evening, they stop her and ask her to join their cause. She refuses and they accuse her of high treason and strip her of her clothing and her memory. They offer to replace her memory with another one and take her breath for genetic testing (102–4). For them, the narrator breathes a lot, which is not only suspicious but also an indication of her guilt. For her, it is only normal that she breathes a lot, especially since her asthmatic son and her husband have occupied her lungs for a long time

(92). They arrest her a second time and will not let her go until she pays with her smile (198). Finally, they stir up public opinion against her, call for the permanent closure of the theatre and for her arrest (200). They break into the theatre only to find no one on stage. The narrator has joined all her shadows and disappeared in the wardrobe.

As mentioned earlier, the protesters act as one group and are diametrically opposed to the narrator on stage. Not only does the group oppose the narrator and the message of tolerance and female awakening she embodies, but also her entire world. It is the ultimate confrontation between different spaces, times and values: between magical and real spaces, between past and present and between conservative and contemporary values. In plain terms, the protesters outside the theatre represent the old-fashioned conservative mentality of patriarchal Lebanese society, and the narrator, with her multiple identities, stands for the problems faced by women in a modern society. The separation of the two worlds is, to a certain extent, clear throughout the text, and the reader is able to differentiate between the real and the magical. As a matter of fact, time is strongly connected to space. When the narrator is on stage, she (and subsequently the reader) is in the magical world. When she is outside the theatre, she is in the real world of the protesters. At the end of the text, however, the lines get blurred, and the two worlds rub up against each other. The result is bloody: the protesters take over the theatre, and the narrator disappears taking the magic with her.

With regards to the audience, at the beginning of the text, no one watches the narrator's performance, but, as the play continues, the audience grows in size, which contributes to the protesters' grievance against the narrator. The interesting point about the audience is the reader's position, because the reader is, in a way, not only the implicit reader of the text but is also placed in the audience. As Wilson argues, 'literary space, in being conceptual, cannot be measured, but it *can* be experienced' (Wilson 1995: 215). This is exactly the position of the reader, who is not only reading the narrator but also attending her performance. The reader thus becomes the spectator of a magical performance and as such is entitled to ask this question: is the narrator mad? While reading/watching this bizarre world unfold, the reader can very well question the narrator's sanity. Is she mad? Is she trustworthy? It is not easy to answer the question, especially given that the narrator has hinted at the beginning of the text that she may be schizophrenic (Yared 2006: 36).

Ultimately, it does not matter whether or not the narrator is mad, particularly since it is impossible for the reader to answer this question. What really matters is the effect produced by her narration and her magical world. By portraying a magical realist world and by being potentially mad, the narrator succeeds in making the reader question the world as he or she knows it and to consider other alternatives.

In examining the history of madness, Foucault (1988) argues that with the rise of Cartesian reason and the contributions of medical and clinical discourses, madness has been oppressed by sovereign reason, or the Western way of thinking. Consequently, madness has been pushed out of the dominant discourse to reflect the voice of the marginalised. In the case of literature, madness functions as a subversive force that makes one question everything: from the narrative voice, to the writing itself, to the world in which the writing takes place (Dow 2009; Felman 1978). To put Foucault's theory in the context of *L'Armoire des ombres*, one could say that the narrator, through her possibly mad narrative, her fragmented sentences, her excessive use of punctuation and her abrupt change of interlocutors, speaks from an outcast position to criticise the dominant patriarchal discourse of Lebanese society during the war and the post-war period.

In fact, magical realism and her possible madness enable her to position herself with the subaltern, to explode the dominant patriarchal narrative and to criticise the existing social order in Lebanon. The reader is confronted with two choices: either join the real world of the protesters when they storm the theatre and accept that after all she is nothing but a crazy narrator, or join her in her magical mad world of shadows. There is not one correct way to read the text and just like Faris (2004) says, the response varies according the reader's cultural beliefs.

Vacarme pour une lune morte and *Les Morts n'ont pas d'ombre* by Vénus Khoury-Ghata

In 1983, Vénus Khoury-Ghata published *Vacarme pour une lune morte* and in 1984 she published its sequel *Les Morts n'ont pas d'ombre*. These are perhaps the darkest books written by Khoury-Ghata and the hardest to comprehend because of their dense literary style and ambiguous plots. These texts, written in similar literary styles that combine elements of magic with grotesque realism, examine the war in Lebanon and expose its insanity. They portray the carnivalesque world of the fictional country of Nabilie where logical rules of time, space, life and death are suspended, and where body parts are described using crude language. They show a world where an old woman gets pregnant from radiation, where a cat swallows a clock and has his pupils replaced by the clock's hands, where fictional diseases like cervical arthrosis, fourmillite and rabia exist, where a woman gives birth to a casserole dish, where a political leader negotiates peace with a dead man, and, finally, where a dead woman asks to have her rocking chair by her grave.

Nabilie, as one can guess, is the French word for Lebanon / Liban spelled backward. Sarah, a Jewish Italian woman, lives in Nabilie and is married to one of the Alpha sons. The Alphas are a wealthy family, very proud of their Phoenician origins and their Christian faith. Mrs Agathe Alpha is Sarah's mother-in-law; she is known for being unfaithful to her husband, Gabriel Alpha. While Sarah's husband and the eldest Alpha son remain unnamed, the middle son is called Robert Alpha. When he becomes the leader of the Christian party, he earns the nickname Chérubin. There is also Tante Léa Alpha, the unmarried old virgin who lives with the Alphas. Sarah, just like her mother-in-law, is unfaithful to her husband. She has different lovers: Max, the Jewish Hungarian violinist, her own brother-in-law Chérubin, Sabbab the Kurdish war lord and head of the political party PKK, a wealthy Arab emir, and Salomon who governs the mountains of Nabilie along with his wife Osiris, his sons and their wives and his two goats Aristote and Xénophobe.

There are other protagonists in the text and their lives are heavily intertwined in the narratives. There is Mme Alma Orefice who is Sarah's mother and Joseph the Alphas' butler and chief of servants and Mr Gabriel Alpha's conscience. The Chinese Master lives in the Alpha's gardener's lodge. Gouraud is another servant living with the Alphas. His only duty is taking care of the shoes Mr Gabriel Alpha bought at Harrods in England for the Queen's coronation. Maryam, also a servant in the Alpha's house, waits for her dead son Jad to return from the grave. Mr Haramon is a southern warlord, and the Hittites, the Philistines and the Hébreux are different war militias. Ararat is the Philistines' leader and Abou-al-Kobh is his right-hand man. Muscadal is Salomon's faithful assistant; he travels the world in an attempt to end the war in Nabilie. Anthébor Friské, the trusted neighbour who has everyone's house keys, eats all the keys and all the furniture when he hears that the neighbourhood might be under attack. The governor of Nabilie is in love with his stamp. The Archimandrite, chief of the Orthodox Church, Monseigneur Hilaire Cappucino, representative of the Vatican, and Barnabé, representative of the Catholic Church, are religious figures in the text. Finally, there is Hama, Salomon's illegitimate daughter, who publicly shames her family by wearing her lover's gold necklace and Loth, Salomon's gay son.

The plot in both texts is very fluid, rapid and difficult to summarise. Both are long series of conflicts between different groups who love and hate each other. Facing these literary puzzles, the one question that comes to mind is why did the author write these two texts with grotesque realism? To say it differently, what does grotesque realism allow the author to accomplish and to reveal to her reader and what are the implications of using grotesque realism in constructing a war narrative? In order to answer these questions, it is important to begin by defining grotesque realism and then move forward to examine its effects in the two novels at hand, *Vacarme pour une lune morte* and *Les Morts n'ont pas d'ombre*.

Before we proceed, it is important to note that since both novels are tailored by the same author and cut from the same cloth, I will examine them together in the section below.

Grotesque Realism according to Bakhtin

The definition of grotesque realism comes to us from Bakhtin in his examination of Rabelais's works, *Rabelais and His World*. Bakhtin analyses the relationship between literature and carnival and shows how in *Gargantua and Pantagruel* Rabelais portrays the carnivalesque spirit through grotesque realism. For Bakhtin, in order to fully comprehend Rabelais, one must go back and study over a thousand years of folk culture and humour. Folk culture and humour essentially mock the austerity of the medieval ecclesiastical institutes and feudal cultures and mimic serious rituals such as the election of a king or queen or the recognition of the victors of tournaments through the humorous figures of clowns, fools, giants, dwarfs and jugglers (Bakhtin 1984: 3–4).

Bakhtin identifies three different forms in which folk culture and humour manifest themselves:

1. *Ritual spectacles*: carnival pageants, comic shows of the market-place.
2. *Comic verbal compositions*: parodies both oral and written, in Latin and in the vernacular.
3. *Various genres of billingsgate*: curses, oaths, popular blazons. (Bakhtin 1984: 5)

Carnival came to embody all these categories. Carnival, for Bakhtin, is neither a spectacle nor an art. It is, instead, life itself. The participants truly live the experiences, free from all the prejudices, rules and conditions of the real world. Carnival is a second life celebrated with different kinds of rituals and feasts. The feast is both a reflection on the spirit of the community but also of time as it is often related to moments of crisis. Carnival thus allows its participants to break away from its time and live in a distorted reality or a 'utopian realm community, freedom, equality, and abundance' (Bakhtin 1984: 9).

This utopian realm available through carnival allows the suspension of all hierarchies that become temporarily void from their traditional significance. It also allows the suspension of time, space and rules. The utopian realm offers therefore 'a parody of the extracarnival life, a world inside out' (Bakhtin 1984: 11). Some elements of carnival stressed by Bakhtin are communal spirit and collective laughter. In fact, carnival laughter is neither reactionary nor individual but rather universal, touching all the carnival's participants. Additionally, carnival contains abusive language, familiar speech, profanities, oaths and other forms of indecent expression, which are all ambivalent in their meanings. Although vulgar and humiliating, their purpose is to diverge from official discourse to create a humorous environment.

Carnival also focuses on the body in conjunction with other themes such as drunkenness, defecation and sexual life. For Bakhtin, these bodily images along with the culture of folk humour give birth to the concept of grotesque realism.[4] The essence of grotesque realism is degradation, which means 'the lowering of all that is high, spiritual, ideal, abstract; it is a transfer to the material, to the sphere of earth and body in the indissoluble unity' (Bakhtin 1984: 20). For Bakhtin, degradation carries two meanings: one is topographical in nature and indicates downward movement or return to earth. In this case, the upward symbolises heaven and consequently the downward refers to earth, grave or womb, to life and death. The second meaning of degradation focuses on the lower stratum which generates a materialising and even more degrading laughter. The belly and the reproductive organs become the focal point of degradation along with themes like defecation, sex, pregnancy and birth.

Effects produced by degradation are not as destructive as one might think. In fact, Bakhtin argues degradation simultaneously allows the return to death and earth but also the return to life through rebirth. Therefore, degradation has a regenerative force:

> To degrade an object does not imply merely hurling it into the voice of non-existence, into absolute destruction, but to hurl it down to the reproductive lower stratum, the zone in which conception and a new birth take place. Grotesque realism knows no other lower level; it is the fruitful earth and the womb. It is always conceiving. (Bakhtin 1984: 21)

Consequently, through degradation, grotesque realism portrays a body that is constantly in motion. It is a body that is regularly changing into something else by aging, procreating or dying. This regular transformation of the body functions also as a reflection on time. Time indicators are frequently present in grotesque realist images through references to historical events or the changing of seasons. They serve two purposes: to ground the grotesque image of the body in a somewhat realistic image and to remind us of the metamorphosis that is about to occur to the body and its biological life.

It is important to add that in folk culture and humour, the grotesque bodily images are depicted in a festive wholeness and with utopian dimensions. The bodily element:

> [I]s presented not in a private, egotistic form, severed from the other spheres of life, but as something universal representing all the people. As such it is opposed to severance from the material and bodily roots of the world; it makes no pretense to renunciation of the earthly, or independence of the earth and the body . . . it is not individualized. The material bodily principle is contained not in the biological individual, not in the bourgeois ego, but in the people, a people who are continually growing and renewed. This is why all that is bodily becomes grandiose, exaggerated, immeasurable. (Bakhtin 1984: 19)

Therefore, the bodily images, although they may look like isolated fragments, are in fact part of a collective image. Contrary to the Renaissance body that stood isolated from the surrounding elements and in the centre of the universe, the grotesque body is a giant body that is in constant transformation and communication with the rest of the world. It is a body with different orifices and organs – such as the mouth, ears, nose, anus and genitals – which collectively allow the body to eat, drink, defecate, have sex, give birth and die.

To sum it up, grotesque realism embodies the carnival with all its elements: it reflects folk culture and humour with community spirit, general laughter and crude language. It offers literary images that are degrading in the sense that they focus on the lower stratum using familiar speech and profanities along with hyperbole, exaggeration, pastiche and other literary figures. It suspends official discourse and highlights the mobility of the body in time and space and shows the ambivalence of the body as both a degenerative and generative body.

By shifting the focus on the body, grotesque realism also allows the destruction of the existing order and the construction of a new one. Bakhtin examines this aspect of grotesque realism in his essay 'Questions of Literature and Aesthetics' where he studies Rabelais's novel and the concepts of time, space and grotesque realism (Bakhtin 1981). As Bakhtin argues, Rabelais writes his novel in reaction to the abuse of the feudal system and religious institutions. As such, he purges his novel from references to real meaning of time, space and human values. Instead, he creates an alternative world that has its own chronotope (or time and space as depicted in the narrative and through language) which destroys the ordinary ties and logical links to the real world and creates a new time, space, and life made out of strange analogies and themes that traditionally do not go together (Bakhtin 1981: 169).

In order to create his own world, Rabelais relies on folklore and antiquity and brings together items that 'had traditionally been kept distant and disunified' (Bakhtin 1981: 170). He also creates different series 'which are at times parallel to each other and at times intersect each other' (170). These series are:

(1) Series of the human body, in its anatomical and physiological aspect;
(2) human clothing series; (3) food series; (4) drink and drunkenness series;
(5) sexual series (copulation); (6) death series; (7) defecation series. Each of

these seven series possesses its own specific logic, and each series has its own dominants. All these series intersect one another; by constructing and intersecting them, Rabelais is able to put together or take apart anything he finds necessary. Almost all the themes in Rabelais's broad and thematically rich novel are brought about via these series. (Bakhtin 1981: 170)

In the first two series, Rabelais makes the body the focal point through which one can see the world. Thus, the world is no longer perceived from a religious point of view according to which the body is sinful and decadent but rather from a material point of view. The world becomes anchored in a new concrete reality that it attached to the body in its different anatomical and physiological elements. The body is portrayed with exaggerated grotesqueness whose imageries reveal gruesome details such as blood, injuries and wounds. Also, it is frequently described in motion, eating, drinking or defecating, or in juxtaposition to various objects or tools like clothing. These remind the reader of the materiality of the body, its temporality, but also its changing nature.

The sex series is the dominant one: 'It appears in a wide variety of forms: from sheer obscenity to subtly coded ambiguity, from the bawdy joke and anecdote to medical and naturalistic discourses on sexual potency, male semen, sexual reproductive processes, marriages and the significance of gender' (Bakhtin 1981: 190).

Death also forms its own series. Often described as a banal incident that occurs in association with other series like food or sex or defecation, death for Rabelais, according to Bakhtin, carries a destructive meaning. It destroys the human body and brings it back to earth. For Rabelais, death is an end in itself; it does not exist in life but rather on the borders of life as an unavoidable and inevitable end. Death is also presented in close relationship with laughter and birth. The 'cheerful death' of Rabelais, as Bakhtin calls it, destroys the seriousness of death and its sober aspect. Its association with life renders it trivial in the sense that both life and death become nothing but one repetitive cycle. However, there are some instances where death is glorified, described in a grotesque fantastic style with a popular epic spirit. In this case, death serves a different purpose, highlights a historical event, and puts the body back in communication with time. In other words, the temporality of the body is momentarily suspended in favor of immortality and historical continuity.[5]

Many of these series have hidden meanings and work on multiple levels. The food and drinking series for instance functions as a criticism of religious institutions and gluttony and drunkenness in monasteries. The defecation series is a statement against the existing order that only focuses on the spiritu- ality of the body and excludes its physicality. Indeed, defecation degrades the body and reduces it to pure flesh. The sex series allows the destruction of the existing social hierarchy and the construction of a new one where indecency becomes the norm and where the private becomes public.

> All these word-linkages, even those that seem the most absurd in terms of the objects they name, are aimed primarily at destroying the established hierarchy of values, at bringing down the high and raising up the low, at destroying every nook and cranny of the habitual picture of the word. But simultaneously he [Rabelais] is accomplishing a more positive task, one that gives all these world-linkages and grotesque images a definite direction: to 'embody' the world, to materialize it, to tie everything in to a spatial and temporal series, to measure everything on the scale of the human body, to construct – on that space where the destroyed picture of the world had been – a new picture. (Bakhtin 1981: 177)

Described in a grotesque realist style, all these series contribute to the demolition of the old world and into the building of a new one where both the body and the soul matter:

> In the process of destroying the traditional matrices of objects, phenomena, ideas and words, Rabelais puts together new and more authentic matrices and links that correspond to 'nature', and that link up all aspects of the world by means of the most marvelous grotesque and fantastic images and combinations of images. In this complex and contradictory flow of images, Rabelais brings about a restoration of the most ancient object-associations; this flow enters one of the most fundamental channels of literary thematics. Along this channel flows a full-bodied stream of images, motifs, plots, fed by the springs of pre-class folklore. The direct association of eating, drinking, death, copulation, laughter (the clown) and birth in one image, in one motif and in one plot is the *exterior* index of this current of literary thematics. The elements themselves that make up the whole image, motif or plot – as

well as the artistic and ideological functions of the entire matrix taken as a whole at various stages of development – both change drastically. Beneath this matrix, which serves as the exterior index, there is a hidden specific form for experiencing time and specific relationship between time and the spatial world, that is, there is hidden a specific chronotope. (Bakhtin 1981: 205)

Ultimately, regarding Bakhtin's reading of Rabelais's works, it is important to bear in mind that carnival in literature is depicted through grotesque realism which focuses on the body in a degrading fashion. When combined with a new chronotope, or a new time and space, with rules that are unknown to our world and with magical elements, grotesque realism allows the destruction of the old existing order and sets in place a new one. This is precisely how grotesque realism operates in the novels *Vacarme pour une lune morte* and *Les Morts n'ont pas d'ombre*, where '[m]etaphorically, the carnivalesque functions as a trope for the parodic subversion of social identity, as a political, psychological, and religious phenomenon' (Lindley 1996: 22).

Grotesque Realism in *Vacarme pour une lune morte* and *Les morts n'ont pas d'ombre*

Just like Rabelais, Vénus Khoury-Ghata wrote *Vacarme pour une lune morte* and *Les Morts n'ont pas d'ombre* as a reaction to her immediate surroundings. She uses grotesque realist images and creates her own rules of time and space and crafts her own values in order to explode the existing order in Lebanon and to replace it with a new one. The new world revealed in Khoury-Ghata's texts becomes available to the reader through different themes, or series, in a manner that corresponds with Rabelais's efforts in his text. However, Khoury-Ghata only uses four of Rabelais's seven series of the body: anatomy, sex, death and defecation.

In the body and anatomy series, the focus is either on the lower stratum, orifices or bodily fluids. For the lower stratum, there are frequent references to the belly, buttocks and feet. The belly appears in connection to pregnancy. For instance, Sarah, the beautiful Jewish Italian woman, wonders whether her belly was only a passage place for her children: 'Mon ventre n'a-t-il été qu'un lieu de passage?' (*Vacarme* 12), and Tante Léa gets pregnant in her old age through radiation from the Chinese master living in her garden lodge, and her belly starts growing every morning by ten millimetres (*Vacarme* 52). Feet make an appearance when Mr Alpha tries to put his shoes on, but his feet are too swollen from the heat. He says that he either needs to shrink his feet to fit in the shoes or to widen the shoes. His servant Gouroud suggests cutting the toes out of the shoes, but Mr Alpha categorically refuses as he bought these shoes in England at Harrods to attend Queen Elizabeth's coronation (*Vacarme* 19–20). The Kurdish fighters, Hamchar and Antar, make references to buttocks to mock their Christian enemies' taste in furniture. For them, Christians have soft buttocks, which explains their choice of furniture. The Kurds' buttocks, conversely, need something very solid to sit on, especially since their testicles are so much heavier than those of their enemies (*Vacarme* 65). References to genitals appear when some French unions call for their country's left wing to help Nabilie end the war by sending the testicles of one hundred leftists. The left wing rejects the idea and claims that their testicles belong to them and them alone (*Vacarme* 93); another example is when Marion, Sarah's servant, compares Sarah's vagina to a hole that devours anyone that comes near it (*Vacarme* 104); and when Barnabé, the young Catholic monk, sees Sarah for the first time, he discovers that his private parts have a function other than urination (*Les Morts* 113).

For the orifices, Sarah's mother is named Alma Orefice and is referred to in both texts as Mme Orefice. Sarah's hateful neighbour is called Edmée LDS or Edmée-à-la-langue de serpillière which is a reference to both her mouth and tongue (*Vacarme* 33). Max's father dies after his ears are cut off. He was an orchestral conductor and when the Soviet army invaded Budapest, he closed his windows and turned his back to the city like any conductor would do except that one bomb took out his right ear and another bomb took out the left. His blood spilled all over the balustrade and dripped into the public square. People wondered if he were Van Gogh which profoundly irritated the sniper who shot him, as his victim became famous. Russian soldiers denied that it was blood spilling in a public place and claimed that it was his brain escaping his body (*Vacarme* 34–5). When the Hittites begin their expansion policy, the authorities ordered all residents to stay awake and to buy clothes pins so they can keep their eyes open (*Vacarme* 136).

For the bodily fluids, there are multiple references to tears, blood and sperm. In talking about her husband, Mme Orefice points out that he cries a lot because he is related to a certain Moses who crossed the Red Sea and started the Wailing Wall (*Vacarme* 32); when Sarah and the Kurdish war-lord Sabbab have sex, Sabbab gives the order to evacuate all residents within one kilometre from his bed so he can ejaculate in all directions, and when Sarah has her period after their twenty-eight days of continuous sex, Sabbab becomes mad at the sight of blood (*Vacarme* 106).

In the sex series, there many references to genitals, copulation and infidelity. Both Agathe Alpha and Sarah have multiple extramarital relations. It is a well-accepted fact that does not shock anyone including the husbands, who in discussing the difference between the two women, admit that Agathe Alpha has a more refined taste than her daughter-in-law Sarah. Agathe's lovers were from France, England and Turkey, as opposed to Sarah whose lover is an insignificant Levantine violinist (*Vacarme* 22). Sarah changes lovers frequently, and she treats her body just like she treats her diamonds. She spreads it around like she spreads her diamonds in different bank accounts (*Vacarme* 38). To aggravate her husband, she walks around the city naked to arouse the sexually frustrated residents. She has sex with her brother-in-law (*Les Morts* 16); she also has sex with Loth, Salomon's son, and during their intercourse he plants a seed of hummus in her belly (*Les Morts* 169). Ararat has a green book on women, according to which every believer should wash his genitals three times after copulating with a woman of his religion and five times after copulating with a foreign woman (*Les Morts* 197).

As for death, it occupies its own space and is heavily present in both texts:[6] Jad, Maryam's son, is executed in the Muslim cemeteries; Jalila finds her husband's and children's bodies cut into pieces and thrown into the river; Ali, the cherry merchant, is killed with five shots in the head since he cannot do the cross sign with his five fingers (*Vacarme* 18); Tante Léa and Mme Alpha die in different circumstances; Sabbab dies from hypertension when peace in Nabilie is signed; and Salomon is killed by one of his goats.

Finally, there is the defecation series. There are multiple references to excrement in association with bodily fluids. In discussing the difference between the Arabs and the Kurds, the narrative voice argues that unlike the Arabs who are spoiled, the Kurds are willing to eat 'la merde salée' or salty excrements in the name of their cause (*Vacarme* 60). When Anthébor's neighbourhood comes under attack, Anthébor grabs a white pillowcase, holds it as a flag and asks the combatants to stop their fighting for the twelve minutes he needs to urinate (*Vacarme* 119). He also gets used to relieving himself in the Alpha's house (*Les Morts* 19). When Max decides to leave Nabilie, he calls it a country with concentrated excrements and sperms with urine essence (*Vacarme* 120); when Muscadal visits different countries to restore peace in Nabilie, he is rewarded with animals that start a defecation war in Nabilie. They urinate and defecate everywhere, which drives the residents of Nabilie mad (*Vacarme* 185); when deprived of weaponry, the Christians and Muslims declare a bacterial war of pollution. They urinate and defecate on each other. The Maronites, who produce more urine than any other community, start their own company to treat the excess of ammoniac in the city. Both communities pollute all the fauna and the flora of Nabilie but leave human beings intact (*Vacarme* 201). Salomon enjoys this pollution war so much he soils himself and says it is more practical (*Vacarme* 202). The Philistines defecate on the Hittites (*Les Morts* 111).

These series do not necessarily stand alone as they are often juxtaposed. Just like Rabelais, Khoury-Ghata creates a combination of themes that traditionally do not go together such as life and death, sex and death, death and defecation, or food and defecation, with the purpose of breaking away from the real world to create her own. In a way, she purges her novel from traditional and logical references and links to the real world to create her own upside-down world. She examines the world of the war through the lens of the human body, its anatomy and its essential functions, and creates her own human race, a race that lives, diets, eats, defecates and gives birth by its own rules. To a certain extent, the narrative becomes impersonal to the reader as it is a long procession of living and dying bodies.

Here are some examples of the series' association: when Sarah and Max are having sex, Max's body is on top of hers, meanwhile the dead bodies of Jad, Jalila's husband and children, and Ali are being found (*Vacarme* 18); Tante Léa is pregnant from the Chinese master but she is also a menopaused virgin (*Vacarme* 53); the city's mosques are as beautiful as the phallus. Built from giant stones and erected between the sky and the earth, they are a cake of excrement mixed with honey which explains all the flies in the city (*Vacarme* 57); Sabbab alternates between killing men and having sex with women (*Vacarme* 62). He kills the gardener in the Alpha's house and plants parsley in his nostrils (*Vacarme* 78); during Ramadan, all fighting activities stop at night since Muslim combatants are breaking the fast. Fighting resumes early in the morning when the Muslim roosters sing (*Vacarme* 80); in describing her bother-in-law, Sarah says that he admits his love to her by spilling blood and killing people (*Vacarme* 181); the war becomes so interesting that it draws the attention of foreign tourists who visit Nabilie for a weekend of war (*Vacarme* 88); Salomon visits Sabbab's tomb and negotiates peace with him (*Vacarme* 139); the city smells like burned cadavers, who in turn smell like grilled kababs (*Vacarme* 149); although Max was killed in the war, his violin keeps playing music (*Les Morts* 152); Sarah wants to add Salomon to her list of lovers since he came back to life after being dead for a while (*Les Morts* 158).

Clearly, all these series focus on the body and its materiality, which goes against the literary tradition inherited from the Renaissance where emphasis is placed on the soul or the mind. As Bakhtin argues, all these series are in a downward movement, which contributes to the debasement of the body and the destruction of the sacred: 'All of them thrust down, turn over, push headfirst, transfer top to bottom, and bottom to top, both in the literal sense of space, and in the metaphorical meaning of the image' (Bakhtin 1984: 370).

Body parts, as depicted by Khoury-Ghata, are mostly exaggerated grotesque images of orifices or convexities such as the mouth, the ears, the eyes or the genitals. They all function as the border between the body and the world; they are the body's extension into the world but also the world's entry way into the body. For instance, Mme Orefice is literally and figuratively the protagonist (or the orifice) through which the action starts or ends. She unexpectedly appears in the plot to link different protagonists or to pit them against each other; Edmée LDS is the mouth that gossips a lot and brings calamity to her community. She brings to mind Bakhtin's description of Lucifer swallowing human bodies (Bakhtin 1984: 325). She is the destructive gaping mouth that eats peace in the world; Max's father survives the Soviet invasion of his city and dies through his ears (*Vacarme* 34–5). Some of the main protagonists, like Sarah, her brother-in-law Robert, Sabbab the Kurdish leader and Salomon the warlord of the mountains, are reduced to their genitals as they enter and exit the world (and the narrative) through their sexes.

Although body parts are described as isolated fragments, and although they give a pixelated image of the protagonists, they remain parts of a larger whole, a body that is interconnected with the rest of the world. The body is therefore, and as Bakhtin calls it, a cosmic body (Bakhtin 1984: 318). This is very apparent in both novels as all protagonists are linked, in one way or another, through their bodies as a whole or through specific parts, such as the genitals, mouth, tongue or ears. Consequently, the body's connection to its immediate surroundings and to other bodies creates a general sense of collectivity. In other words, all bodies and all their parts are in the war together.

Furthermore, all these images of the body in their different associations and with their various functions of urination, defecation and sexuality allow a literal debasement of the body but also establish an intimate link with the cycle of life and death. In other words, the messages they embody are ambivalent because they are simultaneously destructive and regenerative. As Bakhtin argues, they signify destruction:

> a grave for the one who is debased. But such debasing gestures and expressions are ambivalent, since the lower stratum is not only a bodily grave but also the area of the genital organs, the fertilizing and generating stratum. Therefore, in the images of urine and excrements is preserved the essential link with birth, fertility, renewal and welfare. (Bakhtin 1984: 148)

Consequently, as a result of the ambivalence of the images, death in grotesque realism is no longer an end by itself, nor inevitable, since the body is constantly renewed by the lower stratum. In the two texts at hand, death is the transition that moves the protagonists in different directions and allows the plot to move forward. It is frequently trivialised, described in a comic or inappropriate way: the burned dead bodies smell like grilled kebab; Sabbab dies of hypertension when he hears of peace in Nabilie; Salomon dies chasing his goat; Mme Alpha dies under the bombs in her bedroom surrounded by her lovers' photos. The death of these protagonists is indefinite (which sounds like an oxymoron) as they all manage to come back to life or to communicate with the livings from their graves: Salomon returns to life after dying for eighteen months; Mme Alpha communicates with her butler Joseph and her son Chérubin and tries to return to earth as her own grandchild; and Sabbab negotiates peace with Salomon from his grave.

In addition to these images of the body, the grotesque is available to the reader through the crude language used to either describe the body in its materiality or to report a dialogue between different protagonists. When Max and Sarah are having sex, they recite passages from *L'Amant de Lady Chatterley* in English: 'Cock [*sic*] is dark and soft and unspeakably warm', says Max, and 'Cun't is it fuck [*sic*]', Sarah asks him (*Vacarme* 90). Profanities and indecency prevail in both narratives and in the protagonists' lives; they are the norm, and no one seems to be shocked by them, which means that decency and modesty do not belong in the world depicted by Khoury-Ghata.

Furthermore, in this world, time and space are magical and they function differently. Time is indicated to the reader through natural elements such as bird migration, change of seasons, lunar cycles and body changes: when the Phéniciens are waiting for the Hébreux to come to Nabilie, they note a massive migration of swallows (*Les Morts* 27); the governor, who is scared of sunlight and spiders, only governs the country at night and in his sleep (*Les Morts* 55, 118); when Mme Alpha dies, she dies twice, once on the night of 10 April 1980, and again the night of 18 March 1981 (*Les Morts* 137). Time is also deeply attached to the war and is at its service. Before Max decides to leave Nabilie, his cat eats a clock. When he tries to evacuate and reaches the country's borders, the cat vomits up the numbers and the clock's hands migrate to his eyes to indicate time. As a result, the border patrol sends them back to Nabilie where they become insomniac from crossing the borders. To 'kill time', they walk at night and accidently contaminate all the fighters who start shooting at different times. Since the war is a precise and synchronised activity, the fighters are forced to sign peace to resynchronise their war time (*Vacarme* 124–5); when the members of parliament meet to discuss peace, they cannot agree on anything and their permanent contradictions contaminate the clock in the centre of the town that starts ringing erratically regardless of the hour (*Vacarme* 131). It is a way to say that in war even time becomes irrational.

Also, in this world, space is visualised differently. The Alphas' house has strange architecture where some rooms are destroyed by the war and yet they continue to be functional and luxurious and occupied by some protagonists. In opposition to the war raging outside, the house has what seems to be a peaceful garden and lodge that was consecutively inhabited by the gardener, the Chinese Master and Max. Another example of strange space is when Monseigneur Hillaire Capuccio describes the Balkan to the governor. Apparently, it is a country with expandable and retractable borders and exists on top of another one. It is also a country that is practically impossible to locate on a map (*Les Morts* 84, 102).

With these magical elements of time and space, along with the body series and the crude language, Khoury-Ghata deconstructs the traditional notions of time, space and life values to create her own chronotope and to construct a new logic according to which a death can occur twice and a cat can speak, have clock hands in its eyes, and can vomit numbers. In other words, everything becomes irrational and changeable, including time, space, human bodies, human language and human values. Even laughter is different in this grotesque world. Traditionally, carnival generates a communal laughter against the comic. However, in this case, laughter itself is emptied of its meaning and subverted to be used as an instrument of war. When Salomon and Chérubin declare war on each other, they use their laughter as weapons (*Les Morts* 139).

In a way, Khoury-Ghata 'carnivalises' the war. If the war kills people in the real world, then carnival could potentially give them a second life,[7] even if it is an upside-down one in which nothing makes sense, not even the rules that were thought to be immutable. Khoury-Ghata creates a world carefully balancing the conventional and the aberrant, the real and the grotesque. This manufactured world criticises the real war raging in Lebanon at the time of the narratives and mocks the different religious communities largely responsible for the war.[8] Most of, if not all, the protagonists have a religion. Some have biblical names such as Sarah, Salomon, Chérubin, Noé and Loth, and some have holy attributes and are proclaimed saints for their actions. For instance, Mme Orefice flies up in the air during intensive bombing and performs miracles (*Vacarme* 73);[9] Sabbab is revered by his Kurdish political party, which asks the pope to canonise him (*Vacarme* 126); and Salomon equates himself with God. When he dies, the villagers make a statue of him that looks like Saint George's (*Vacarme* 201–2), and when he comes back to life, he compares himself to Lazarus (*Les Morts* 205). The narratives also satirically depict religious institutions or establishments: the Orthodox archbishop is always sleeping (*Vacarme* 67, 74), the Catholic one is busy fornicating with Mme Orefice in a confessional position and the erected mosques are compared to a phallus (*Vacarme* 57). The number forty, which is an important number in the Old and New Testament, appears in the narratives with other biblical references: the bombing of the city lasts for forty days (*Vacarme* 69), the rain lasts for forty days and nights (*Vacarme* 95), the villagers expect a flood and Noé builds an ark and, finally, the Hébreux wait for the Messiah (*Les Morts* 20).

It is important to say that both novels do not necessarily mock religion, but rather the way it is practised in Nabilie. In Khoury-Ghata's grotesque world, religion becomes the door for destruction and fuel to war, which explains the subtle references to biblical and historical destructive moments such as the flood, the crucifixion of Jesus, the death of Saint Sebastien and the number forty. The protagonists clearly embody different religious communities and represent real life political leaders from Lebanon, but the author defies the reader to actually make that connection. Not only does she challenge the reader but also accuses him or her of imagining the correlation. In the epigraph to *Vacarme pour une lune morte,* she says '[s]erait coupable – comme moi – d'imagination quiconque reconnaîtrait dans ce livre des personnages connus'.

In a way, Khoury-Ghata creates a carnivalesque war with grotesque realist images, and this carnivalesque space becomes a 'malleable space, in which activities and symbols can be inflected in different directions' (Dentith 1995: 75). To say it differently, the carnivalesque space as used by Khoury-Ghata has three different functions, all challenging to the reader: first, it destroys the world as we know it in time and space, mocks the sacred and human values and promotes indecency; secondly, it defies gender rules in two different ways; and thirdly, it resists the reader's easy comprehension of narratives.

Indeed, the defiance of gender roles and the resistance to easy understanding are the result of the world's destruction in time and space. As we have already demonstrated, Khoury-Ghata creates a grotesque world to criticise the war in Lebanon. She portrays an upside-down world where the sacred is mocked and logic is suspended. However, in doing so, she transgresses both gender and readership rules. For gender rules, Khoury-Ghata defies them in her capacity as a writer for she writes grotesquely and in crude language which goes against Bakhtin's observation that crude language belongs to the male realm (Bakhtin 1984: 319). Furthermore, historically, the grotesque has been associated with the female body.[10] As a result, carnival becomes the perfect venue for the public celebration of the female body. As Bakhtin points out, this appears in Rabelais's writing where the focus is on the female body for its generative and degenerative qualities. However, Khoury-Ghata breaks away from this tradition that frequently restricts the grotesque to the female body and expands it to all protagonists regardless of their gender. She also uses the grotesque to widen the space that is traditionally assigned to women in patriarchal society. As such, women in the grotesque realist world can be indecent and speak freely of their sexuality. Grotesque realism allows a reversal of the order of things, the private becomes public and the public becomes private which, in its own odd way, can be empowering to women and can put 'women on top' as Natalie Zemon Davis (1975) argues.

As for the readership, when opening a text, the reader can usually assume that it will be readable or intelligible. In other words, the text will make sense. Susan Rubin Suleiman argues that for a text to make sense, it must follow fundamental rules of readability:

> [P]rinciple of noncontradiction (an event cannot occur and not occur at the same time, a thing cannot exist and not exist at the same time), the notions of temporal succession and causality (events follow each other and are related to each other consequentially), a belief in the solidity of the phenomenal world (a table is a table is a table), and a belief in at least a relative unity of the self (a name designates a person who has certain fixed characteristics and a set of identifiable ancestors). (Suleiman 1981: 19)[11]

These rules do not necessarily apply to these two narratives as grotesque realism renders them difficult to comprehend. Facing this inaccessible fortress of a text, the reader feels assaulted and lives the narrative as an aggression (Laurent 1976, qtd in Sulemein 1981: 270). Consequently, the reader declares the text to be 'unreadable', which automatically strikes the text with death. For Barthes, there is a solution for this problem. In fact, in *S/Z* he makes the distinction between 'the readable' and the 'writable', and by 'writable' he means 'unreadable' (as pointed out by Suleiman). He argues that the only way to interpret a 'writable' text is through jouissance or pleasure in reading, even when the narrative goes against the logical rules (Barthes 1974: 5). In other words, the reader should enjoy the text, reading it with pleasure rather than questioning it. But what if the reader does question it? In that event, Barthes argues, it is irrelevant because the reader is already a mad person:

Imagine someone (a kind of Monsieur Teste in reverse) who abolishes within himself all barriers, all classes, all exclusions, not by syncretism but by simple discard of that old specter: *logical contradictions*; who mixes every language, even those said to be incompatible; who silently accepts every charge of illogicality, of incongruity; who remains passive in the face of Socratic irony (leading the interlocutor to the supreme disgrace: *self-contradiction*) and legal terrorism (how much penal evidence is based on a psychology of consistency!). Such a man would be the mockery of our society: court, school, asylum, polite conversation would cast him out: who endures contradictions without shame? Now this anti-hero exists: he is the reader of the text at the moment he takes his pleasure. Thus the Biblical myth is reversed, the confusion of tongues is no longer a punishment, the subject gains access to bliss by the cohabitation of languages *working side by side:* the text of pleasure is sanctioned by Babel. (Barthes 1975b: 3–4)

To question the text rather than read it with pleasure is not a statement on the madness of the text but rather on the madness of the reader. Truly grotesque realism flips everything; the rogue, the clown and the fool make more sense than the reader.[12]

In both novels, Khoury-Ghata not only creates a grotesque world with porous boundaries between the real and the unreal, the spiritual and the material and the traditionally accepted and rejected, but also creates a world where she (the author) as well as her protagonists defy the rules of gender and defy the reader. For the reader to enter this world, he or she must accept their own madness. Consequently, everything related to these two texts is turned upside down: time, space, human values, language, the author herself for creating such texts, and the reader for reading such texts. Everyone is contaminated by the grotesque realist and carnivalesque spirit.

Facing this general contaminating hysteria, some questions remain. We saw that the grotesque body is an ambivalent body for its generative and degenerative attributes. Is it possible to say that Khoury-Ghata, in using grotesque realism, destroys the world as we know it and creates the world of war in the hope that it regenerates into something else? The endings or the lack of endings in both texts suggest otherwise. They seem to imply that the plots will go on and on forever, imprisoned in an endlessly repetitive cycle.[13] From the end of the narratives, we return to the beginning with the titles of the narratives: *Vacarme pour une lune morte* and *Les Morts n'ont pas d'ombre*. Both contain the word death, and both leave little room, if any, for optimism. Additionally, Faris argues that the absence of an ending to a narrative not only postpones closure but also allows for chaos to win (Faris 1982: 811). Does chaos win in Khoury-Ghata's narrative?

Finally, Natalie Zemon Davis argues that carnival brings temporary release from social hierarchy as it takes place with the acceptance of church and state. Women during that period can be unruly. However, outside carnival, an unruly woman can bring destruction and the only way to avoid that is by returning to the natural order of things. So 'a world-turned-upside down can only be righted' (Davis 1975: 131). The question then would be, can this world be changed? In the case of war and as depicted by Hyam Yared and by Vénus Khoury-Ghata, one might be inclined to say no.

Notes

1 When asked about the process of cultural change, transformation and hybridity, Homi Bhabha explains the third space:

> [F]or me the importance of hybridity is not to be able to trace two original moments from which the third emerges, rather hybridity to me is the 'third space' which enables other positions to emerge. This third space displaces the histories that constitute it, and sets up new structures of authority, new political initiatives, which are inadequately understood through received wisdom. (Bhaba 1994: 211)

See Rutherford 1990: 207–21; Huddart 2006.

2 One could give the example of the movie *Groundhog Day* where Phil, played by Bill Murray, finds himself stuck in the same time and the same place.

3 For more information on the story of Cinderella and gender role, see Platt 2007: 32–53.

4 Or the genre of grotesque realism. See Todorov (1975) for the definition of genre.

5 On the relationship between the grotesque body and history, see Dentith 1995: 82.

6 In an interview with Bernard Mazo, Vénus Khoury-Ghata says: 'Je fais de la mort un espace de vie. Les morts se nourrissent de l'odeur de notre pain, boivent les

vapeurs de nos sources, vivent sur notre vacarme. J'avais besoin de le croire pour me consoler de la perte de mon mari et de la perte de 200 000 Libanais tués par la guerre' (Mazo 2002: 28).

7 As mentioned earlier, Bakhtin argues that carnival is not just art. It is life itself as it gives its participants a second chance to live again (Bakhtin 1984: 9). Arthur Lindley argues that to say that carnival gives us life back or makes us feel alive again means that we were dead at some point (Lindley 1996: 19). In the case of Khoury-Ghata, carnival allows her to bring dead people or people who are doomed to die back to life in the violent context of war.

8 Rabelais as discussed by Bakhtin uses grotesque realism to criticise religion. For more on the topic of religion in the Bakhtinian thought see Bagshaw (2013).

9 It is important to note that Mme Orefice's flying and sainthood play an important role in increasing her grotesqueness. In fact, Mary Russo, in examining the philobatic body, argues that the flying body transgresses space as it is launched in the air and it is floating free from all attachments. In that sense, it defies the materiality of the body and attempts to remind the viewers of the spirituality of the body. However, the philobatic body, especially of a female performer, comes back to earth erected like a phallus. If it surpasses its materiality, it is only for a short period of time. Therefore, the flying body is a grotesque body. Its grotesqueness gets accentuated when it is a female performer who makes a spectacle out of herself (Russo 1994: 34–41). So in the case of Mme Orefice who flies away during the forty days of bombing, one can argue that it was her attempt of escaping the grotesque to return to the realm of refinement. However, she had to come back to earth and thus return to her own materiality and grotesque body. As for her sainthood, Laurie Finke (1988) shows how women in medieval times, in order to escape male oppression and church authority, claimed mystical experience which allowed them to surpass their bodies as grotesque. The female body, in medieval times, was the site of power struggle: it was the link to the divine through the mystical experience but it was the site of sin and degradation. This reading of women's mystical powers in the medieval time could be applied to Mme Orefice in her claim of sainthood. It was her way, once again, of escaping her grotesque material body. She claimed a relationship with the divine and performed miracles in his name. However, everything else in the text indicates her degrading and sinful nature.

10 For more information on the link between the grotesque and the female body, see Russo 1994; Lindley 1996.

11 It is important to note that Suleiman discusses the fundamental rules of

readability in the particular case of avant-garde texts. However, the rules are transferable to grotesque realist narrative. For more on the avant-garde, see Poggioli 1968; Suleiman 1990.

12 In the essay 'Questions of Literature and Aesthetics', Bakhtin argues that the carnivalesque figures of the rogue, the clown and the fool may push the reader to question the author's authority, when in fact, they are aiding the author to expose private matters (Barthes 1981: 160).

13 For more on ending in narrative, see Kermode 2000.

Conclusion

The diverse corpus examined in this book shows the reader the original ways by which Lebanese women writers of French expression construct war narratives to oppose the war, criticise patriarchal values and to defend women's rights. Contrary to what classical narratology claims, this corpus demonstrates how the structure of the narrative informs, influences and, at times, creates meaning which, in return, relies on the structure to convey its message.

Classical narratology examines a narrative scientifically. It is not concerned with moral issues or with the production of meaning; instead, it speaks in favour of rigid structural elements that exist in every narrative and that transcend or exist irrespective of it. To a certain extent, there is truth in this statement. In any given narrative, there will be a narrative voice (in any or all of its various forms). However, as postclassical narratology argues, it would be a mistake to examine the structure independently of its content and the context in which it exists.

Throughout the book, I argue that it is certainly useful to examine the narrative voice from the classical narratology point of view. This allows us, for instance, to borrow some of Genette's categories in order to identify the voice's point of view and position it with regard to the story, whether the voice is speaking from inside or outside the story, or whether the voice is telling its own story or the story of others. However, this scientific examination of the voice is dry and does not take into account the context in which the narrative exists.

Examined through the postclassical narratological lens, the narrative voice carries multiple meanings: it is the feminine 'I' that transgresses male space to speak up, to defy conservative traditions and to defend women's rights; it is the feminine 'I' that bears witness to its trauma and the trauma of others; it is the historian postcolonial feminine 'I' that rewrites history from her own perspective since history has for long been written by colonialist males; and it is the humanist postmodern omniscient narrator that deliberately monopolises the voice in an attempt to understand what is happening in the war and to impose a message of peace and love when no one is listening.

As for the narrative body, although the concept itself did not necessarily interest narratology, I argue that it is an alternative form of voice. And, even without a voice, the body speaks; it performs women's voices in armed conflicts. As seen in the second part of the book, the body is loaded with meaning: it is the evil silent body that brings great calamity into the city; it is the sick and disabled female body that reflects deep emotional distress; it is also the magical and the grotesque female body that exists in the margins of society, and that functions according to surreal rules of time, space and reason. In her struggle against war and conservative society, the female protagonist speaks with her body, and its performance cannot be ignored as it becomes an alternative voice on which narrative structure is built and through which meaning is conveyed.

From this study, two important questions arise: in the context of interdisciplinary narratology, can we speak of trauma narratology, and what role, if any, does the language of expression play in war narratives?

In Chapter 1 and as a brief reminder, Caruth argues that Freud defines trauma as the unexpected encounter with an event that the mind misses but then repeatedly attempts to grasp. As such, trauma is repetitive in the sense that, through dreams or other conscious or unconscious acts, the brain continuously attempts to understand painful past events. Trauma is also amnesiac and inexpressible. Trauma survivors find it hard to remember what happened, and when they do, they find it hard to put it in words. Finally, trauma is often collective as one person feels responsible for others and speaks in their names. Trauma, in all these traits, becomes the expressive or performative language by which the victim bears witness. Trauma is therefore its own language, available to the reader either through a narrative voice or a narrative body. Since narrative is constructed through language, it is legitimate to speak of a trauma narratology alongside feminist, postcolonial and postmodern narratology.

In his defence of postcolonial narratology, Gerald Prince shows how concepts like space, time, characters, events and structure vary in meaning from classical to postclassical/postcolonial narratology. To give a few examples: classical narratology examines these elements from an objective point of view and consequently asks scientific questions: are time and space mentioned in the narrative? Is time linear or cyclic? Does the plot occur in one space or multiple? What is the distance between the narrative space and the characters? Are they inside or outside that space? Do events occur one time or multiple times? Are they told by an inside or outside character or voice? In contrast, in postcolonial narratology these items are not just observed for scientific purposes, but they are examined to search for a meaning keeping in mind the binary colonial – postcolonial power struggle. Time, for example, is not just acknowledged but it is interpreted in relation to this bipolar dimension. Language, according to Prince, is also an important element to be considered. He says that:

> special attention could be given to the nature of the narrator's language in order to specify whether that language is (supposed to be) written, uttered, signed, or unexpressed, whether it is the same as that of the narratee and the characters, or whether it is that of the colonizer, that of the colonized, a creolized compound of the two, or none of the above. One might, in addition, concentrate on whether it is native to the narrator; whether it contains regionalisms, dialect turns, neologisms, nonstandard or incorrect forms; to what extent, and in what circumstances, it involves code switching, using words or phrases from a different linguistic code; whether these words or phrases are (indirectly) translated or left untranslated. (Prince 2005: 377)

Postcolonial narratology considers the context in which a narrative takes place as well as the language that builds that narrative. Taking into account the particular context of war and taking trauma into consideration as a form of language, we ask if it is possible to speak of trauma narratology. If so, do the elements enumerated by Prince carry different meanings in a war narrative? What about language? If trauma is by its own merit a language by which the victim bears witness, can it therefore help but create the category of war or trauma narratology?

On the surface, there are multiple answers to these questions. On the one hand, as the corpus here has shown, it is possible to argue in favour of trauma narratology since space, time, characters, events and structure are utilised to build war narratives, and to carry significance in the context of war. In fact, their goal differs from the one advanced by postcolonial narratology. If these elements aim to structure a narrative in order to reflect a colonial-postcolonial struggle, they may have a different purpose in the case of a war narrative particularly if the narrative deals with a civil war with no colonial component. Additionally, the elements mentioned above might be utilised to expose or address trauma, to help survivors make sense of their experiences in speaking of painful memories and to testify.

While it holds that postcolonial narratology with its elements can be inclusive of trauma narratology, the inverse is not necessarily true. In other words, a postcolonial narrative can speak of trauma and/or of war, but a trauma narrative may not necessarily be inserted into a colonial-postcolonial dynamic. As such, trauma narratology should be its own category.

However, while there is no doubt that narratology is becoming increasingly interdisciplinary, this may create a redundancy in the field as it overlaps with feminist, postcolonial and postmodern narratologies as well as others. As Roy Sommer (2007) points out, many of the contextual narratologies overlap precisely because of the kinship between the various contexts. Additionally, one can argue that trauma narratology can be studied under what Nünning identifies as cognitive and reception theory-oriented narratology (with the focus on psychoanalytical narrative theories) or the linguistic approach to narratology (Nünning 2003: 250).

Finally, I will not go as far as Nilli Diengott (1988) and call for a pure form of objective narratology, one that is not contaminated by contextual narratology. However, to borrow Wallace Martin's expression (in his description of the omniscient narrator), narratology might become the 'dumping-ground' filled with different contextualised and overlapping narratologies (Martin 1986: 146). In fact, there is a legitimate concern of over-stretching the field.

As for the second question and as highlighted in the Introduction, this book focuses only on war narratives written in French, and does not engage in the discussion of the choice of the language of expression for several reasons: first, the concept of Francophonie has been widely discussed, approved, rejected, altered and stretched. And while there might be more to say about it, this book chooses not to dwell on the conversation more than necessary. Second, Amal Amireh (1996) deplores the fact that Arab women writings are often and very reductively appreciated for their courage to speak up rather than their literary quality. Consequently, she calls for a serious study of this literature. Responding to this call, this book engages in a literary analysis that does not stop at the language of expression as it is time to push the conversation forward, and make peace with the fact that some Lebanese writers speak and write in French, and others do so in other languages such as Arabic and English.

Additionally, and in many cases, the choice of language is personal and is related to the writer's life circumstances. Many of them live in France and are French citizens like Andrée Chedid and Vénus Khoury-Ghata, for example. Evelyne Accad had a Swiss French mother, spoke French at home and admits not having learned Arabic well (Heistad et al. 2004: 26).

One must acknowledge that language reflects personal, cultural and national identity. As such, it carries a political weight. Consequently, the choice of one language over the other may be highly problematic; this is particularly true in the Maghreb where, due to a heavy colonial history, there has been a push to Arabise the countries and to stop using French, as it is viewed as the language of the former colonisers. In Algeria, for example, writers were and continue to be divided into two camps: the first camp defends the Arabic language. Some see the choice to write in French as a denial of the writers' Arabic and Islamic identities and as a continuation of the neo-colonial agenda in the region. Some writers, like Tahar Ouettar (1936–2010), have argued that Algerian writers who write in French should lose their Algerian citizenship. Under such high pressure, Rachid Boudjedra (b. 1941), who started writing in French, shifted to Arabic because he considered Francophonie responsible for preventing the separation of the Arabic language from a religious connotation and away from conservatism. Ahlam Mosteghanemi (b. 1953) was the first Algerian woman to write a novel in Arabic and is proud of her choice to write exclusively in her native language. As for the second camp, they consider French to be part of their cultural heritage. Writers like Mohamed Dib (1920–2003) and Kateb Yacine (1929–89) argue that it belongs to them. Yacine calls the French language his 'butin de guerre' or spoil of war (Kilanga-Musinde et al. 2010: 263).

In Lebanon, the language of expression is certainly not devoid of political meaning. In some circles, it is considered either a sign of an elitist rejection of Arabic identity in favour of an imported Western colonial one, or a representation of the upper class. Nevertheless, despite these representations, French remains generally accepted as a part of life. As I highlighted in the Introduction, for miriam cooke, the French language continues to be widely spread in Lebanon due to the Christian pro-French majority but also for the lack of serious resistance and advocacy for the Arabic language. As such, Lebanon has an easy affiliation with the language, and the Lebanese use it by choice (cooke 1996: 142).

Therefore, instead of asking whether language plays a role in war narratives, one should ask whether there are differences in writing trauma and war narratives in French and Arabic (since Arabic is Lebanon's native and official language). As such, the conversation is moved from the why of the French language to the how; how is French different from Arabic in the context of war narratives?

Immediately, some general differences surface between writing trauma and war narratives in French and Arabic: in general, writing in Arabic may sound more authentic for some as it opens the door for native expressions and dialect (very frequently novels of Arabic expression contain dialogues in local dialects). To borrow from Prince's above-mentioned general comment on postcolonial narratology, writing in Arabic allows for regionalisms, dialect, local expressions and code switching to be visible. These linguistic nuances may not appear in a text originally written in French (or any foreign language, for that matter) or translated into French.

Writing in French exposes women writers to accusations of being orientalist and neo-colonialist as they may seem like they are contributing to the Western anti-Islamic discourse. These accusations may be true in some cases. However, in general, postcolonial writers were able to dodge and combat them by claiming ownership of the colonial language. Jane Hiddleston discusses the dilemma faced by postcolonial intellectuals. Typically, they are the people who benefited from a colonial education. 'They are the products of the *mission civilisatrice*, yet they are, at the same time its lucid but complicit opponents' (Hiddleston 2014: 1). They use the colonial language, a heritage that is not theirs, but that shaped them and became part of their identities, to rebel against colonial values. As such, their writings reflect dilemmas and innovations particularly in the ways they had to redefine their own identities, humanity and culture, all while using the French language. In short, they had to re-appropriate the language to make space for their own cultural legacies (Hiddleston 2014: 1–4). Hiddleston focuses on writers like Senghor (1906–2001), Césaire (1913–2008), Fanon (1925–61), Amrouche (1906–62), Feraoun (1913–62) and Yacine (1929–89). In comparison, it is possible to say that Lebanese women writers decolonised the French language by claiming it and making it their own in writing war narratives. Their stories are often penetrated by Arabic words – especially terms of endearment, local expressions and images – that simultaneously reveal the writers' awareness of writing in a colonial language, but also their willingness to innovate and personalise it in addressing issues of war and trauma. This process of language appropriation reminds us of Vénus Khoury-Ghata's statement on writing Arabic in French: '[m]es dialogues sont de l'arabe écrit en français. J'ai intégré la langue arabe dans la langue française: la forme de la phrase est française mais le contenu est arabe' (qtd in Darwiche Jabbour 2007: 89).

As such, it is possible to say that in their war narratives of French expression, Lebanese women writers decolonised the French language and inserted Lebanese dialect and Arabic language in French; they revolutionised the French language by introducing native terms, expressions and images to its lexicon. They fought to carve a personalised space which subsequently allowed them to diversify the language and fight against its homogenisation.[1]

To sum it up, two differences emerge. Arabic may allow more room for authenticity in writing trauma, and French may be viewed as a colonialist orientalist language of expression even though Lebanese women writers claimed it as their own and decolonised it. For sure, these differences call for a more in-depth study as there are many variables at play (different writers with different circumstances and contexts), but for now they appear to be minimal and can be further attenuated through translation. Lawrence Venuti (2013) points out the shift that occurred in the field of translation studies and allowed to better incorporate cultural differences and nuances. In the 1990s, translation studies were mostly focused on linguistics, which led to the assimilation or marginalisation of cultural differences in the receiving text. For Venuti, this instrumental approach is very narrow as it relies exclusively on understanding a language without consideration for contextual factors or for what is lost from the source text.

According to Venuti, nowadays translation cannot just be understood as a domesticating process; it must be seen as a cross-cultural ethical communication that preserves certain elements from the source text. His method, while it defends linguistic fluency, argues in favour of the 'foreignizing effects' which allows the transmission of a foreign concept or a non-standard use of a term into translation. Borrowing Gilles Deleuze and Félix Guattari's term, Venuti advances that this method allows the deterritorialising of the text as it opens the door for a minority text or language to exist in a majority, dominant or mainstream space (Venuti 2013: 2). Consequently, Venuti's method allows for a translated text to preserve, to a certain extent, the authenticity of the original text. Additionally, the availability of a novel in multiple languages helps dissipate the accusation of orientalism. Aware of the value of translation and of its progression, many women writers had their war narratives translated from Arabic into French or English (or vice versa) Some have contributed to the translation of their own works, like Hanan Al-Shaykh and her novel *Hikayat Zahra* or *The Story of Zahra*, while others, like Ahlam Mosteghanemi, had their works retranslated into multiple versions. In fact, her novel *Dhakirat el Jassad* was translated into English in 2003 by the American University in Cairo as *The Memory in the Flesh*; it was retranslated in 2013 with Bloomsbury as *The Bridges of Constantine*. When asked during an interview about the new version, Mosteghanemi admits that the American University in Cairo rushed the translation and focused only on linguistics. She says:

> I really wanted the translator to be a poet, so that he or she would have expertise in translating poetry and not just translating at the level of word for word, not just a text translator but a more precisely literary translator. The beauty of a text gets lost in a word for word translation and as a result, it loses much of its meaning. Those who read in two languages grasp the difference between the original text and the translated. These readers can sense and understand that there is something missing in the translation. The most striking example of this for me was the poet and publisher Nizar Qabbani, may Allah have mercy on him, who used to say to me 'Whenever I read a

translated text, I feel like going crazy'. This is because the music of the text has disappeared through translation into English or French, and as such, the writing no longer signifies anything nor motivates anybody. This is why, for me, the translator must be a poet because when the text impresses him, he can translate it wonderfully. (Baaqeel 2015: 146–7)

There is no doubt that translation serves as a bridge between different languages and reduces the gap between them. In the case of Lebanese women's war narratives, it opened the door for a wider audience. In many ways, it also 'deterritorialised' the narratives by allowing the source text to exist in a dominant culture. Despite its benefits, one last question remains: can trauma be translated?

Note

1 French authorities are taking steps in order to recognise the continuous diversification of the French language. Recently, the Ministry of Culture, in collaboration with the Ministry of Europe and Foreign Affairs, the Institut Français, the International Organization of La Francophonie, the Académie des Sciences d'Outre-Mer, TV5 Monde, the Agence Universitaire de la Francophonie and the University of Lyon 3 Jean Moulin, worked on producing a digital dictionary that reflects the diversity of the French language in the world. This dictionary considers expressions and terms from different francophone regions. Available at <https://www.youtube.com/watch?v=BYsNTjWLOkM&fbclid=IwAR27jsg1rkzpwG8YBl_Yjm7VyZ2zF5fgO1xT7bdlXzWy_TfRaLHZB56PhCw> (last accessed 12 January 2020).

Bibliography

Abou, Sélim (1962). *Le bilinguisme arabe-français au Liban. Essai d'anthropologie culturelle.* Presses Universitaires de France.

Accad, Evelyne, Anne Craver and Christiane Makward (2013). *Andrée Chedid, Je t'aime: hommages, souvenirs et lettres.* Alfabarre.

— (2006). *Coquelicot du massacre. Poppy from the Massacre*, trans. Cynthia Hahn. Édition Bilingue. L'Harmattan.

— (2001). 'On Sexuality and war', *Guns & Roses*, 2.1 (2001), <http://www.littlemag.com/jan-feb01/evelyne.html> (last accessed 22 August 2016).

— (1997). 'A(e)ncre sans(g) censure', *Présence Francophone*, 51 (1997), pp. 7–22.

— (1993). 'Rebellion, Maturity, and the Social Context. Arab Women's Special Contribution to Literature', *Arab Women. Old Boundaries, New Frontiers*, ed. Judith E. Tucker. Indiana University Press, pp. 224–53.

— (1990). *Sexuality and War. Literary Masks of the Middle East.* New York University Press.

— (1988). *Coquelicot du Massacre.* L'Harmattan.

Aczel, Richard (1998). 'Hearing Voices in Narrative Texts', *New Literary History*, 29.3 (1998), pp. 467–500.

Adnan, Etel [1977] (2010). *Sitt Marie Rose.* Tamyras.

— (1982). *Sitt Marie Rose.* Translated from the French by Georgina Kleege, Post-Apollo Press.

Aldea, Eva (2011). *Magical Realism and Deleuze. The Indiscernibility of Difference in Postcolonial Literature.* Continuum International Publishing Group.

Alexander, M. Jacqui and Chandra Talpade Mohanty (2010). 'Cartographies of Knowledge and Power. Transnational Feminism as Radical Praxis', *Critical Transnational Feminist Praxis*, ed. Amanda Lock Swarr and Richa Nagar. State

University of New York Press, pp. 23–46.

— (1996). *Feminist Genealogies, Colonial Legacies, Democratic Futures*. Routledge.

Amireh, Amal (2005). 'Bearing Witness: The Politics of Form in Etel Adnan's *Sitt Marie Rose*', *Critique: Critical Middle Eastern Studies*, 14.3 (2005), pp. 251–63.

— (1996). 'Publishing in the West: Problems and Prospects for Arab Women Writers', *Al Jadid*, 2.10 (27 March 2012), <http://www.aljadid.com/content/publishing-west-problems-and-prospects-arab-women-writers> (last accessed 1 August 2019).

Amnesty International (2018). 'Lebanon: Parliamentary vote a historic victory for thousands of relatives of the missing', 13 November, <https://www.amnesty.org/en/latest/news/2018/11/lebanon-parliamentary-vote-a-historic-victory-for-thousands-of-relatives-of-the-missing/> (last accessed 1 August 2019).

Aristotle (1953). *Generation of Animals*, trans. A. L. Peck. Harvard University Press.

Ashplant, T. G., Graham Dawson and Michael Roper (2000). 'The Politics of War Memory and Commemoration: Contexts, Structures and Dynamics', *The Politics of War Memory and Commemoration*, ed. T. G. Ashplant, Graham Dawson and Michael Roper. Routledge, pp. 1–86.

Aziz, Désirée (1995). *Le Silence des cèdres*. Robert Laffont.

Baalbaki, Layla (1958). *Ana Ahya (I Live)*. Dar Majallat Shi'ir.

Baaqeel, Nuha (2015). 'An Interview with Ahlam Mosteghanemi', *Women, A Cultural Review*, 26.1–2 (2015), pp. 143–53.

Badran, Margot (1993). 'Independent Women: More Than A Century of Feminism in Egypt', *Arab Women: Old Boundaries, New Frontiers*, ed. Judith E. Tucker. Indiana University Press, pp. 129–48.

Badran, Margot and miriam cooke (1990). *Opening the Gates. An Anthology of Arab Feminist Writing*. Indiana University Press.

Bagchi, Alaknanda (1996). 'Conflicting Nationalisms: The Voice of the Subaltern in Mahasweta Devi's *Bashai Tudu*', *Tulsa Studies in Women's Literature*, 15.1 (1996), pp. 41–50.

Bagshaw, Hilary B. P. (2013). *Religion in the Thought of Mikhail Bakhtin. Reason and Faith*. Ashgate.

Bakhtin, Mikhail (1984). *Rabelais and His World*, trans. Hélène Iswolsky. Indiana University Press.

— (1981). *The Dialogic Imagination. Four Essays by M. M. Bakhtin*, ed. Michael Holquist, trans. Caryl Emerson, Michael Holquist. University of Texas Press.

Bal, Mieke (1997). *Narratology: Introduction to the Theory of Narrative*, 2nd edn. University of Toronto Press.

Barthes, Roland (1978). 'The Death of the Author', *Image – Music – Text*, trans. Stephen Heath. Hill & Wang, pp. 142–9.

— (1976). *Sade/Fourier/Loyola*, trans. Richard Miller. Johns Hopkins University Press.

— (1975a). 'An Introduction to the Structural Analysis of Narrative', trans. Lionel Duisit. *New Literary History*, special issue: On Narrative and Narratives, 6.2 (1975), pp. 237–72.

— (1975b). *The Pleasure of the Text*, trans. Richard Miller. Hill & Wang.

— (1974). *S/Z*, trans. Richard Miller. Hill & Wang.

— (1968). 'L'Effet du réel', *Communications*, 11 (1968). Recherches Sémiologiques le Vraisemblable, pp. 84–9.

— (1966). 'Introduction à l'analyse structurale des récits', *Communications*, 8 (1966), pp. 1–27.

Bartky, Sandra Lee (1997). 'Foucault, Femininity and the Modernization of Patriarchal Power', *Writing the Body. Female Embodiment and Feminist Theory*, ed. Katie Conboy, Nadia Medina and Sarah Stanbury. Columbia University Press, pp. 129–54.

Bell, Rudolph M. (1985). *Holy Anorexia*. The University of Chicago Press.

Benveniste, Émile (1966). *Problèmes de linguistique générale*. Gallimard.

Bhabha, Homi K. (1995). *The Location of Culture*. Routledge.

Biddle, Arthur W., Gloria Bien, miriam cooke, Vinay Dharwadker, Roberto Gonzàlez Echevarrí, Mbulelo Mzamane, Angelita Reyes (1995). *Global Voices. Contemporary Literature from the Non-Western World*. Blair Press Book.

Blaik Hourani, Rida (2017). 'A Call for Unitary History Textbook Design in Post-Conflict Era: The Case of Lebanon', *The History Teacher*, 50.2 (2017), pp. 255–84.

Bordo, Susan (1997). 'The Body and the Reproduction of Femininity', *Writing the Body. Female Embodiment and Feminist Theory*, ed. Katie Conboy, Nadia Medina and Sarah Stanbury. Columbia University Press, pp. 90–110.

— (1993). *Unbearable Weight. Feminism, Western Culture, and the Body*. University of California Press.

— (1987). *Flight to Objectivity. Essays on Cartesianism and Culture*. State University of New York Press.

Bouchard, Danielle, et al. (2010). 'Continuing Conversations. Critical Transnational Feminist Praxis Contributors', *Critical Transnational Feminist Praxis*, ed. Amanda Lock Swarr and Richa Nagar. State University of New York Press, pp. 206–18.

Bourget, Carine (2010). *The Star, the Cross and the Crescent Religions and Conflicts in Francophone Literature from the Arab world*. Lexington Books.

Boustani, Carmen (2016). *Andrée Chedid. L'Écriture de l'amour. Biographie.* Flammarion.

Braidotti, Rosi (1997). 'Mothers, Monsters, and Machines', *Writing the Body. Female Embodiment and Feminist Theory*, ed. Katie Conboy, Nadia Medina and Sarah Stanbury. Columbia University Press, pp. 59–80.

Brissette, Pascal (2002). 'Le Lecteur en procès: analyse rhétorique du modèle judiciaire dans *Les Confessions* de Rousseau', *International Review of Literary Studies*, 57.3 (2002), pp. 181–96.

Brownmiller, Susan (1984). *Femininity*. Linden Press / Simon & Schuster.

Brumberg, Joan Jacobs (1988). *Fasting Girls. The Emergence of Anorexia Nervosa as a Modern Disease*. Harvard University Press.

Bruyère, Vincent (2012). *La Différence francophone. De Jean de Léry à Patrick Chamoiseau*. Presses Universitaires de Rennes.

Butler, Judith (1998). 'Selections from *Gender Trouble*', *Body and Flesh. A Philosophical Reader*, ed. Donn Welton. Blackwell Publishers Inc., pp. 27–44.

Carpentier, Alejo (1975). *The Kingdom of This World*, trans. Harriet de Onis. Penguin Modern Classics.

Caruth, Cathy (2013). *Literature in the Ashes of History*. Johns Hopkins University Press.

— (1996). *Unclaimed Experience. Trauma, Narrative, and History*. Johns Hopkins University Press.

Casper, Monica J. and Eric H. R. Wertheimer (2016). 'Within Trauma: An Introduction', *Critical Trauma Studies: Understanding Violence, Conflict and Memory in Everyday Life*. New York University Press, pp. 1–16.

Chatman, Seymour (1978). *Story and Discourse: Narrative Structure in Fiction and Film*. Cornell University Press.

Chedid, Andrée (2000). *Le Message*. Flammarion.

— (1989). *The Return to Beirut*, trans. Ros Schwartz. Serpent's Tail.

— (1985). *La Maison sans Racines*. Flammarion.

Chernin, Kim (1985). *The Hungry Self. Women, Eating, and Identity*. Times Books.

— (1981). *The Obsession. Reflections on the Tyranny of Slenderness*. Harper & Row.

Cixous, Hélène (1986). 'Sorties: Out and Out: Attacks/Ways Out/Forays', *The Newly Born Woman*. Hélène Cixous and Catherine Clément; trans. Betsy Wing. University of Minnesota Press, pp. 63–134.

Clavaron, Yves (2018). *Francophonie, postcolonialisme et mondialisation*. Classiques Garnier.

Cohen, Jeffrey Jerome (1999). *Of Giants, Sex, Monsters, and the Middle Ages*. University of Minnesota Press.

cooke, miriam (2016). 'Women and the Arab Spring: A Transnational, Feminist Revolution', *Women's Movements in Post-'Arab Spring' North Africa*, ed. Fatima Sadiqi. Palgrave, pp. 31–44.

— (1997). *Women and the War Story*. University of California Press.

— (1996). 'Mothers, Rebels, and Textual Exchange. Women Writing in French and Arabic', *Postcolonial Subjects. Francophone Women Writers*, ed. Mary Jean Green, Karen Gould, Micheline Rice-Maximin, Keith L. Walker and Jack A. Yeager. University of Minnesota Press, pp. 140–56.

— (1994–5). 'Arab Women Arab Wars', *Cultural Critique*, 29 (1994–5), pp. 5–29.

— (1987). 'Women Write War. The Centering of The Beirut Decentrists', *Centre for Lebanese Studies*, Papers on Lebanon, 6 (1987), pp. 3–22.

— (1982). 'Beirut . . . Theatre of the Absurd . . . Theatre of Dreams . . .: The Lebanese Civil War in the Writings of Contemporary Arab Women', *Journal of Arabic Literature*, 13 (1982), pp. 124–41.

Cooper, Brenda (1998). *Magical Realism in West African Fiction. Seeing with a Third Eye*. Routledge Research in Postcolonial Literatures.

Corvellec, Hervé (2011). 'The narrative structure of risk accounts', *Risk Management*, 13.3 (2011), pp. 101–21.

Culler, Jonathan (2004). 'Omniscience', *Narrative*, 12.1 (2004), pp. 22–34.

Daly, Brenda O. and Maureen T. Reddy (1991). *Narrating Mothers – Theorizing Maternal Subjects*. University of Tennessee Press.

Darwiche Jabbour, Zahida (2007). *Littératures francophones du Moyen-Orient. Égypte, Liban, Syrie*. Collection dirigée par J-F Durand et Th. Galibert, Les Écritures du Sud.

Davis, Natalie Zemon (1975). 'Women on Top'. *Society and Culture in Early Modern France. Eight Essays by Natalie Zemon Davis*. Stanford University Press, pp. 124–52.

Dawson, Paul (2013). *The Return of the Omniscient Narrator. Authorship and Authority in Twenty-First Century Fiction*. Ohio State University Press.

De Beauvoir, Simone (1989). *The Second Sex*, trans. H. M. Parshley. Vintage Books.

Dentith, Simon (1995). *Bakhtinian Thought. An Introductory Reader*. Routledge.

Derrida, Jacques (1990). 'Structure, Sign and Play in the Discourse of the Human Sciences', *Writing and Difference*, trans. Alan Bass. Routledge, pp. 278–94.

D'haen, Theo L. (1995). 'Magical Realism and Postmodernism: Decentering Privileged Centers', *Magical Realism. Theory, History, Community*. Duke University Press, pp. 191–208.

Diengott, Nilli (1988). 'Narratology and Feminism', *Style*, 22 (1988), pp. 42–51.

Djebar, Assia (1999). *Ces Voix qui m'assiègent ... En marge de ma francophonie*. Albin Michel.

Douglas, Mary (2002). *Purity and Danger. An Analysis of Concept of Pollution and Taboo*. Routledge.

Dow, Suzanne (2009). *Madness in Twentieth-Century French Women's Writing. Leduc, Duras, Beauvoir, Cardinal, Hyvrard*, ed. Peter Collier. Peter Lang, Modern French Identities, vol. 76.

Duffy, Brian (1994). 'Notes sur l'identité et la causalité dans *Les Confessions* de Jean-Jacques Rousseau', *French Studies Bulletin*, 50 (Spring 1994), pp. 8–11.

Edkins, Jenny (2003). *Trauma and the Memory of Politics*. Cambridge University Press.

Eggert, Jennifer Philippa (2018). 'Female Fighters and Militants During the Lebanese Civil War: Individual Profiles, Pathways, and Motivations', *Studies in Conflict & Terrorism*, 41 (2018), pp. 1–31. Available at <https://www.tandfonline.com/doi/full/10.1080/1057610X.2018.1529353 (last accessed 16 July 2019).

El-Hage, Anne-Marie (2019). 'Adoptés du Liban: une association dénonce un véritable trafic d'enfants durant plus de 40 Ans', *L'Orient Le Jour* [Beirut], 22 June, <https://www.lorientlejour.com/article/1175883/adoptes-du-liban-une-association-denonce-un-veritable-trafic-denfants-durant-plus-de-40-ans.html> (last accessed 1 August 2019).

Fanon, Frantz [1961] (2002). *Les Damnés de la terre*. La Découverte/Poche.

— (1967). *Black Skin, White Masks*, trans. Richard Philcox. Grove Press.

— (1963). *The Wretched of the Earth*, trans. Constance Farrington. Grove Press.

Faris, Wendy B. (2004). *Ordinary Enchantments. Magical Realism and the Remystification of Narrative*. Vanderbilt University Press.

— (1995). 'Scheherazade's Children: Magical Realism and Postmodern Fiction', *Magical Realism. Theory, History, Community*. Duke University Press, pp. 163–90.

— (1982). '1001 Words: Fiction Against Death', *The Georgia Review*, 36.4 (Winter 1982), pp. 811–30.

Fayad, Mona (1995). 'Reinscribing Identity: Nation and Community in Arab Women's Writing', *College Literature*, 22.1, issue on Third Women's Inscriptions, pp. 147–60.

Felman, Shoshana (1978). *La Folie et la chose littéraire*. Éditions du Seuil.

Finke, Laurie (1988). 'Mystical Bodies and the Dialogics of Vision', *Philological Quarterly*, 67.1 (Winter 1988), pp. 439–60.

Fisk, Robert (2001). *Pity the Nation: Lebanon at War*. Oxford University Press.

Flax, Jane (1990). *Thinking Fragments. Psychoanalysis, Feminism and Postmodernism in the Contemporary West*. University of California Press.

Flores, Angel (1995). 'Magical Realism in Spanish American Literature', *Magical Realism. Theory, History, Community*, ed. Lois Parkinson Zamora and Wendy B. Faris. Duke University Press, pp. 109–18.

Fludernik, Monica (2005). 'Histories of Narrative Theory (II): From Structuralism to the Present', *A Companion to Narrative Theory*, ed. James Phelan and Peter J. Rabinowitz. Blackwell Publishing Ltd, pp. 36–59.

— (2000). 'Beyond Structuralism in Narratology: Recent Developments and New Horizons in Narrative Theory', *Anglistik*, 11.1 (2000), pp. 83–96.

Foster, Thomas (1995). 'Circles of Oppression, Circles of Repression: Etel Adnan's *Sitt Marie Rose*', *PMLA*, 110.1 (1995), pp. 59–74.

Foucault, Michel (1995). *Discipline & Punish: The Birth of the Prison*, 2nd edn, trans. Alan Sheridan. Vintage Books.

— (1988). *Madness and Civilization. A History of Insanity in The Age of Reason*, trans. Richard Howard. Vintage Books.

— (1980). *Power / Knowledge. Selected Interviews & Other Writings 1972–1977*, ed. Colin Gordon, trans. Colin Gordin, Leo Marshall, John Mepham, Kate Soper. Vintage Books.

Gaard, Greta (2010). 'New Directions for Ecofeminism: Towards a More Feminist Ecocriticism', *Interdisciplinary Studies in Literature and Environment*, 17.4 (2010), pp. 643–65.

Gafaïti, Hafid (1996). *Les Femmes dans le roman algérien*. L'Harmattan.

Garland Thomson, Rosemarie (1997a). *Extraordinary Bodies: Figuring Physical Disability in American culture and Literature*. Columbia University Press.

— (1997b). 'Feminist Theory, the Body and the Disabled Figure'. *The Disability Studies Reader*, ed. Lennard J. Davis. Routledge, pp. 279–92.

Gauthier, Xavière and Anne Rivière (1982). 'Des Femmes et leurs œuvres', *Magazine Littéraire*, 180 (1982), pp. 36–41.

'Gender Equality Top 100. The Most Influential People in Global Policy 2019', *Apolitical*, <https://apolitical.co/lists/gender-equality-100/> (last accessed 16 July 2019).

Genette, Gérard (1988). *Narrative Discourse Revisited*, trans. Jane E. Lewin. Cornell University Press.

— (1983). *Nouveau discours du récit*. Éditions du Seuil, Collection Poétique.

— (1972). *Figures III*. Éditions du Seuil, Collection Poétique.

Germain, Christine (1985). 'Andrée Chedid', *Auteurs Contemporains*, ed. Jean-Claude Polet. Didier Hatier, pp. 67–90.

Ghandour, Sabah (2002). 'Hanan al-Shaykh's *Hikayat Zahra*. A Counter Narrative and a Counter-History', *Intersections Gender, Nation, and Community in Arab Women's Novels*, ed. Lisa Suhair Majaj, Paula W. Sunderman and Therese Saliba. Syracuse University Press, pp. 231–49.

Gibson, Andrew (1996). *Towards A Postmodern Theory of Narrative*. Edinburgh University Press.

Gilbert, Paula Ruth (2103). 'Préface' in *Rebelles et criminelles chez les écrivaines d'expression française*, ed. Frédérique Chevillot and Colette Trout. Rodopi, pp. 7–11.

Goffman, Erving (1963). *Stigma. Notes on The Management of Spoiled Identity*. Simon & Schuster.

Goodheart, Eugene (2004). *Novel Practices. Classic Modern Fiction*. Transaction Publishers.

Grewal, Inderpal, and Caren Kaplan (2001). 'Global Identities: Theorizing Transnational Studies of Sexuality', *GLQ: A Journal of Lesbian and Gay Studies*, 7.4 (2001), pp. 663–79.

Gymnich, Marion (2002). 'Linguistics and Narratology: The Relevance of Linguistic Criteria to Postcolonial Narratology', *Literature and Linguistics: Approaches, Models, and Applications. Studies in Honor of Jon Erickson*, ed. Marion Gymnich, Ansgar Nünning, Vera Nünning. Wissenschafter Verlag, pp. 61–76.

Haddad, Joumana (2010). *I Killed Scheherazade. Confessions of an Angry Arab Woman*. Dar Al Saqi.

Halbwachs, Maurice (1992). *On Collective Memory*, ed., trans. and with an Introduction by Lewis A. Coser. University of Chicago Press.

Hamdar, Abir (2014). *The Female Suffering Body. Illness and Disability in Modern Arabic Literature*. Syracuse University Press.

Harrison, Nicholas (2019). *Our Civilizing Mission. The Lessons of Colonial Education*. Liverpool University Press.

Hartman, Michelle (2014). *Native Tongue, Stranger Talk. The Arabic and French Literary Landscapes of Lebanon*. Syracuse University Press.

— (2002). *Jesus, Joseph and Job. Reading Rescriptings of Religious Figures in Lebanese Women's Fiction*. Reichert Verlag.

Haugbolle, Sune (2005). 'Public and Private Memory of the Lebanese Civil War', *Comparative Studies of South Asia, Africa and the Middle East*, 25.1 (2005), pp. 191–203.

Hayek, Caroline (2019). 'Faire reconnaître le viol de guerre est très important pour les survivants', *L'Orient Le Jour* [Beirut], 8 March, <https://www.lorientlejour.com/article/1160670/-faire-reconnaitre-le-viol-de-guerre-est-tres-important-pour-les-survivants-.html> (last accessed 1 August 2019).

Heavy, Emily (2015). 'Narrative Bodies, Embodied Narratives', *The Handbook of Narrative Analysis*, ed. Anna De Fina and Alexandra Georgakopoulou. Wiley Blackwell, pp. 429–46.

Hegel, Georg W. F. (1967). *Hegel's Philosophy of Right*, trans. T. M. Knox. Oxford University Press.

Heistad, Deirdre Bucher, Sharon Meilahn-Swett and Bartley Meinke (2004). 'Entretien avec Evelyne Accad', *Evelyne Accad: explorations*, ed. Deirdre Bucher Heistad. L'Harmattan, pp. 17–40.

Herman, David (1999). 'Introduction: Narratologies'. *Narratologies: New Perspectives on Narrative Analysis*, ed. David Herman. Ohio State University Press, pp. 1–30.

Hiddleston, Jane (2014). *Decolonizing the Intellectual. Politics, Culture, and Humanism at the End of the French Empire*. Liverpool University Press.

Huddart, David (2006). *Homi K. Bhabha*. Routledge, Critical Thinkers.

Hunt, Nigel C. (2010). *Memory, War and Trauma*. Cambridge University Press.

International Center for Transitional Justice (ICTJ) (2014). *Failing to Deal with The Past. What Cost to Lebanon?* <https://www.ictj.org/publication/failing-deal-past-what-cost-lebanon> (last accessed 1 August 2019).

Jakobson, Roman (1963). *Essais de linguistique générale*, trans. Nicolas Ruwet. Les Éditions de Minuit.

Jeannelle, Jean-Louis (2007). 'Où en est la réaction sur l'autofiction?', *Genèse et autofiction*, ed. Jean-Louis Jeannelle and Catherine Viollet. Bruylant-Academia, pp.17–37.

Kaedbey, Deema and Nadine Naber (2019). 'Reflections on Feminist Interventions within the 2015 Anticorruption Protests in Lebanon', *Meridians: feminism, race, transnationalism*, 18.2 (2019), pp. 457–70.

Keen, Suzanne (2015). 'Intersectional Narratology in the Study of Narrative Empathys', *Narrative Theory Unbound*, ed. Robyn Warhol and Susan S. Lanser. Ohio State University Press, pp. 123–46.

Kermode Frank (2000). *The Sense of An Ending. Studies in the theory of Fiction*. Oxford University Press.

Khoury-Ghata, Vénus (2013). 'En Forme de Kaléidoscope', *Défense et illustration de la langue française aujourd'hui*. Gallimard, pp. 59–62.

— (1998). *Une Maison au bord des larmes*. Éditions Balland.

— (1992). *La Maîtresse du Notable*. Seghers.

— (1984). *Les Morts n'ont pas d'ombre*. Flammarion.

— (1983). *Vacarme pour une lune morte*. Flammarion.

Kilanga-Musinde, Julien, Naïm Kattan, Jean Pruvost, Geneviève Goubier and Ambroise Queffélec (2010). 'Pourquoi choisir le français comme langue d'expression litteraire?', *La langue française: de recontres en partages: Quatriemes Lyriades de la langue française*, ed. Françoise Argod-Dutard. Presses universitaires de Rennes, pp. 251–70. Available at <http://books.openedition.org/pur/32828> (last accessed 13 August 2021).

Knapp, Bettina L. (2001). 'Review of *Le Message* by Andrée Chedid', *World Literature Today*, 75.1, pp. 136.

— (1986). 'Review of *La Maison sans racines* by Andrée Chedid', *World Literature Today*, 60.2 (1986), pp. 357–8.

Knapp, Bettina L. and Chedid Andrée (1984). 'Interview avec Andrée Chedid', *The French Review*, 57.4 (1984), pp. 517–23.

Kosofsky Sedwick, Eve (1985). *Between Men. English Literature and Male Homosocial Desire*. Columbia University Press.

Kristeva, Julia (1994). 'Bulgarie, ma souffrance', *Kristeva*, <http://www.kristeva.fr/bulgarie.html> (last accessed 9 August 2019).

— (1982). *Powers of Horror. An Essay on Abjection*, trans. Leon S. Roudiez. Columbia University Press.

Lang, Felix (2015). *The Lebanese Post-Civil War Novel. Memory, Trauma, and Capital*. Palgrave Macmillan. Palgrave Studies in Cultural Heritage and Conflict.

Langellier, Kristin M. and Eric E. Peterson (2004). *Storytelling in Daily Life. Performing Narrative*. Temple University Press.

Lanser, Susan (2013). 'Gender and Narrative', *The Living Handbook of Narratology*, ed. Peter Hühn, John Pier, Wolf Smid and Jörg Schönert. Hamburg University Press, <https://www.lhn.uni-hamburg.de/node/86.html> (last accessed 26 July 2019).

— (2010). 'Are We There Yet? The Intersectional Future of Feminist Narratology', *Foreign Literature Studies*, 32 (2010), pp. 32–41.

— (1995). 'Sexing the Narrative: Propriety, Desire, and the Engendering of Narratology', *Narrative*, 3.1 (January 1995), pp. 85–94.

— (1992). *Fictions of Authority: Women Writers and Narrative Voice*. Cornell University Press.

— (1986). 'Toward a Feminist Narratology', *Style*, 20 (1986), pp. 341–63.

Laurent, Jenny (1976). 'La stratégie de la forme', *Poétique*, 17 (1976), pp. 270–81.

Le Bris, Michel, Jean Rouaud and Alain Mabanckou (2007). 'Pour une "Littérature-Monde" en Français', *Le Monde*, 15 March, <https://www.lemonde.fr/livres/article/2007/03/15/des-ecrivains-plaident-pour-un-roman-en-francais-ouvert-sur-le-monde_883572_3260.html> (last accessed 19 July 2019).

Lejeune, Philippe (1980). *Je est un autre. L'Autobiographie de la littérature aux médias*. Éditions du Seuil.

— (1975). *Le Pacte autobiographique*. Éditions du Seuil.

Levi, Primo (1989). *The Drowned and the Saved*, trans. Raymond Rosenthal. Vintage.

Leys, Ruth (2007). *From Guilt to Shame. Auschwitz and After*. Princeton University Press.

— (2000). *Trauma. A Genealogy*. University of Chicago Press.

Lindley, Arthur (1996). *Hyperion and the Hobbyhorse. Studies in Carnivalesque Subversion*. University of Delaware Press.

Linkhorn, Renée (2002). 'Review of *Le Message* by Andrée Chedid', *The French Review*, 76.1 (2002), pp. 143–4.

— (1990). *The Prose and Poetry of Andrée Chedid. Selected Poems, Short Stories, and Essays*. Summa Publications.

— (1985). 'Andrée Chedid: quête poétique d'une fraternité', *The French Review*, 58.4 (1985), pp. 559–65.

Maalouf, Muriel (2015). 'Invité culture. *Les Absents* premier roman de Georgia Makhlouf', *Radio France* Internationale, 30 June 2014, <http://www.rfi.fr/emission/20140630-absents-premier-roman-georgia-makhlouf> (last accessed 27 June 2019).

Makhlouf, Georgia (2019). 'Re: *Les Absents*'. Received by Mireille Rebeiz, 11 May 2019.

— (2014). *Les Absents*. Rivages/L'Orient des Livres.

Makhlouf, Georgia, Dominique Eddé and Tahar Ben Jelloun (2013). 'Portrait, hommage à Andrée Chedid', *Andrée Chedid, Je t'aime: hommages, souvenirs et lettres*. Alfabarre, pp. 101–13.

Malti-Douglas, Fedwa (1991). *Woman's Body, Woman's Word: Gender and Discourse in Arabo-Islamic Writing*. Princeton University Press.

Martin, Wallace (1986). *Recent Theories of Narrative*. Cornell University Press.

Mazo, Bernard (2002). 'Entretien avec Vénus Khoury-Ghata', *Sud Autre. Cahiers Trimestriels*, 19 (2002), pp. 26–32.

Mejcher-Atassi, Sonja (2006). 'Breaking the Silence Etel Adnan's *Sitt Marie Rose* and *The Arab Apocalypse, Poetry's Voice – Society's Norms: Forms of Interaction Between Middle Eastern Writers and Their Societies*, ed. Andreas Pflitsch and Barbara Winckler. Reichert, pp. 201–10.

Mendel, Gérard (1980). 'La Violence est un langage', *Violences et non-violence: raison présente*, 54.2 (1980), pp. 37–54.

Mezei, Kathy (1996). *Ambiguous Discourse: Feminist Narratology and British Women Writers*. University of North Carolina Press.

Migraine-George, Thérèse (2013). *From Francophonie to World Literature in French. Ethics, Poetics, and Politics*. University of Nebraska Press.

Miraglia, Anne-Marie (1998). 'Le temps et ses reflets dans *La Maison sans racines* d'Andrée Chedid', *Francofonia*, 35 (1998), pp. 17–33.

Morreall, John (1994). 'The Myth of the Omniscient Narrator', *The Journal of Aesthetics and Art Criticism*, 52.4 (1994), pp. 429–35.

Moura, Jean-Marc (2007). *Littératures francophones et théorie postcoloniale*. Quadrige/ Presses Universitaires de France.

Murr-Nehmé, Lina (1987). *Comme un torrent qui gronde*. Ishtar.

Nagar, Richa and Amanda Lock Swarr (2020). 'Theorizing Transnational Feminist Praxis', *Critical Transnational Feminist Praxis*, ed. Amanda Lock Swarr and Richa Nagar. State University of New York Press, pp. 1–22.

Nalbantian, Suzanne (2003). *Memory in Literature. From Rousseau to Neuroscience*. Palgrave Macmillan.

Nielsen, Henrik Skov (2010). 'Natural Authors, Unnatural Narration', *Postclassical Narratology. Approaches and Analyses*, ed. Jan Alber and Monika Fludernik. Ohio State University Press, pp. 275–301.

Nora, Pierre (1989). 'Between Memory and History: *Les Lieux de Mémoire*', *Representations*, 26 (1989), pp. 7–24.

Ochs, Elinor and Lisa Capps. 'Narrating the Self', *Annual Review of Anthropology*, 25 (1996), pp. 19–43.

Ofeish Sami and Sabah Ghandour (2001). 'Transgressive Subjects: Gender, War, and Colonialism in Etel Adnan's *Sitt Marie Rose*', *Etel Adnan. Critical Essays on The Arab-American writer and Artist*, ed. Lisa Suhair Majaj and Amal Amireh. McFarland & Jefferson, pp. 122--36.

Olson, Barbara K. (2006). 'Who Thinks This Book? or Why the Author/

God Analogy Merits Our Continued Attention', *Narrative*, 14.3 (2006), pp. 339–46.

Orbach, Susan (1986). *Hunger Strike. The Anorectic's Struggle as a Metaphor for our Age.* W. W. Norton & Company.

Nünning, Ansgar (2003). 'Narratology or Narratologies? Taking Stock of Recent Developments, Critique and Modest Proposals for Future Usages of the Term', *What Is Narratology? Questions and Answers Regarding the Status of a Theory*, ed. Tom Kindt and Hans-Harald Müller. Walter de Gruyter, pp. 239–75.

Page, Ruth E. (2006). *Literary and Linguistic Approaches to Feminist Narratology.* Palgrave Macmillan.

Pearman, Tory Vandeventer (2010). *Women and Disability in Medieval Literature.* Palgrave Macmillan.

Phelan, James (2011). 'Rhetoric, Ethics, and Narrative Communication: Or, From Story and Discourse to Authors, Resources, and Audiences', *Soundings: An Interdisciplinary Journal*, 94.1/2 (2011), pp. 55–75.

— (2005). *Living to Tell About it: A Rhetoric and Ethics of Character Narration.* Cornell University Press.

Plato (1993). *Phaedo*, ed. C. J. Rowe. Cambridge University Press.

Platt, Justin (2007). 'Breaking the glass slipper: Changing cultural norms and the Cinderella Story', *The Rutgers Journal of Comparative Literature*, 8 (2007), pp. 32–53.

Poggioli, Renato (1968). *The Theory of the Avant-Garde*, trans. Gerald Fitzgerald. The Belknap Press of Harvard University Press.

Poniewozik, James (2000). 'TV Makes a Too-Close Call', *Time*, 20 November 2000, pp. 70–1.

Prince, Gerald (2005). 'On a Postcolonial Narratology', *A Companion to Narrative Theory*, ed. James Phelan and Peter J. Rabinowitz. Blackwell Publishing Ltd, pp. 372–81.

— (1982). *Narratology: The Form and Functioning of Narrative.* Mouton Publishers.

Radstone, Susannah (2007). 'Trauma Theory: Contexts, Politics, Ethics', *Paragraph*, 30.1 (2007), pp. 9–29.

Ramazanoğlu, Caroline (ed.) (1993). *Up Against Foucault. Explorations of some Tensions between Foucault and Feminism.* Routledge.

Reisert, Joseph R. (2000). 'Authenticity, Justice, and Virtue in Taylor and Rousseau', *Polity*, 33.2 (Winter 2000), pp. 305–30.

Rice, Alison (2004). 'Les Air(e)s du temps: Evelyne Accad et l'écriture de deux femmes du monde « Arabe », Andrée Chedid et Assia Djebar', *Evelyne Accad: Explorations*, ed. Deirdre Bucher Heistad. L'Harmattan, pp. 81–94.

Rich, Adrienne (1995). *Of Woman Born: Motherhood as Experience and Institution*. W. W. Norton & Company.

Roger, Alain (1984). 'Le Je paranoïaque', *Le Personnage en question*. Université de Toulouse-Le Mirail, pp. 45–53.

Rothberg, Michael (2009). *Multidirectional Memory. Remembering the Holocaust in the Age of Decolonization*. Stanford University Press.

Russo, Mary (1994). *The Female Grotesque: Risk, Excess and Modernity*. Routledge.

Russo, Richard (2001). 'In Defense of Omniscience', *Bringing the Devil to His Knees. The Craft of Fiction and the Writing Life*, ed. Charles Baxter and Peter Turchi. University of Michigan Press, pp. 7–18.

Rustum Shehadeh, Lamia (1999). *Women and War in Lebanon*. University Press of Florida.

Rutherford, Jonathan (ed.) (1990). 'The Third Space: Interview with Homi K. Bhabha', *Identity: Community, Culture, Difference*. Lawrence & Wishart, pp. 207–21.

Said, Edward W. (2002). *Reflections on Exile: And Other Essays*. Harvard University Press.

— (1979). *Orientalism*. Vintage Books.

Saint-Augustine (2016). *The Confessions of Saint Augustine*, trans. Edward Bouverie Pusey. Digireads.com Publishing.

Salem Manganaro, Elise (1995–6). 'Negotiating Feminist Ideologies within Lebanese Women's Writings', *Bāhithāt*, 2 (1995–6), pp. 163–74.

Sarhan, Carla (2013). 'L'Enseignement des littératures francophones dans les universités libanaises. État des lieux, représentations et perspectives', *Francophonies d'Europe, du Maghreb et du Machrek. Littératures et Libertés*, ed. Marc Quaghebeur. Peter Lang, pp. 161–84.

Seidenberg Robert and Karen DeCrow (1962). *Panic and Protest in Agoraphobia. Women Who Marry Houses*. McGraw Hill Book Company.

Shildrick, Margaret (2002). *Embodying the Monster: Encounters with the Vulnerable Self*. Sage.

Silverman, Kaja (1989). 'White Skin, Brown Masks: The Double Mimesis, or with Lawrence in Arabia', *Differences*, 1.3 (1989), pp. 3–54.

Slemon, Stephen (1995). 'Magic Realism as Postcolonial Discourse', *Magical Realism. Theory, History, Community*, ed. Lois Parkinson Zamora and Wendy B. Faris, Duke University Press, pp. 407–26.

Sommer, Roy (2007). 'Contextualism Revisited: A Survey (and Defense) of Postcolonial and Intercultural Narratologies', *Journal of Literary Theory*, 1.1 (2007), pp. 61–79.

Sontag, Susan (2004). *Regarding the Pain of Others*. Penguin.

Stanley, Liz (1992). *The auto/biographical I. The Theory and Practice of Feminist Auto/Biography*. Manchester University Press.

Starobinski, Jean (1971). *Jean-Jacques Rousseau: la transparence et l'obstacle*. Gallimard.

— (1970). *L'Œil vivant II. La relation critique*. Gallimard.

Sternberg, Meir (2007). 'Omniscience in Narrative Construction: Old Challenges and New', *Poetics Today*. International Journal for Theory and Analysis of Literature and Communication, 28.3 (2007), pp. 683–794.

Suhair Majaj Lisa (2002). 'Voice, Representation, and Resistance: Etel Adnan's *Sitt Marie Rose*', *Intersections Gender, Nation, and Community in Arab Women's Novels*, ed. Lisa Suhair Majaj. Syracuse University Press, pp. 200–31.

Suhair Majaj Lisa and Amireh Amal (2001a). 'Introduction: Biographical and Career Highlights', *Etel Adnan. Critical Essays on The Arab-American writer and Artist*, ed. Lisa Suhair Majaj and Amal Amireh. McFarland & Jefferson, pp. 15–24.

— (2001b). 'Preface: Situating Etel Adnan in a Literary Context', *Etel Adnan. Critical essays on the Arab-American writer and Artist*, ed. Lisa Suhair Majaj and Amal Amireh. McFarland & Jefferson, pp. 1–15.

Suleiman, Susan Rubin (1990). *Subversive Intent: Gender, Politics, and the Avant-Garde*. Harvard University Press.

— (1981). 'The Question of Readability in Avant-Garde Fiction', *Studies in 20th Century Literature*, 6.1 (1981), *Getting the Message: On the Semiotics of Literary Signification*, pp. 17–35.

Taylor, Charles (1992). *Grandeur et misère de la modernité*, trans. Charlotte Melançon. Bellarmin.

Talpade Mohanty, Chandra (2003). 'Under Western Eyes: Feminist Scholarship and Colonialist Discourses', *Feminism Without Borders. Decolonizing Theory, Practicing Solidarity*. Duke University Press, pp. 17–42.

The Holy Bible (1952). Revised Standard Version, Thomas Nelson & Sons.

'The 100 World's Most Influential Arab Women 2017. Joumana Haddad', *Arabian Business*, 27 June, <https://www.arabianbusiness.com/revealed--100-world-s-most-influential-arabs-2017-678773.html?itemid=678673> (last accessed 16 July 2019).

Theweleit, Klaus (1987). *Male Fantasies, Vol 2: Male Bodies – Psychoanalyzing the White Terror*, trans. Erica Carter and Chris Turner. University of Minnesota Press.

Todorov, Tzvetan (1975). *The Fantastic. A structural Approach to a Literary Genre*, trans. Richard Howard. Cornell University Press.

— (1969). *Grammaire du « Décameron »*. Mouton Publishers.

Touya de Marenne, Eric (2011). *Francophone Women Writers. Feminisms, Postcolonialisms, Cross-Cultures*. Lexington Books.

Trilling, Lionel (1972). *Sincerity and Authenticity*. Harvard University Press.

Valassopoulos, Anastasia (2007). *Contemporary Arab Women Writers. Cultural Expression in Context*. Routledge.

Velguth, Madeline (1985). 'Le Texte comme prétexte: Jacques Derrida lit *Les Confessions* de Rousseau', *The French Review*, 58.6 (May 1985), pp. 811–19.

Venuti, Lawrence (2013). *Translation Changes Everything. Theory and Practice*. Routledge.

Viollet, Catherine (2007). 'Troubles dans le genre. Présentation', *Genèse et autofiction*, ed. Jean-Louis Jeannelle and Catherine Viollet. Bruylant-Academia, pp. 7–13.

Waddell, Kaveh (2018). 'The Desperate Search for Lebanon's Mass Graves. Everyone knows someone who went missing. But they don't speak about these things', *The Atlantic*, 22 April, <https://www.theatlantic.com/international/archive/2018/04/lebanon-civil-war-burial-missing/558632/> (last accessed 1 August 2019).

Walsh, Richard (2010). 'Person, Level, Voice. A Rhetorical Reconsideration', *Postclassical Narratology. Approaches and Analyses*, ed. Jan Alber and Monika Fludernik. Ohio State University Press, pp. 35–57.

Walters, Margaret (2005). *Feminism. A Very Short Introduction*. Oxford University Press.

Warhol, Robyn R. (2012). 'A Feminist Approach to Narrative', *Narrative Theory: Core Concepts and Critical Debates*. David Herman, James Phelan, Peter J. Rabinowitz, Brian Richardson and Robyn Warhol. Ohio State University Press, pp. 9–13.

— (1989). *Gendered Interventions: Narrative Discourse in the Victorian Novel*. Rutgers University Press.

Warren, Karen J. (1997). 'Introduction', *Ecofeminism: Women, Culture, Nature*, ed. Karen J. Warren. Indiana University Press, pp. xi–xvi.

Weed, Elizabeth (2012). 'The Way We Read Now', *History of the Present*, 2.1 (2012), pp. 95–106.

Welldon, Estela V. (1988). *Mother, Madonna, Whore: the Idealization and the Denigration of Motherhood*. Free Association Press.

Wendell, Susan (1996). *The Rejected Body. Feminist Philosophical Reflections on Disability*. Routledge.

Wheatley, Edward (2010). *Stumbling Blocks Before the Blind. Medieval Constructions of a Disability*. University of Michigan Press.

Willis, Mary-Angela (2004). 'La Guerre civile et le rôle de la femme', *Evelyne Accad: explorations*, ed. Deirdre Bucher Heistad. L'Harmattan, pp. 173–88.

Wilson, Rawdon (1995). 'The Metamorphoses of Fictional Space: Magical Realism', *Magical Realism. Theory, History, Community*. Duke University Press, pp. 209–34.

Winter, Jay and Emmanuel Sivan (1999). 'Setting the Framework', *War and Remembrance in the Twentieth Century*, ed. Jay Winter and Emmanuel Sivan. Cambridge University Press, pp. 6–39.

Yared, Hyam (2012). *La Malédiction*. Éditions des Équateurs.

— (2006). *L'Armoire des ombres*. Sabine Wespieser Éditeur.

Young, Iris Marion (1990). *Throwing Like a Girl and Other Essays in Feminist Philosophy and Social Theory*. Indiana University Press.

— (1998). 'Pregnant Embodiment', *Body and Flesh. A Philosophical Reader*, ed. Donn Welton. Blackwell Publishers Inc., pp. 274–85.

Zalzal, Zéna (2016). 'Hyam Yared: nous sommes tous des comateux!', *L'Orient Le Jour* [Beirut], 23 January, <https://www.lorientlejour.com/article/966352/hyam-yared-nous-sommes-tous-des-comateux-.html> (last accessed 18 July 2019).

Zamora, Lois Parkinson and Wendy B. Faris (eds) (1995). 'Introduction: Daiquiri Birds and Flaubertian Parrot(ie)s', *Magical Realism. Theory, History, Community*. Duke University Press, pp. 1–11.

Zeidan, Joseph T. (1995). *Arab Women Novelists. The Formative Years and Beyond*. State University of New York Press.

Index

Abou, Sélim, 44n6
Accad, Evelyne, 23, 24
    on Adnan, Etel, 82n14, 99
    characters, 112–13
    on Chedid, Andrée, 93
    Coquelicot du massacre, 109–18; feminine
      'I', 111–12, 113–14, 116–17; hope,
      115; music, 115–18; narrative voice,
      110–12, 115; structure, 110; title,
      109–10
    and language, 209
    and narrators, 92, 94
Aczel, Richard, 11
Adnan, Etel, 23, 24
    Sitt Marie Rose: death, 77–8; feminine
      'I', 49, 50, 68–78; masculinity, 68–9,
      72–3, 74–5; narrative voices, 72;
      pro-Palestinian position, 76, 99; time
      distortion, 71
agoraphobia, 159n16
Aldea, Eva, 163, 164, 167
Alexander, M. Jacqui, 16
Algeria: language, 45n8, 209
Amireh, Amal, 4, 68, 76, 209
Amnesty International, 33
anorexia, 148, 149
Arab Feminist Union, 27
Arab nationalism, 27
Arab Spring, 28
Arab Women's Solidarity Association
    (AWSA), 27

Arabic language, 20, 21, 22, 26, 209, 210,
    211
Ashplant, T. G., et al., 34
Awakening of the Arab Girl (cultural
    movement), 27
Aziz, Désirée, 23, 99

Baalbaki, Laila, 28, 45n9
Badran, Margot, 25, 30, 45n11
Bakhtin, Mikhail
    on bodies, 195, 196
    on carnival, 186, 203n7, 204n12
    on crude language, 199–200
    on degradation, 186–7
    on the grotesque, 161–2
    on grotesque realism, 185–91
    on omniscience, 86
Bal, Mieke, 2
Barakat, Hoda, 28
Barthes, Roland, 84, 89, 157n2, 200–1
Bartky, Sandra Lee, 137–8, 159n14
Baz, Jurji Niqula, 27
Beirut
    American University, 32
    march for peace (1984), 94
    Martyrs' Square, 36
    Al-Nahda al-Nisaiyyah fi Bayrut (the
      Women's Renaissance in Beirut), 27
    siege of (1982), 32
    Syrian Protestant College (later American
      University of Beirut), 27